Slow Places in Béla Tarr's Films

The Intersection of Geography, Ecology, and Slow Cinema

Clara Orban

LEXINGTON BOOKS
Lanham • Boulder • New York • London

Published by Lexington Books
An imprint of The Rowman & Littlefield Publishing Group, Inc.
4501 Forbes Boulevard, Suite 200, Lanham, Maryland 20706
www.rowman.com

6 Tinworth Street, London SE11 5AL, United Kingdom

Copyright © 2021 by The Rowman & Littlefield Publishing Group, Inc.

All rights reserved. No part of this book may be reproduced in any form or by any electronic or mechanical means, including information storage and retrieval systems, without written permission from the publisher, except by a reviewer who may quote passages in a review.

British Library Cataloguing in Publication Information Available

Library of Congress Cataloging-in-Publication Data

Names: Orban, Clara Elizabeth, 1960– author.
Title: Slow places in Béla Tarr's films : the intersection of geography, ecology and slow cinema / Clara Orban.
Description: Lanham : Lexington Books, [2021] | Includes bibliographical references and index. | Summary: "This book explores Hungarian filmmaker Béla Tarr's approach to creating geographies of indifference through slow cinema techniques. Author Clara Orban utilizes close readings of the films, relevant poems, a thorough filmography, and an interview with Tarr in her analysis"—Provided by publisher.
Identifiers: LCCN 2021022455 (print) | LCCN 2021022456 (ebook) |
 ISBN 9781793645647 (cloth) | ISBN 9781793645654 (epub) |
 ISBN 9781793645661 (paper)
Subjects: LCSH: Tarr, Béla, 1955—Criticism and interpretation. | Tarr, Béla, 1955—Interviews. | Motion picture producers and Directors—Hungary.
Classification: LCC PN1998.3.T363 O73 2021 (print) | LCC PN1998.3.T363 (ebook) | DDC 791.43023/3092—dc23
LC record available at https://lccn.loc.gov/2021022455
LC ebook record available at https://lccn.loc.gov/2021022456

Contents

List of Illustrations		vii
Acknowledgments		ix
1	Introduction: Tarr in the Anthropocene	1
2	Slow Cinema, Tarr's Places, and Hungarian Cinema	15
3	The Claustrophobic Indoors	41
4	The Empty Outdoors	81
5	Animals	107
6	Short Films and Segments: Further Experimentation	125
7	Conclusion: Visions of Loneliness	145
Appendix A: Petőfi Poems		151
Appendix B: Transcript of Interview with Béla Tarr		171
Filmography		179
Bibliography		193
Index		201
About the Author		209

Slow Places in Béla Tarr's Films

List of Illustrations

Figure 1.1	Maloin with the Signal Box in the Background	10
Figure 2.1	Claudia and Sandro with Etna in the Background	22
Figure 2.2	A Crosswalk That Becomes an Abstract Figure	24
Figure 3.1	The Television in *Family Nest*	49
Figure 3.2	The Cluttered Apartment in the Background	51
Figure 3.3	The Pullout Couch, Tennis Racket, and Objects	52
Figure 3.4	The Washing Machine Ride	54
Figure 3.5	The Stone Walls behind the Unhappy Couple	56
Figure 3.6	Objects in the Bourgeois Apartment	57
Figure 3.7	Washing in the Hut	64
Figure 3.8	Eclipse in the Kocsma	70
Figure 3.9	The Asylum	74
Figure 4.1	An Elegant Square and a Whale Trailer	89
Figure 4.2	Irimiás and Petrina in the Forest	96
Figure 4.3	Coal Buckets Out the Window	98
Figure 4.4	Wind and a Well	101
Figure 5.1	The Coal Pit Pack	111
Figure 5.2	Cows	115
Figure 5.3	Chickens in Budapest	120
Figure 5.4	A Birdcage by a Window	123
Figure 6.1	Tension in the Hotel	127
Figure 6.2	The Open Road	130
Figure 6.3	A Ruined Church and Field	130
Figure 6.4	Waiting for a Handout	141

Acknowledgments

This project comes from a very personal space: my love of the arts and literature, my love of cinema, and my Hungarian roots. As a professor of Italian and French, I began working on cinema as part of my scholarly interest. I was able to teach courses on Italian films at DePaul University, which led me to delve more deeply into Michelangelo Antonioni's works, among others. My Italian heritage has always been entwined with my professional aspirations and thanks to my mother's enthusiasm and passion for the arts it became a calling for me. My Hungarian roots were less prominently influential in my professional life, given the simple fact that Italian was the language we spoke at home, while my contact with Hungarian was limited to moments when my father talked to his siblings, or when we attended events in the Chicago Hungarian community. My interest in Hungarian started there, but it was not until adulthood that I accelerated my Hungarian exploration.

I was first introduced to Béla Tarr's films at Facet Multimedia in Chicago, one of the premiere art house theaters that showed *Werckmeister Harmonies* when it first came out. This film was a revelation. Already interested in Antonioni's cinema, I realized an affinity between the two directors. It was not until later, upon reading the increasing materials about slow cinema, that I made the connection. I loved both these filmmakers because they made films that were like books. While Hollywood exploited film's potential for movement and fast pacing to the extreme, these filmmakers and others like them demanded that we take our time to really see what was in front of us. They brought pacing back to a level where contemplation can replace adrenaline rush in helping the mind synthesize images. I continue to discover new films, new filmmakers, and new approaches that are witness to this tradition of emphasizing the "art" in art house cinema.

There are many individuals whose energy and knowledge helped move this project to completion. First, I would like to thank the people at Facets Multimedia Chicago. The founder, the late Milos Stehlik, made films such as the ones I consider here accessible and continued to ensure that cinema remained an art form and not just a form of entertainment. As I researched information for the book, staff members were able to find rare titles and encouraged my exploration. I would like to thank them all for their knowledge and expertise in international cinema.

I am grateful to DePaul University's University Research Council for leaves of absence that helped me begin work on Hungarian cinema, and then to transform a more shapeless study into the current work on Tarr. My students, especially those in Italian cinema, engaged with me in exploring films that kept my scholarly interest peaked. Heather Jagman of DePaul University's library helped me find a rare translation of poems from Hungarian to English, and then to uncover authoritative originals for those same poems. In appendix A, I include these texts, recited in Tarr's short films *Journey on the Plain*, which I believe will for the first time allow us to better understand this film and its lyricism. I have included a published translation of the poems with some additions from the subtitles if there were differences.

Jessica Tepper of Lexington Books led the project through completion and believed in it. I owe her and her staff at Lexington a great debt of gratitude.

My father's memory resonates in these pages. He encouraged me to the scholarly life and was happy to learn I had begun working on Hungarian language skills (still a work in progress). I wish we could meet to converse, to have a lesson in Hungarian, now. I thank my other Hungarian language partners over the years, here in Chicago, Etelka Tatar who began my formal lessons in Hungarian. In Hungary, Ferenc Bihari not only patiently listened to Hungarian sentence fragments as my teacher but also provided much-needed proofreading of Hungarian words in this text. Their patience was endless and the process of studying a new language made me a better teacher. It reminded me how hard, but rewarding, learning a second language can be. My cousin Anna sleuthed some definitions, which helped in the final phases of writing this book.

Appendix B includes a transcription of an interview I was able to conduct with Béla Tarr himself. My deep gratitude to Tamara Nagy of the National Film Institute/Filmarchive in Budapest who helped us get in touch. Mr. Tarr graciously answered my naïve questions, steering me right, providing context, and giving me a glimmer of his post-COVID-19 future. It was a privilege to speak with him, and if this book can add something to our understanding of his extraordinary career, it will have been worthwhile. I thank him profusely for allowing this stranger to ask him about his films.

Finally, Elliot has been the inspiration of all my work, scholarly or not. His encouragement meant I could take risks, move beyond "my comfort zone," and I am a better person for it. I hope that over the course of the last third of a century I have been able to repay him.

Previously published material from the following book and articles that I have written has been graciously granted permission from the publishers to be reprinted in this book. For further reading, please refer to the following sources:

Orban, Clara. "When Walls Fall: Families in Hungarian Films of the New Europe." In *Popular Cinemas in East Central Europe. Film Cultures and Histories*. Edited by Dorota Ostrowska, Francesco Pitassio, and Zsuzsanna Varga. 248–262. London and New York: I.B. Tauris, 2017. Used by permission of Bloomsbury Publishing Plc.

———. "Antonioni's Women Lost in the City." *Modern Language Society* 31, no. 2 (Autumn 2001): 11–28.

———. "Contextualizing History in Hungarian Films of the New Millennium." *AHEA E-Journal of the American Hungarian Educators Association* 6 (Fall 2013). Accessed 18 February 2021, http://ahea.net/e-journal/volume-6-2013/7.

Chapter 1

Introduction
Tarr in the Anthropocene

Like its culinary counterpart, Slow Food, slow cinema has become a way of watching the world go by more slowly, a mindful approach to moving pictures. Not really a movement, filmmakers from many different countries and even different decades created films that emphasize the passage of time. Before the term was used, Michelangelo Antonioni employed long takes to unfold stories of isolated characters who live anxious lives. Ingmar Bergman, Andrei Tarkovsky, Theo Angelopoulos, and Miklós Jancsó have all been associated with and considered proponents of slow cinema. Among the cinematic masters of slow cinema, Hungary's Béla Tarr stands out as one of the directors who most consistently and effectively used the slow camera in explorations of the human condition.

Often in slow cinema, the spaces inhabited by isolated characters unfold as though in real time, the camera lingering on the natural contours of places, landscapes, animals, and other elements of what we might call the "natural world." Furthermore, the characters' isolation comes to the foreground because they are surrounded by bleakness, emptiness, and lonely landscapes. The damaged environment in which Tarr's films often unfold may not always be directly damaged by human interactions. Characters rarely appear scarring the landscapes, killing wildlife, or harming natural habitats. And yet the ruined, pock-marked land, the crumbling villages, and the muddy fields have, by implication, been ruined by human neglect. The ecological reality of Tarr's geographic locations implies the negative influence humans have had, an underlying concept of what we now call the Anthropocene. It is possible to read into these spaces an ecological significance, where the Anthropocene becomes an environmental nightmare. Tracing one film after another to identify types of locations in Tarr's films proves useful as a way to understand how human behavior conditions our physical reality.

As described in scientific and social-scientific debates, the Anthropocene would demarcate the evolutionary era when human beings' influence shaped the geographic, physical, and ecological realities of the globe. Paul J. Crutzen, the Nobel Prize-winning atmospheric chemist, coined the term "Anthropocene" at a conference in Cuernevaca, Mexico, in 2000. During a discussion of the Holocene, a period referring to the post-glacial epoch of the past ten to twelve thousand years and probably first proposed by Sir Charles Lyell in 1833, Crutzen suggested we have now surpassed the Holocene and find ourselves in the Anthropocene. Crutzen and Eugene F. Stoermer provided a short, written description of this idea in a newsletter, noting the numerous atmospheric, oceanographic, and geological changes that humankind's short appearance on earth have produced over the past 50,000 years, namely "the anthropogenic emissions of CO_2." They assign a date, perhaps arbitrary, they admit, to the beginning of the most profound changes, the latter part of the eighteenth century, a period during which the effects of human activity became particularly noticeable (Crutzen and Stoermer 2000, 17). This idea of humankind's impact has penetrated and, in turn, had a profound effect not only on the interdisciplinary science that Crutzen and his colleagues practice but also on other forms of scholarly endeavor. As the concept has evolved over the following decades, it has also become an important measure of the negative impact humans can cause. In the preface to his contribution on the Anthropocene, Christian Schwägel insists that it can trigger strong ethics-driven reactions and strong impulses toward caring.

Analyses of this important concept have been applied to the arts, and even most importantly for us, to Tarr's production. Franklin Ginn sums up the Anthropocene in his article describing Tarr's *The Turin Horse*'s (*A torinói ló* 2011) apocalyptic vision, which for Ginn comes from the fantasies of the Anthropocene, the new geological epoch in which humans become the planetary force. Ginn summarizes that:

> For some, the Anthropocene signals a final enclosure of politics and culture within ecology; a new geopolitics in which Earth is the sovereign authority and humans are inmates of a planet-sized camp in a permanent state of emergency. For others, it is an occasion to double down on techno-hubris and call forth more fevered bouts of rationality and management . . . . Only once we can measure, read, and therefore sense how the Earth has become sensitive do we enter the Anthropocene. (2015, 352)

In Ginn's reading of Tarr's *The Turin Horse*, the film shows the limits of the Anthropocene, the limits of being human and the future of life after the Anthropocene, as do all allusions to an apocalyptic future. In the end, it is also the characters' loneliness, their inability to assist one another, that brings about their fate.

The Anthropocene has become a framework within which to examine human activity, including cultural production. Tarr's films include landscapes, villages, and even animals, which show the negative effects of human influence on nature and other creatures. In turn, the characters portrayed in his films are themselves neglected, scarred, and indifferent, mostly incapable of genuine emotional responses or altruistic behavior. Ultimately, Tarr's characters are lonely, distant from each other with little commonality and the spaces they inhabit both mirror and accentuate the separation. Furthermore, Tarr's preferred technique accentuates this dynamic. As we discuss Tarr's work, landscapes, places, inanimate objects, and their relationship to humans take on heightened significance precisely because the slow camera lingers on them and lengthens their presence before the viewer. In an interview on the importance of places in his work, Tarr himself states, "every place has a face. Places are main characters"[1] (Maury and Zuchuat 2016, 14).[2] This examination of Tarr's body of work will offer new ways of understanding Tarr's significance to world cinema and to the place cinema can have in explorations of the human condition.

I will argue that it is precisely Tarr's slow camera that allows us to contemplate the places in his films, which become in many cases indictments of human activity and its futility in the face of social and political constraints. Human relationships are very often flawed in Tarr's films. Personal relationships are damaged by the social structures in place that dictate human activity. Materialism, deceit, repression, violence, mistrust, and alienation erode human interactions. Corinne Maury argues that Tarr moves us "from an ontology to a cosmology associated with a heaviness that weighs down and petrifies beings" (2016, 45).[3] While Tarr's films remain a-political (he rarely mentions specific places, regimes, personalities, or concepts in his films) one can read a critique of political systems from communism to European Union membership and beyond into his works if studied chronologically. The slow camera allows us to see the intrinsic difficulties that structures put on individual human activity and how they shape humans' relationships to each other, and by extension, to the world around them.

Tarr has been studied also as a Hungarian director whose works reflect and echo many of the themes prevalent in Hungarian national cinema. Isolation, overtly political overtones, allusions to totalitarian regimes, and exploration of some of the degradations communism brought to Hungary have remained important undercurrents in Tarr's work. Critical appraisals have focused on understanding the possible political motives behind his filmic choices. Studies of individual films, as well as more comprehensive surveys of his oeuvre, reconnect Tarr to the trajectory of Hungarian cinema, relating his work to those of contemporaries such as István Szabó. Tarr's work contrasts with Szabó's and aligns with Jancsó's through the use of slow cinematic long takes, which give a relentlessly static pace to the films. His narratives are also allusive, and therefore political or social equivalences between his films and Hungarian (or international) realities are more obscure.

The focus of this exploration into Tarr's work will concentrate less on parallels with national or international auteurs, or on any historical or social-scientific readings, and more on the thematic connections between his stylistic concerns and his portrayal of the physical environment. Tarr's mise-en-scène will be the locus of our discussion and on how the setting can be read thematically. Perhaps neither his preference for long takes, still cameras, and other directorial choices often associated with slow cinema nor his extensive portrayal of landscapes in his films stems from Tarr's national perspective. However, combined, all these elements intertwine to make Tarr's recognizable style.

The intersection of geography, ecology, and slow cinema brings us to an important possibility for contemplating Tarr's work. Ecological readings of literary and artistic works, through ecocriticism, show how man's intervention in the natural world influences it. Geographic readings of places in literary works, or within a series of works, to examine the significance of place, are explored in geocriticism. Many scholarly contributions to understanding Tarr have touched on aspects of his use of spaces, of his insistence on long takes which puts him squarely within the group of filmmakers linked to slow cinema, but a study specifically of Tarr's use of spaces, of animals, and how his slow cinema techniques generate meaning from these images provides new territory. This study will continue the work already begun by geo- and ecocriticism scholars in an attempt to shed some light on the interconnectedness of geography, ecology, and slow cinema in the works of this Hungarian cinematic master by mapping types of spaces and creatures that appear throughout his filmic career.

OVERLAPPING TERRITORIES

Tarr's work's insistence on places and objects, brought into focus and lingered upon, creates a geography and ecology of places in connection with human activity. Mise-en-scène by definition includes a location in which the staged representation takes place, so exploring the actual or man-made environment surrounding a filmed action is a necessary part of all film analysis. Even in experimental surrealist or dadaist films, where lines or objects rotate in space to create hallucinatory effects (I am thinking here of Man Ray's *Emak Bakia* or other shorts films), the physical space surrounding the objects constitutes a geographic location. In the overwhelming majority of films, however, of all genres, these staged locations are meant to refer to a recognizable type of geographic ecological reality.

Natural locations can sometimes be exploited to serve an extra-diegetic purpose. Cliched examinations of nature can be implicitly activated to rally the viewer, where characters "fight against nature," "work with it," "tame it," "let it overcome," and so on. As an example, the ways in which nature was portrayed in the cinematic genre of Westerns played an important part in the metaphorical reading of these films as enactments of nation building. Deborah A. Carmichael shows how, in John Ford's *Stagecoach* (1939), the coach with its inhabitants is a microcosm. The mise-en-scène accentuates the struggle of the settlers against nature. The coach is depicted rolling along overshadowed by looming rock formations and harsh landscapes, showing the ominous surroundings as antagonists. In the end, humans triumph having conquered nature and the nation is built.

This facile equivalence of nature as a force to dominate does not appear in Tarr's films. He does not portray humans building, burning, chopping down, or otherwise modifying the landscape. Often, the damage has been done before the film begins. We witness only the ruined landscapes and come to understand the human realities as a fait accompli. Estelle Bayon nuances our understanding of Tarr's stance on the ecology because: "Tarr's ecological preoccupation as shown in his cinema has nothing to do with alarmist stances about danger to the environment. It is the *vision* of a doomed landscape which translates to the serious, but vain, attempt to dwell in the world" (2016, 56).[4] To Bayon, Tarr's films are not environmental but ecological; they concern the earth rather than the environment: "It seems that Béla Tarr's ecological process resides in the cinematic access to a vision of ecological disaster that renders the world's uninhabitability, the impossibility of *remaining* within it" (2016, 49).[5] In particular,

> It's less a question of showing the landscape than of showing its disappearance, to remember that the world cyclically and inexorably changes. Béla Tarr's cinema cannot be limited to a pessimistic contemplation of humans and their environment, it is rather ecological resistance. (Bayon 2016, 52)[6]

Tarr brings us to the time after the destruction and shows us how we arrived at the calamity.

What Bayon alludes to is the potential for an ecocritical reading of Tarr's films. While we will not propose a rigid theoretical interpretation here, it may be useful to review some theories that align well with an exploration of slow spaces. William Rucekert first used the term "ecocriticism" in a 1978 essay, "Literature and Ecology: An Experiment in Ecocriticism." Ecocritical approaches to film and other media have accelerated after the turn of the millennium. Furthermore, ecocriticism seems to be of interest to a fair number of geologists and geographers as well as literary and film scholars. With ecocriticism, some forms of ethical stance lend themselves very well. The European Association for the Study of Literature, Culture and Environment, the professional organization for those interested in exploring ecocritical perspectives, notes that "the common ground on which all strands of ecocriticism stand is the assumption that the ideas and structures of desire which govern the interactions between humans and their natural environment (including, perhaps, most crucially, the very distinction between the human and the non-human) are of central importance if we are to get a handle on our ecological predicament." Ecocriticism provides frameworks for exploring the natural world as portrayed in film and literature, but Tarr's films rarely put the viewer into the center of a debate about our ecological predicament. We have already despoiled our surroundings, and this demoralizing environment mirrors our neglect of human relationships. Adrian J. Ivakhiv writes about the ecologies of the moving image, and he wishes to remind us, through the use of the term "ecologies," of the context within which the images in the film were created. He notes that the movements of the moving image "unfold in a series of contexts—that is, in relational ecologies that connect us all the way back to the places from which their raw materials were sourced and where they were crafted into manufactured works" (2013, 5). Perhaps these comments could guide an analysis of Tarr's geographic locations and their ecological implications. The natural world exists outside the human not only as an oppositional force to be nurtured, or tamed, or subjugated but also as a reflection of the human. Tarr's places manifest this dual exteriority and interiority. Tarr suggests that our geographic condition mirrors our human conditions just as this ecological framework and the Anthropocene itself suggest a human influence on the epoch.

Closely related to ecocriticism, geocriticism studies places in literary and artistic works. Geocritical approaches to a text do not necessarily relate the locations to current ecological concerns about destruction and possible salvation of the natural world by humans. Instead, within an artistic work, one is led to compare locations from one work to the other to understand its importance. In some senses, like a geographic survey, the reader plots out the places in a series of texts from the same author, for example, to see patterns and recognize important thematic connections. These patterns can create a map to visually plot out spatial or thematic relationships. Maps allow for bringing our external reality into focus before our eyes, and hopefully mapping types of locations in Tarr's films will help us understand larger concerns in his films. Building off one of the mainstays of literary scholarship—reading places in the text to understand their importance—the geocritical approach brings a social-scientific framework to the process and brings fresh perspectives to reading texts and images. In 2007, Bertrand Westphal noted that "Geocriticism is not confined to the study of the representation of the Other, perceived in a monological environment" (2007, 113). It involves the confrontation of several points of view and assures that the representation of space comes from reciprocal creation and is not simply a one-way activity. The geocritical approach shows that spaces are often transgressive, crossing the boundaries of established norms while also reestablishing new relations among people, places, and things. Tarr's work does lend itself to this type of examination since there are some types of physical landscapes that recur in several of his films: "the claustrophobic apartment" or "the deserted square" reappears in several films, and may provide a map indicative of human activity. Through the slow camera lens, these places and their emptiness increase feelings of isolation, of desperation. Tarr's scarred landscapes contain traces of previous human interaction and show the transgressions of peoples that continue to influence the current situation.

Some of the most promising scholarly frameworks for a study of Tarr reside at the intersection of geo- and ecocriticism. Robert T. Tally Jr. and Christine M. Battista's introduction to the volume on the connection between eco- and geocriticism desires to show that "space is of the upmost social important . . . . While distinctive in meaningful ways, both ecocriticism and geocriticism share a concern for the manner in which spaces and places are perceived, represented, and ultimately used." The authors see that once stable, fixed spatial and environmental markers are increasingly showing their volatility and thus undermining the distinction between the social and the natural worlds (2016, 2). The present circumstances show the artificiality of the current organization of real and imagined spaced (2016, 3). They present overlapping territories and provide the intersection between mapping and ecology (2016, 7). They state that the geocritical approach, born more of cartography and other now-surpassed geographic iconographic techniques such as the inherently colonial aspect of map making, often lacks the political overtones of the ecocritical approach.[7] For Tally and Battista, "a jointly ecocritical and geocritical approach offers a more sophisticated line of inquiry that examines the intersections between mapping and ecology" (2016, 7) thus bringing the political back into the intersection between space, place, mapping, and literature. Continuing in an effort to link eco- and geocritical approaches, Eric Prieto states that "Westphal, and those of us working in his wake, build on this cross-disciplinary effort to bring together humanistic and social scientific modes of inquiry" (2016, 22) showing that a discussion of the meaning spaces contain can benefit from a multidimensional, theoretically polyvalent approach. Tarr's films allow spaces to resonate with meanings and they can be categorized and assessed as reflections of the humans that inhabit them. His visual insistence on certain types of landscapes, places, and objects allows us to find a framework for understanding his films through their places.

The emphasis on mapping in geocriticism proves important for the current project. It allows a visualization of recurring elements, their shape, and their nuances from film to film. These spaces often contain humans who become part of the mapped landscape elements. As geocriticism allows us to do, we can trace how the same locations (the cramped apartment, the forest) recur, modulate, but often mirror the anguished existences of the film's characters. And no matter how filled with animate beings, these spaces reinforce the loneliness and isolation of the characters more often than not. Almost never spaces of quiet contemplation, revelry, or happiness, spaces become loci for loneliness.

As we will see in this study, Teréz Vincze gives primacy to space in Tarr's films. She notes that both his cinematic language and his artistic concept assign a significant role to three-dimensional space, which is revealed through long, complicated camera movements paying special attention to landscapes and the environment (2012, 20). Even his cameraman noted that in this relationship to space, he and Tarr connected:

> According to Kelemen, the secret of the success of the creative relationship between them is that, among other things, they share a very similar sensual relationship to physical space. The relationship between the human body and space, as well as the coordination of all this with the movement of the camera, is the essence of their joint work; these are the kind of problems they talk about while making the film, never about intellectual, philosophical issues. (2012, 21)[8]

As we shall see in the next chapter, this connection, and the reality of locations both man-made and natural, is enhanced through the slow camera.

Ginn's examination of *The Turin Horse* referenced earlier sees the film's connection to real-world ecological issues, for example, the damaging power of fossil fuels alluded to with the omnipresent lamp, and the general absence of the sun, shrouded in wind-blown dust. Ginn looks at the horse at the center of the film and its interaction with humans and declares it really signals our capitulation to fate as it is the first creature in the film to stop eating, a precursor to the humans' lack of food and therefore the total darkness that envelopes the screen at the end. He sees a philosophical turn to this film which may be indicating we need to rise up to fight the forces against us. The Anthropocene as an epoch has at its center the destruction of humans and of the natural world as we have known it. We are doomed, as the characters in this film are doomed, unless there is action to stop the destruction. Tarr might not go as far as Ginn in his ecological activism, but Ginn's contention that the earth has become sensitive remains true to Tarr's ruined, rain-drenched places, inhabited by beaten-down, lonely people.

OUR ROADMAP

The framework provided earlier allows us to contextualize the discussion that will unfold in subsequent chapters. This book has as its intention to talk about ecologically and geographically meaningful elements in Tarr's oeuvre from the aspect of place, spaces, and time. For that reason, the chapters are organized according to a logic of spaces.

The next chapter will discuss Tarr's filmic career in part within the scope of Hungarian cinema (although by no means an attempt at an exhaustive review). As we shall see, he produced feature films, a TV series, and a few shorts.[9] He declared his retirement in 2011, but in 2019 produced a documentary, *Missing People*. This film presents a genre departure for Tarr and will be considered only briefly. In the interview he granted for this book, he mentions other new installations and projects. This chapter will also provide a quick review of slow cinema techniques and other slow cinema masters, including Antonioni, Bergman, Tarkovsky, Jancsó, and Angelopoulos, to allude to how they dealt with ecological and geographical realities in their films.

The following chapter will talk about indoor spaces, the kinds that tend to be part of Tarr's works. In all his films, he often uses similar types of indoor spaces to highlight the plight or the defects of the people who inhabit them. We shall examine works from ecological and geocritical perspectives, whether it be looking at how nature is portrayed, or exploring how ecology becomes the subject of the work of art. Tarr's films tend to be set in certain types of interior spaces that recur from film to film, spanning the decades, and the repetition of these spaces from one film to the other makes them part of Tarr's filmic mapping. Dwellings, stark or luxurious apartments, taverns (*kocsmak*), and bureaucratic offices make up the majority of Tarr's interiors. In a very few films, signal boxes (figure 1.1)[10] or barns create liminal spaces to be inhabited on the fringes of primary dwellings.

The humans and animals that live and work there are influenced by their narrowness or expansiveness, and their poverty or relative luxury, and the people, in turn, influence their surroundings. Tarr's camera lingers on objects in disarray, the haggard faces of people, and their worn-out condition. The signal boxes and barns tend to be spaces into which humans intrude and where they cannot set down roots. Barns and their very sparse animal inhabitants create a space for human-animal interaction in heightened desperation. Interior spaces create an ecology of claustrophobia, in some sense, as characters struggle to escape, or remain trapped, by their surroundings.

Figure 1.1 Maloin with the Signal Box in the Background. Screen capture October 7, 2020. *The Man from London* DVD.

Outdoor spaces take up the following chapter, where we also tend to see some recurrences. Tarr's landscapes, often sparse and forbidding, are set in a very dreary reality. Be they natural spaces or open fields, forests, or man-made outdoor spaces like central squares and gravel-filled lots, their desolation emphasizes human misery. From winter fields filled with mud lying fallow, to roads going nowhere toward a gray horizon, to town squares in the fog, these nearly empty spaces fill his films with foreboding and allow the viewer to see how humans are dwarfed and, in some sense, doomed before they even act.

Animals are present in his films and their repeated appearance and limited variety leads to the potential for symbolic meaning. Since Tarr's films often explore the existential difficulties between humans, the animals in his films are almost always domestic. These fellow creatures who inhabit the same dreary geography provide a possible added ecological reading of his films. Animals mirror the unhappiness of the characters. Barking dogs in the coal pit in *Damnation* (*Kárhozat* 1987), the dead whale lying in the trailer in the town's central square in *Werckmeister Harmonies* (*Werckmeister harmóniák* 2000), the almost ten-minute-long sequence of cows in the rain in a muddy field to begin *Satan's Tango* (*Sátántangó* 1994), and the "star" of his last film *The Turin Horse* fit into the deserted, desolate spaces and interact, or ignore, humans to round out an ecology of Tarr's filmic geography.

In the next chapter, I look at some of Tarr's non-feature productions, which show similarities and differences from the other works under consideration. Two short films, *Hotel Magnézit* (1978) and *Journey on the Plain* (*Utazás az*

Alföldön 1995), provide very different mise-en-scènes. The first, produced before the fall of communism, continues Tarr's use of stark interiors with claustrophobic enclosures that mirror, or exacerbate, the loneliness of the characters trapped in the hotel. *Journey on the Plain* superimposes the words of one of Hungary's greatest Romantic poets, Sándor Petőfi, as a mournful counterpoint to the summer's richness. Here nature is real, not constructed, as the camera lingers on different landscapes. Both of these films stand alone but continue and extend the theoretical issues presented in the chapters exploring his feature films.

Tarr also produced two short films that were episodes in longer feature films: a segment in *City Life* (1990) entitled *The Last Boat* (*Az utolsó hajó*), and *Prologue*, an episode in *Visions of Europe* (2004). *The Last Boat* journeys along the Danube, ferrying passengers as twilight closes the horizon from view. *Prologue* presents a single shot in which a line of mostly men is queuing for a handout, a reflection on Hungary's admission, along with nine other countries, to the European Union in 2004. Bringing himself out of self-imposed retirement, Tarr produced a documentary, *Missing People*, in 2019. Even in this film ostensibly portraying "reality," Tarr focuses his lens on issues that have filled his feature films and his shorter works. Examining these non-feature Tarr creations will provide important contrasts to his full-length films, but the undertone remains the difficulties of human relationships and how geographical and ecological elements reflect and refract those difficulties.

A note on titles: in this study, I will refer to Tarr's films by the titles usually used in English after having noted the original Hungarian. *Sátántangó* is often referred to in English as *Satantango* without accent marks. In keeping with full translations for the other film titles, I will refer to it as some other studies do, *Satan's Tango*. Also, I will use transliterations into the Latin alphabet to cite the Greek or Russian titles of films originally written in the Greek or Cyrillic alphabets.

Besides an appendix of poetry, a conclusion and a bibliography, the manuscript will include a filmography with details of the films Tarr directed. The filmography will make it possible to move right into the topics at hand in the chapters with only minimal paraphrasing of plots or film specifics and will hopefully be useful to those readers who may be less familiar with Tarr's works. For the first time to my knowledge in a study on Tarr's films, I reproduce the full Hungarian texts and English translations of Petőfi's poems narrating *Journey on the Plain* in appendix A, listed in the order in which they appear in the film (which is not their chronological order of composition or their alphabetical order). These poems also appear in the bibliography in the order in which they appear in the film. In this way, analysis of these poems will follow the logic Tarr anticipated by placing them where he did in the film.

Appendix B includes an interview I had with the director late in the process of revising this book. This interview confirmed some of my readings, and also opened my eyes to an important potential emphasis of this work: loneliness reappears in so many of his works, in different ways. This isolation I now see is exacerbated by the physical spaces the characters inhabit. We can provide a map of these places because variations of the same types of structures or outdoor locations reappear from film to film. This will allow us to show continuity in his work in a way that some studies de-emphasize in favor of highlighting changes in Tarr's directorial style and techniques through phases of his career. As I learned in the interview, some locations and films were born of grief, longing, or loneliness. Tarr insisted with me, has always insisted, that rhetorical devices are the purview of literature and that films are real. I will respect in great part this vision, providing a map rather than a symbolic connection between films. Mapping the types of structures, the varieties of landscapes, and the limited number of animals in his films—a taxonomy of sorts to use a scientific rather than a literary term—will allow us to see deeply into the human interaction with what surrounds us.

I hope readers will find this list and these chapters useful as they come with me to briefly inhabit Tarr's slow spaces and their geographies of indifference.

NOTES

1. Translations of critical works in French not yet available in English are mine, as are some film dialogue quotes from the Italian, as noted throughout the book. The translator of Hungarian articles is noted in the bibliography.

2. Tout lieu a un visage . . . Le lieu est un personnage principal.

3. D'une ontologie à une cosmologie, associé à une pesanteur qui engourdit et pétrifie les êtres.

4. Le souci écologique du cinéma de Béla Tarr n'a-t-il rien des problématiques alarmistes sur la mise en danger de l'environnement. Il est la *vision* d'un paysage en perdition, lequel traduit la tentative sérieuse, quoique vaine, de demeurer au monde.

5. Il semble que la démarche écologique de Béla Tarr réside dans cet accès, par l'image cinématographique, à une vision du désastre écologique en ce qu'il rend sensible la déshabitation du monde, l'impossibilité d'y *demeurer*.

6. Il s'agit moins d'enregistrer le paysage que sa perte, pour se souvenir que le monde se *métamorphose* de manière cyclique, inéluctablement. Le cinéma de Béla Tarr, qu'on ne saurait limiter totalement à la contemplation pessimiste de l'humain et de son environnement, se fait alors résistance écologique.

7. Brian Friel's play *Translations* (1980) is an example of the literary critiques of mapmaking. In the play, British mapmakers come to an Irish village to chart the location, which amounts, however, to "translating" the places into English and thus erasing them as places with autochthonous meaning.

8. Szerinte a kettőjük közti alkotói kapcsolat sikerének titka, hogy többek között nagyon hasonló a fizikai térhez kötődő érzéki viszonyuk. Az emberi test és a tér viszonya, valamint mindennek a kamera mozgásával való összehangolása a lényege közös munkájuknak, ilyen jellegű problémákról beszélgetnek a film készítése során és sohasem intellektuális, filozófiai kérdésekről.

9. The present study includes films that Tarr directed, but not all those in which he was involved.

10. In *The Man from London*, the structure in which Maloin watches over the harbor and train has been translated alternately as a "lighthouse," "tower," or "signal box" (figure 1.1). In Georges Simenon's novel on which the film is based, *L'Homme de Londres*, Maloin climbs a ladder to get to his workplace, "le perchoir" because "il était aiguilleur" (the perch/station/He was a rail switcher) (9). Maloin's workspace differs from that of others who also work in "une cabine vitrée" (a windowed cabin) because he works in a "gare maritime" (maritime station) rather than a railway train station. For that reason, I will use "signal box" to refer to the structure where Maloin works, based also on Erik Beranek's translation in Jacques Rancière's *Béla Tarr, The Time After* (translations by Clara Orban).

Chapter 2

Slow Cinema, Tarr's Places, and Hungarian Cinema

By extending the temporal vector in his films, Tarr's long takes, developed over the course of his career, allow the viewer to contemplate the geographic contours and locales in his works. These locations provide an ecology of human relationships in the sense that they reflect human dynamics, and the interconnectedness of humans to their surroundings and to each other. Slow cinema techniques allow Tarr to emphasize places and the creatures that inhabit them. Jacques Rancière has masterfully traced the temporal vector in Tarr's works, shaping his reading on archetypes and stylemes. This especially useful approach brought to light the importance of slow cinema as a vehicle through which we watch Tarr's world unfold (Rancière 2013). This world is also shaped by recurring locales, somewhat limited in their scopes as characters find themselves in places that seem to be variations on an ontological theme.

Emphasis on physical space and how humans interact reveals meanings structuring the human relationships in the films. It also allows for examination of how interior and exterior space constructs, constricts, restricts, or nurtures interactions between humans and other creatures. Taking inspiration from David Ingram, we could ask about the uses of animals in these movies—are they seen as themselves or only in their utility for human beings (food, transportation, etc.) (143). The basis for an analysis of Tarr's geography and its ecological implications is the continuous use of long takes, an important element of slow cinema.

Chapter 2

SLOW CINEMA

Slow cinema and the extension of time in film places emphasis on physical space. Our attention is drawn to the object on which the camera lingers. Film's inherent movement provides an ideal medium in which to elongate time because only the progression of stills through time provides the illusion of movement. The ancient notion of unities of time, place, and action already wished to distill the audience's perception of time to create the illusion of reality. Aristotle's *Poetics* provided the first interpretation of unities, an idea that was brought to one of its most developed levels in the French classical theater of Jean Racine and Pierre Corneille. Theatrical productions that provided unity would allow the spectator to enter into the theatrical universe and be included within the three walls of the theatrical stage by being immersed in the same spatiotemporal framework of action. Plays which provide action that takes place in a limited number of spaces and seemingly within a few hours allow for the illusion of reality because the time the audience spends in front of the performance corresponds to the time during which the action takes place. The limited locales allow for the illusion of inhabiting the space on stage. In the same way, the minimal editing and framing typical of slow cinema allows the "action" to pass before the viewers eyes as if in real time. Sequences where the static camera records the action passing before it allow the audience to perceive what a solitary stationary observer would from a limited point of view. Tarr, and other slow cinema masters, allow the viewer's gaze to concentrate, often simulating real time.

Slow cinema is a term used to describe the work of certain filmmakers who emphasize time, who make time noticeable. Not really a structured movement such as neorealism, some characteristics of these films include the length of the shot, use of ambient noise or field recordings, and a sense of mystery. In *Motion(less) Pictures*, Justin Remes notes that slow cinema, "motion pictures without motion," usually features no camera movement and little or no movement within the frame. This type of cinematic construction blurs the lines between moving and static arts (Remes 2015, 3). His study credits Walter Ruttmann's *Weekend* (*Wochenende* 1930) as the first truly "slow" cinematic creation. He reminds us that stasis was part of cinema from its earliest inception, even in the Lumière brothers' first short (Remes 2015, 5).

Tiago de Luca and Nuno Barrados Jorge in their "Introduction" to the book *Slow Cinema* note:

> Though slowness may be identified as a constitutive temporal feature of previous films, schools and traditions, the notion has gained unprecedented critical valence in the last decade. One of the first to coin the expression "cinema of slowness" was the French film critic Michel Ciment in 2003, citing as

exemplary of this trend directors such as Béla Tarr (Hungary), Tsai Ming-liang (Taiwan) and Abbas Kiarostami (Iran). (2016, 1)

Quoting Matthew Flanagan, they also recognize in this type of cinema "'the employment of (often extremely) long takes, de-centered and understated modes of storytelling, and a pronounced emphasis on quietude and the everyday'" (1).

Tarr's name appears very often in studies of slow cinema, and he is identified as one the most important contemporary master of the style. Ira Jaffe, for example, examines Tarr's work in the context of his overall exploration of slow cinema. Jaffe notes that slow movies are slow by virtue of their visual style and thematic structure; they do not represent a genre but rather a cinema of modestly fixed camera, taciturn, isolated characters, and vague narrative, long or super long takes, action unfolding in real time, framed tableau shots, hyperrealism, and de-dramatization. Jaffe concentrates part of his study specifically on Tarr and notes that, different from some other directors known for their slow cinematic contributions, Tarr's characters often reside in nameless wastelands. Tarr tends to make films in which individuals and societies do not easily improve their lot (Jaffe 2014, 14). Yet in Tarr's stringent cinema "not just time looms larger as action is displaced or diminished; cinematic form itself comes to the fore in a new way. A cut, camera move, slant of light, the texture of a wall, the posture of a character—all become more prominent, and afford the pensive spectator rare insight and pleasure" (Jaffe 2014, 14). For example, when discussing *The Turin Horse*, Jaffe notes that "the pace of the film rarely quickens and the sense of weightiness and confinement persists. One reason is that the camera usually moves slowly" (2014, 162) and Tarr has indicated he favors the long take because its continuity matches that of real life (2014, 164).

Vincze has examined Tarr films as slow cinema, noting that the terminology itself—slow, contemplative, and so on—focuses on painting a mood (2012, 6). Already with the release of Tarr's *Damnation*, "contemplative" was chosen as a label (Vincze 2012, 8). Slow film minimizes areas of dramatic tension and saturation of plot and story with action, and can also lead in the direction of a kind of transcendence (Vincze 2012, 9). She states that

> What is a kind of religious reverence for the Russians, for Tarr is a state of mind resulting from a respect for the elements, earth, water, wind, the power of a penetrating gaze on objects and human bodies, and the almost hypnotic state thus aroused in the viewer: secularized contemplation as opposed to religious devotion. (Vincze 2012, 10)[1]

Slow cinema descends from modernism with its tendency toward minimalism, which Vincze see in Tarr's work as well.

The relationship between Tarr's films and any political realities has been alluded to often. Tarr has been an outspoken critic of the both the communists and then the postcommunist Fidesz government, and he spoke passionately about repressive treatments he received even in the United States during our interview. The political implications of slow cinema have been explored in studies about both Tarr's films and those of other slow cinema directors. One risk for Jaffe is that this may make characters become passive victims (2014, 164). If characters can be made into passive victims of circumstances, this could lead to a political reading of slow cinema. Lutz Koepnick points out that "aesthetic slowness hangs on to the promise of contingency—freedom, indeterminism, surprise, and wonder—while challenging how today's culture of speed, ubiquitous computing, and neoliberal deregulation has appropriated contingency as one of its primary ideological building blocks, as part of a new language of inevitability" (2014, 14). The political implications of slow cinema, alluded to here, recur in several studies. As we shall see, Hungarian films, Tarr's included, have often been read through a historico-political framework, at times as resistance, compliance, or reassessment of the country's communist past. The agentless victimization potentiated by slowing down the camera could suggest the powerlessness of people governed by a totalitarian regime. Many analyses consider the political possibilities of slow cinema based on aesthetic qualities. Lúcia Nagib finds a political dimension to slow cinema from Japan and notes that "modernity" is the political project of slow cinema. The very notion of a slow cinema carries within it the presupposition of a fast cinema against which it can be contrasted, which provides an "advantageous alternative" (Nagib 2016, 26). Asbjørn Grønstad notes that, in its contrast to commercial filmmaking, slow cinema can constitute a political gesture, and the divergent cinematic styles constitute a stylistic and conceptual macro-structure within which questions of aesthetic and ethical value might be framed (2016, 275). The prominent place history and politics plays in Hungarian cinema's trajectory somewhat goes counter to Tarr's filmic world. Tarr remains problematic as a historical or political commentator for he himself disavows metaphorical readings of his works. Still, in several of his films, it is possible to detect meta-meanings from the seemingly atemporal and dislocated ambiance.

A more recent study links aesthetic and political analyses of slow cinema and Tarr's work. Rancière writes of Tarr's use of cinema and shows him as inherently committed: "one of the filmmakers most committed to making time the very stuff of cinematic fiction" (2016, 245). In *Werckmeister Harmonies*, for example, Rancière sees that Tarr takes characters "abandoned by history . . . and he gives them back their capacity and their dignity by a certain way of making them turn and of turning with them" (2016, 259). From this, he concludes:

The poetics and the politics of Tarr's films, then, are connected by way of two principles. Firstly, they break the monotonous narration of the "post," thought of as a homogenous time in which everything turns at the same rhythm in the same circle. Instead they construct a dissensus, an opposition to two sensible worlds, which reopens time as the site of the possible. (Rancière 2016, 260)

Rancière understands Tarr's stance here not only as a filmic and artistic gesture but also as a consistent political statement. A world depicted moving in real time, in contrast to the hyper-speed of Hollywood action films, presents a contrasting worldview that could allude to a different understanding of reality, a conscious counter-choice to what is presented as an inevitable accumulation of reality. Whether political or not, Tarr decelerates films, allowing us to contemplate, to emphasize, and perhaps to act.

SLOW CINEMA EXAMPLES—
BEFORE AND BEYOND TARR

While we have seen that critics trace slow cinema back at least to the 1930s, we can find evidence of films that may have influenced Tarr beginning in the late 1950s. In many of these works, geography unfolds through slow cinema to show how places shape human activity and mirror it to some degree. Important filmmakers famous for their extensive use of long takes previous to Tarr became influences on his work. Here we will only be able to touch on some examples, in similar trajectory to the work András Bálint Kovács provided when examining Tarr's early years (2013, chapter 2).

Bergman's 1957 films, *The Seventh Seal* (*Det sjunde inseglet*) and *Wild Strawberries* (*Smultronstället*), very different in tone and narrative from one another, both include scenes emphasizing geographical spaces that provide similarities to the Hungarian filmmaker. In *The Seventh Seal*, extended takes of the wild coastline behind Death and Block, the knight Crusader returned from the Holy Land, is one of cinema's most exceptional scenes. At various other moments, the slow pace the camera establishes—as a flagellants' procession moves through town; as an actor, his wife and child make their way in a wagon reminiscent of the biblical Flight from Egypt; and during the final "dance of death" as Death takes Block after winning his chess match against the knight—provides evidence that the slow camera is crucial to the success of this film.

Similarly, in *Wild Strawberries*, long takes of Professor Isak Borg's dream sequences in which he relives his youth, sees again his love interest lost to his brother, his family home, and comes to reconcile with his past at the end of the movie provide the slow pacing that makes this healing unfold before the viewer and bring Borg's emotional redemption to the audience. While the human movements in Bergman's masterpieces are what he "slows down" with his camera, the physical landscapes in which these scenes unfold reinforces the feeling of time standing still. The expansive, unchanging forests, the seascapes stretching to the horizon, extend our gaze outward, a form of perspectival slowness. The large, unchanging scenery focuses us on the totality rather than allowing us to move from one visual element to the other. These backdrops reinforce and work with the slow camera as they will in Tarr. In Bergman's films from the late fifties, we already see the importance of slow takes as a way to create not only mood but also a kind of real time for the viewer.

Antonioni also lingered over places and spaces especially in some of his films from the 1960s. His career began during the tail end of neorealism, and during the 1960s evolved to include his signature stark, sleek, and cold settings. Antonioni used geographical and material realties and slow camera techniques to great advantage, frequently favoring long takes, with important moments filmed with a static camera. His films often explore the anxieties of Italy's economic boom years, the early sixties, and the malaise of spiritual and emotional meaninglessness primarily of Italy's middle and upper classes. Vincze connects Tarr to Antonioni noting their similar approach to

> analytical minimalism as represented by Antonioni is characterized by long takes that unfold lean compositions, the accompanying sense of continuity, the inverted dramatic construction that reduces the dramatic tension, and the eponymous analytic nature, which is represented on the one hand by favoring geometric compositions and on the other, by analytically separating various dimensions (background against actors, plot against the viewer's perception of time). (2012, 11)[2]

In Antonioni's films, places, whether famous landmarks or anonymous landscapes, reflect the characters' isolation, fears, and rootlessness.

Outdoor urban landscapes dominate Antonioni's spaces, but they are often contrasted to rural or natural locales. Each film features different cities, to different ends. As an example, Antonioni's trilogy from the 1960s provides similarities to Tarr's work. In the first film of the trilogy,[3] *The Adventure* (*L'avventura*), Antonioni features medium-sized Italian cities in Sicily, ending in Taormina. In the other two works, *Night* (*La notte*) and *The Eclipse* (*L'eclisse*), he presents Italy's two largest urban centers, Milan, and Rome, respectively. Antonioni's use of recognizable cities is largely in contrast to Tarr, who often situated his films in anonymous villages. Antonioni's critique of contemporary Italy is highlighted by his emphasis on immediately recognizable urban areas. These cities are juxtaposed in the films with natural or seminatural setting such as parks, golf courses, woods, desolate islands, and deserted landscapes. Frank P. Tomasulo notes the tension between the city and its inhabitants as a central nexus of the filmmaker's work: "thematically, all of the endings manifest some aspect of the Levi-Straussian binary opposition of Nature versus Civilization" (Tomasulo 1983, 134). The interaction of the characters within these different environments is of utmost importance to understanding how the city works within the framework of Antonioni's films.

The first film of the trilogy, *The Adventure*, relates the anxiety of the modern condition as seen through the sterile existence of a group of mostly young, wealthy people. The first scene shows a location that cannot be precisely identified: a diplomat's villa on the outskirts of Rome. An empty background dominates, and the diplomat's daughter Anna is framed against this largely empty landscape consisting of scrub grass, a gravel road, and a partially built housing development in the distance. The natural setting here provides a contrast to the impending, encroaching modernity of the housing project. In apparent contrast to this anonymous location, Anna and her friend Claudia go to Rome to pick up Sandro, Anna's date. Yet, as is often the case in Antonioni's films, even the big city is portrayed as empty. While waiting for the lovers, Claudia is framed in the center of the empty piazza below the apartment, swinging her purse with abandon as she waits by the car.

The trio and friends cruise to the Eolian Islands where Anna's disappearance forms the central narrative, and the islands represents a natural landscape, empty, and wild. Marcia Landy notes that "the island signifies how conventional forms of interaction are pushed to their limit and introduces the major investigative axis of the film—the crisis of representation, involving a reassessment of relations between men and women and their sense of milieu" (2000, 299–300). In an important early long take sequence, the characters walk slowly around the island, looking out over the cliffs toward the ocean, in a scene reminiscent of Luchino Visconti's *The Earth Trembles* (*La terra trema* 1947) in which the camera lingers on the profiles of village women looking out over the wind-swept cliff toward the sea where their men struggle in their fishing boats against the storm. Antonioni's camera watches from a distance and lengthens our view of the friends' search, which heightens the viewer's anxiety. As was the case with Bergman, the natural, physical setting, urban or rural, unfolds slowly and reinforces the emptiness of human relationships.

Deserted urban settings reappear in a village in the mountains that Claudia and Sandro mistake for Noto, the city for which they are searching. As Tomasulo has noted, this town near Caltanisetta has a "near-Surrealist" feel: "a latter-day ghost town, an architectural cemetery built as an experiment in 'functional' Fascist architecture during World War II" (1993, 6). Claudia calls through the closed shutters of a house in the town, only to receive an echo in reply. Sandro, the architect says: "I ask myself why they built it," to which she answers, "It isn't a city, it's a cemetery."[4] Antonioni again slows down the camera to emphasize the desolation of this scene, where the village provides a contrast both to Rome and to the unbuilt landscape of the Eolian Islands; it represents an urban setting that is depopulated.

Perhaps the most discussed scene, the last one, best exemplifies Antonioni's slow camera. The two lovers find themselves facing the bay watching Mount Etna on the horizon (figure 2.1).

Sandro is seated on a bench as Claudia approaches. She stands behind him and begins to extend her hand to caress his head, but does not do so. The camera is in extreme close-up to the hand after having panned toward the couple. The camera then slowly moves out again and we lose sight of the pair as they retreat in the distance, never having moved from their positions relative to one another. The single shot here highlights and accentuates the affective distance between these two lovers and their subsequent alienation, but it is Etna that dominates the frame. The physical markers of their surroundings, the dormant but internally smoldering volcano, represent the pair's internal conflict.

As was the case with *The Adventure*, *Night* highlights an empty landscape, populated only by two people growing apart emotionally but desperate to reconnect physically. For Peter Bondanella, "characters are treated as if they were objects, captured as often by their reflection in a window or mirror as by a direct shot; they are observed in a number of different environments: modern homes, urban buildings, gardens" (1995, 214). This reification of the individual is the result of the bleakness and artificiality of modern

Figure 2.1 Claudia and Sandro with Etna in the Background. Screen capture October 7, 2020. *L'avventura* DVD.

relationships reflected in the bleakness of both the city and the quasi-rural landscapes. For Tomasulo, the film's initial sequence, an elaborate downward crane shot filmed from a descending elevator on the outside of Milan's glass Pirelli Building, epitomizes a contemporary urban hell (1993, 7). As in *The Adventure*, the final scene shows the two lovers alone in a deserted setting. Giovanni (Pontano) and his wife Lidia sit on the lawn at dawn having come from a party where the emotional distance between them reached its peak. They stare, defeated expressions on their faces, as the camera zooms slowly outward. They, like Sandro and Claudia in the previous film, disappear as the camera continues its slow, continuous movement. Once again Antonioni's slow sequencing forces the viewer to gaze upon the ruins of a human relationship. Similar to Tarr's works, in *Night*, human loneliness is mirrored in the empty, manicured landscape as the two people lose their individual traits to be swallowed up by their environment.

The Eclipse features Rome and its stock market as the center of its stylized universe. The city becomes almost an abstract landscape in the director's hands. Buildings and streets are filmed so that their geometric characteristics come to the fore, and the near-absence of people in many outdoor shots increases the physical realities of the materials used to create the architectural spaces emphasized with shots of piles of bricks, construction drums, and so on. Antonioni heightens the abstract nature of the city by highlighting its most futuristic parts: the EUR complex and the mushroom-shaped water tower. Similar to *The Adventure*, streets are almost entirely deserted. Even the natural settings are again very artificial, emphasized when Piero's car falls into the artificial lake in the EUR. All of these architectural elements combine to create a sense of alienation and estrangement. Joan Esposito notes that the prefabricated Palazzo dello Sport in the EUR district, where many of the film's scenes were shot, with its ultra-modern sterile buildings, alludes to the difficulties of emotional relationships in modern times (1984, 31–32). Artificiality and emptiness constitute the modern landscape of commercial Rome.

The last scene of *The Eclipse*, like *The Adventure* and *Night*, provides lingering shots but the camera accelerates to create anxiety from random, ordinary objects (figure 2.2).

These final shots contain almost no humans and instead focus on the crosswalk stripes at an intersection, the corner of an apartment building, a drainpipe spout, and other objects of urban daily life that become abstract objects as they envelope the screen. This particular segment could be a cross between slow cinema and the types of avant-garde experimentations of Ray and Hans Richter. Bondanella reminds us that lack of communication remains at the heart of this film in which phones ring unanswered, and characters are photographed through barriers of all kinds: windows, doors, and so on (1995, 216).

24   *Chapter 2*

Figure 2.2   A Crosswalk That Becomes an Abstract Figure. Screen capture October 7, 2020. *L'eclisse* DVD.

The trap in which Vittoria feels herself, the relationship she cannot shape to her designs, is visually represented by a series of lined objects. The city element most indicative of the relationship of the two characters are the white lines at the cross walk of their usual meeting place at the end of the film. They go forward but lead nowhere, part of a series of prison-bar landscape elements, such as the recurrent window blinds, or the stack of bricks arranged at the building site, seemingly trapping the characters within them.

Antonioni's relationship to objects exemplified in his interior shots hints at the potential significance of interior space. In *The Adventure*, one particularly long take occurs when Sandro goes to the police station in Milazzo to file a missing person's claim. He tracks down Claudia at the train station where she is waiting, alone, framed sitting at the extreme edge of a bench in the corner of the waiting room, distractedly flipping newspaper pages. The frame squeezes Claudia into a corner of the room, overwhelmed. In *Night*, interior spaces are again filled with material goods and Antonioni focuses on them by slowly following characters as they interact, or ignore, those objects. In this way, the alienation of materialism becomes apparent. Even the writer's book-filled home seems devoid of intellectual life once the artist has become a celebrity, and his art has been commercialized. In *The Eclipse*, Vittoria also feels unsure of herself within four walls while Piero dominates interiors. In the opening scenes, as Vittoria breaks her engagement to Riccardo, she fingers some objects in his house, but she mostly paces the room aimlessly. The camera slowly follows her as she ambles from one piece of furniture to the other and in so doing provides an almost tactile presence of material objects before the viewer. The glacial speed of the camera is vital to allow us to contemplate those objects. Twice, she goes to the window to look out as though searching for air and light. The discomfort the viewer feels is made greater by the use of slow camera work.

Antonioni underscores the impossibility of communication by using long outdoor shots with lingering views of characters. Kevin Moore has noted, "to be alienated in an Antonioni film is to be resentfully situated in an overtly industrialized, capital-intensive world that fails to provide a nurturing environment in which the emotions might flourish" (1995, 23). This exploration of Antonioni's films from the 1960s provides a historical link to Tarr's work. Antonioni, like Tarr, reacted to his historical circumstances by using slow cinema techniques and placing characters in physical locations that would accentuate their loneliness. Antonioni's films most often portray upper-middle-class Italians in the economic boom years, and their emotional emptiness contrasts with and is accentuated by the locations in which they find themselves. The slow camera's lingering eye heightens the viewer's discomfort witnessing these often-meaningless interactions. Tarr's focus mostly remains on the less privileged classes of communist-controlled Hungary, with only a few films situated in a middle-class milieu. The fact that his films, especially his earlier ones, look at life in a totalitarian regime make discussions of class somewhat problematic. Also, while Antonioni anchors these three early works in urban Italy by including visual references to monuments, it is difficult to say exactly what the setting is for many of Tarr's films. Still Antonioni's groundbreaking examinations of Italy during the 1960s through slow cinema provide a prelude to Tarr's filmic contributions. Antonioni's exterior and interior spaces all contribute to the malaise that characters feel because of their alienated relationships, a feeling that is accentuated and created using the slow camera.

Like Tarr, Tarkovsky's films provide potential political undertones, often so strong his works were banned in the Soviet Union. Tarr and Tarkovsky continue to be compared: J. Hoberman marked the 2020 streaming release of *Damnation*, noting that Tarr's film "owes something to Andrei Tarkovsky's dank, majestic *Stalker* in its rapt attention to a despoiled landscape, etched on the screen with fastidious black-and-white cinematography" but noted that Tarr is mordant where Tarkovsky is mystical, making *Damnation* something of a meteorological event according to Hoberman (2020). Vincze also noted the connection as well as a nuanced difference between the two directors' approach to the transcendental:

> Tarr's films do not transcend their subject matter. For example, long, continuous movements were necessary not for metaphysical abstraction (as in Tarkovsky) or for the perception of abstract choreographies of human relations (as in Jancsó), but to involve the viewer. Tarr's primary goal does not seem to be an approach to transcendence, but to human experience, to experiencing the—often very depressing—conditions of "being in it." (2012, 14)[5]

Tarkovsky's films such as *Andrei Rublev* (1966), *Solaris* (1972), *Mirror* (*Zerkalo* 1975) and *Stalker* (1979) all explore the aesthetic and political potential of slow cinema while working under Soviet domination.[6] *Andrei Rublev*, a historical drama, became one of the Tarkovsky's most important slow cinema masterpieces. Influenced probably by a great conational precursor, Sergei Eisenstein's *Alexander Nevsky* (1938),[7] Tarkovsky recounts the life of Rublev (1360–1430), a fifteenth-century icon painter, in a series of episodes each introduced by intertitles on screen noting the timeframe.[8] Long takes in this film serve to highlight important moments in the story arch, but the lingering camera often accentuates the pain and misery of the peasants in the film.

An underlying theme of the film becomes the suffering of peasantry and the importance of imagery, including religious, to provide moments of higher spirituality. This misery is set within the context of an endless, mystical, desolate landscape that becomes abstract as the camera makes its way slowly across the frame. In the prologue with a balloonist flying over the landscape, the camera remains trained on the river and riverbank, mostly seemingly devoid of humans or animate objects. The arrival of boats punctuates the scene, but the aerial view makes the human intrusion seem infinitesimal. Horses play an important role in this film as well, and the camera marks them by lingering on them, such as in one scene where a saddleless horse rolls around on the riverbanks. Horses are engines of destruction as well when the Tartars come to raid the churches and destroy the Russian peasants. The camera focuses on these images. These slow scenes are all the more pronounced because the battle scenes use fast-paced editing to produce a sense of violence. In this historical drama, the populations' suffering is accentuated through the use of the slow camera, as will be the case in Tarr, although within a less obviously historical context.

We could here read a critique of capitalism in Tarkovsky's work, and it would bring us back to some larger considerations about slow cinema, Tarr, and his colleagues. Tally and Battista point out that some critics of the Anthropocene want to pinpoint the real engine behind the environmental crisis: capitalism (2016, 6). Zoran Samardzija explains the durational aesthetic we see in Tarr, as well as Tarkovsky, as a way to represent "modes of reconciling with the communist past while overcoming the problem of capitalist realism" (2020, 91). In that way, Samardzija sees that slow cinema cannot only provide a rejection of Hollywood, for that would obscure a range of political and aesthetic discourses. For him, Tarkovsky's rejection of montage cinema was more a critique of Eisensteinian cinema than of Hollywood (2020, 91). For Tarkovsky, consumer capitalism and technological progress are at the root of modern life's spiritual malaise (Samardzija 2020, 94) and *Andrei Rublev*'s rich tapestry brings these thematic threads together.

Solaris seems like a vastly different film, reminiscent of Stanley Kubrick's *2001: A Space Odyssey* (1968). The slow camera in a sci-fi film seems like a strange combination, but Tarkovsky mainly uses this technique to contrast the dacha and the Russian countryside with the futuristic space station. In opening and nearly closing shots, Tarkovsky's camera focuses on vegetation in water, the vibrant greens and blues contrasting with the browns of the river bottom and bank. The camera moves out to reveal a country house where Dr. Kelvin's father lives. Bálint Kovács compares natural elements in Tarr to Tarkovsky and concludes there is no exact or measured representation of the environment:

> Different from Andrei Tarkovsky's works, where the frequent presence of these elements is transcendent, rain in Béla Tarr's films is what it is for the homeless: it makes life difficult. Wind is what it is for the poor: it dries up wells and renders movement difficult. Mud is what it is: the absence of paved roads slows down travel. These natural elements undeniably belong to a real context, but their presence is so amplified that they become surreal. (2016, 31)[9]

This waterscape becomes like an abstract painting, the timelessness of the rural reality contrasting with the improbability of the space station. As was the case in *Andrei Rublev*, Tarkovsky trains the slow camera on the land to emphasize the smallness of the human condition.

In *Mirror*, Tarkovsky produces a different sort of work, with an autobiographical element. Once again, however in moments when the camera slows down, the viewer sees the landscape in panorama or in close-up, an almost abstract reality that emphasizes the timelessness of nature in a world where man's destruction is ever present. Fixed scenes in which Tarkovsky focuses on the early years in the countryside include ripe fields, tall grasses, and flower-filled meadows. In the beginning, characters watch the landscape from afar, and at the end, mother and children walk through the landscape as the film closes. In both instances, the land serves as witness to human activity, unchanged even though humans have ravaged the country. In what we shall see is reminiscent of Tarr, Tarkovsky's slow camera works alongside the geographic locations of the film to produce a timeless, and timely, quality.

Water, puddles, and extended takes of natural scenery continue in *Stalker*, this time in a futuristic setting depicting a dystopian restricted area, "the zone." Stalkers bring people to this area clandestinely to arrive at the room where wishes are fulfilled. A writer trying to overcome writer's block and a physicist-professor hoping to win the Nobel Prize from discoveries made in the zone come instead to realize they are powerless. In the meantime, the stalker himself goes mad, returning to his homelife in the dismal urban environment. Arriving near the zone, the trio find themselves in verdant fields with flowers, a joyous contrast to the stark reality of their industrial wasteland. The meadows, trees, and natural areas before arriving at the destroyed urban-scape and tunnels that constitute the zone are lovingly brought into focus with an almost still camera that follows the three as they move closer to the openings that will bring them to the zone. As a contrast, the camera tightly, unflinchingly follows the three as they move, single file, through the rubbish-festooned tunnel toward the room where their quest will end. Jean-Marie Samocki compares Tarr to Tarkovsky, noting that Tarr was fascinated by decomposition: "it is not the resurgence of a more or less Tarkovskian postapocalyptic strain that we find here. It is rather beyond that world, beyond that quest common to the characters in *Stalker* who brave death thanks to their power of refusal" (2016, 62).[10] Once arrived, and once they realize that they will not make their wishes come true in the room, the three sit, dejected, on the floor of the ruined space as the rain begins to pour through the roof. The camera watches them and slowly zooms out as they remain staring at the ground. Tarkovsky's camera in several of his important films from the 1960s and 1970s resembles Tarr's style and camera work.

Fellow Hungarian Jancsó, a filmmaker whose long career included a period immediately preceding Tarr's first film release, provided other important slow camera films that can be considered in this context. Tarr counted Jancsó among his greatest influences and had a small role in his 1986 film *Seasons of Monsters* (*Szörnyek évadja*). In an interview at the Cork Film Festival, Tarr said that he perhaps related most to Jancsó among Hungarian filmmakers, although disavowing any direct connection. Two of Jancsó's major films from the mid-1960s can serve as precursors for the development of his film style. *The Round Up* (*Szegénylegények* 1966) is set in an important period of Hungarian history, 1848, the year of the failed revolution against the Habsburg Monarchy, which did, however, lead to Hungary's gaining a measure of autonomy from Austria.[11] Many of Jancsó's films recreate historically significant periods but rarely are these films attempts to provide a recreation for its own sake, or as a way to enflame nostalgia or reminiscence. Instead, he extracts meanings from these important moments, which the viewer can often see as barely veiled reference to Jancsó's own time. Bálint Kovács notes Jancsó as an important model for Tarr:

> The plots, as well as the landscapes, are marked by strong local color (the *puszta*, the steppes of the Hungarian plains) and situated in a precise historical time. The world and the stories represented remain timeless, a-historical, transposable into any region and any timeframe. Just as in Béla Tarr, temporal and geographic ambiguity, between universalism and regional individuality, opens diverse interpretive possibilities and allows these films to make sense to spectators from any corner of the globe. (2016, 33)[12]

The voiceover at the beginning situates the viewer in 1848 but the narrative begins twenty years later, following the life of Hungarian revolutionary Lajos Kossuth. The film revolves around the Hungarian government's attempts to stamp out all rebellious units of followers of the exiled Kossuth through "round ups," where captured revolutionaries are taken to a stark prison, chained and beaten, where their women come to give them food only to be killed themselves. Despite the fast editing of many of the fight and battle scenes, the film still contains many long takes of prisoners made to wait in the rain, women being stripped before being beaten, prisoners lined up against walls, and so on. These moments serve to accentuate the characters' suffering and project it on to the audience. Jancsó also provides ample long takes of fields and the countryside as a way perhaps to emphasize that human brutality cannot defeat the land that all sides are fighting to defend.

The Red and the White (*Csillagosok, katonák* 1967), a Russian-Hungarian coproduction, proves a landmark of a new way to produce and market films, although the film itself was initially banned in the Soviet Union upon release. Another historical period of great importance to Hungary provides the focus here, the end of World War I. Set in 1918, the film explores the tenuous relationship of Hungarian troops that came to aid in the Russian civil war, still raging a few years after Lenin's takeover. The film's setting is the Volga River valley. After having secured a victory in Russia itself and assassinated the Russian Czar Alexander II and his family, the Bolsheviks, buoyed by the end of the war, continued to look for areas where they could export the communist system. Hungarian troops intervening in Russia were linked to the short-lived Béla Kun communist revolution in Hungary. Having been defeated in the war and in 1920 to see its empire dissected, Hungary found itself without a solid system of government at the end of the conflict. Kuhn and his supporters, heavily inspired by the newly entrenched communist regime in Russia, established communism in Hungary. The short-lived experiment in Bolshevik government ended with Kun interned by the Austrian government.

This film explores the opportunistic collaboration between Hungary and Russia, when Red communists and White czarists were still fighting one another. Jancsó's camera lingers over the fields where combat takes place, showing the fighters as minuscule actors far in the distance from the camera. As it did in *The Roundup*, the landscape—this time the Volga valley—seems impervious to the fighting and the dying, the one constant element in an otherwise chaotic and futile vision of human carnage. Firing squads execute men for taking liberties with the civilian population, and in this film, both sides are brutal with each other and with their own men. The hospital, which should provide a respite, becomes a strange dance parlor, with troops ordering nurses into the woods so they can waltz with them. This scene parodies the refinement and gentility of the Habsburg and European elite classes in the face of a world that is crumbling. In fact, the fighting could be seen as a futile attempt by the upper classes to maintain their lifestyles, and the strange dance scene shows how this world is moving away from them and that its gentility was really all a façade, quite literally a sick joke. In this film, the ripe fields, the beautiful landscapes, the rivers, and woods provide a backdrop of natural beauty that show the timelessness of the world that will continue to flourish even after the humans have erased all traces of themselves. According to László Strausz, "In *The Red and the White*, the impersonal, geometrical long takes critique the concept of collective identity, which according to Communist ideology is the subject of history" (2009, 41). He argues that in Jancsó's communist-era films, the impersonal long takes eliminate the possibility of individuality. This is a characteristic that Tarr, too, uses to great advantage.

Angelopoulos's career spanned many of the same later years as other directors under consideration here, but his untimely death in 2012 cut short the completion of his intended trilogy. Andrew Horton describes Angelopoulos, saying: "foremost among those contemporary filmmakers who consciously, consistently, and creatively produce films that strive to maintain the pleasures of slowness is the Greek film director Theo Angelopoulos, whose films help us experience and better appreciate a unique sense of space and place, one bridging past, present, and mythical time, which his characters—and thus his audiences—inhabit" (2010, 23). In *Landscape in the Mist* (*Topio stin omichli* 1988), his first film to be distributed in the United States, we view through a lingering camera that allows us to experience the pain of the children's journey. Voula, a pre-teenager, and her younger brother try to get to Germany to see their father who their mother has said lives there. Their journey takes them in trains, from where they are ejected for not having a ticket, to many lonely roads where they find people who will help them and who will harm them. Orestis, a young theater performer, finds them and joins their journey as he awaits his impending military service. When they leave each other, the children are picked up by a truck driver who rapes Voula. The pair again find Orestis but are separated for good when the children take another train for Germany, this time with a ticket that Voula paid for by asking a soldier also waiting for a train for money (the implication being that she would prostitute herself, but the soldier cannot go through with it, leaving her money behind). The children get off the train at the border when the announcement comes that there will be a passport control, at which point they try to cross the river that constitutes the border under the watchtower. As the screen goes dark, we hear a shot as the searchlight has spotted the boat. The two awaken in a dense fog but they say they are across the river in Germany, while Alexis tells Voula a story that "in the beginning was darkness." As the fog lifts they see a solitary, lush tree on the horizon in a beautiful grassy, meadow which they go to hug as the camera stays stationary.

Throughout this film, both the stationary camera and the slow camera work as a way to focus our attention on the landscapes both natural and man-made. The beautiful landscapes of the title contrast to the industrial construction sites, open roads, and highways that make up the majority of the film's settings. The slow camera allows us to contemplate what is happening off the screen, and on what might be happening but away from our eyes. The children's eye view is mimicked in the way the camera lingers on places and oddities such as the statue hand floating in the bay that is subsequently lifted via helicopter and taken back presumably from where it came. This scene reminds us of the opening sequence of Federico Fellini's *La dolce vita*, where Marcello flies in a helicopter transporting a statue of Christ toward the Vatican, and we follow its surreal movement over the rooftops of modern Rome, complete with sunbathing beauties that wave and mouth greetings to Marcello, who mouths back "I can't understand."[13] The melding of old and new, the layering of Rome through the centuries, brings us to the modern consumeristic emptiness that Fellini will be criticizing in this film. In the same way, the hand in the bay in *Landscape in the Mist*, closing around an absent object as though it were a claw, begins to fly above the landscape, above the clouds, while Orestis and the children watch it get smaller on the horizon. This "hand of God" cannot hold, cannot grasp, cannot caress, cannot comfort, just as there is no Germany, there is no father waiting to bring them to his home. This ruined human artistic creation exemplifies the damaged human lives, an echo of the dynamic in Tarr's films.

In 2004, Angelopoulos's *Weeping Meadow* (*To livadi pou dakryzei*) began the planned three-film sequence with a story that resonates with ancient Greek myths. Forced to flee Odessa after the Bolshevik takeover in 1919, a family of Greeks traveling to Thessaloniki finds a girl beside the body of her dead mother. They take Eleni with them as they resettle in Greece. As a teenager she and her adopted brother, Alexis, begin an affair that results in the birth of twin boys who are adopted out of the family immediately. Now widowed, her adopted father plans to marry her, but on her wedding day Eleni and Alexis, a talented accordionist, escape with the help of other musicians. They find their children and continue to move.

History again breaks up the family, as Alexis (a modern Apollo or perhaps Orpheus) is invited to America to play just as World War II looms in Greece, with fascist and anti-fascist forces facing off in the towns. Angelopoulos brings a timeless quality to his historically situated film through possible allusions to Greek mythology—twins on opposite sides of the war, a father whose music could "charm the stones," a weeping mother wailing for her children. His use of slow camera work, especially during scenes near the river, accentuates this metaphysical quality. Very long takes unfold of Spyros, the father, wading through the river where he sees Eleni's wedding dress caught in reeds, a ruse to allow the lovers to escape. And then again, long takes are used when Spyros dies and Eleni, Alexis and their two children come back to the hostile village for his burial on a barge that slowly makes its way toward the houses as the camera moves closer to the gruesome site that turned the villagers against them: Spyros hung the village sheep by their necks to a tree thus destroying the village's future in a rage for having been spurned. The final scene, of Eleni hovering over the body of her man, wailing to the wind and the sea is also a heart-wrenching allusion to classical tragedy. As is the case often in Tarr, human relationships in Angelopoulos's works unfold against an impervious background, slowly revealing natural landscapes that witness the downfall.

This brief discussion of other slow cinema masters allows us to provide the grounding for a discussion of Tarr's slow cinema and how his examination of spaces evolves from important preoccupations in Hungarian cinema. His films feature spaces that accentuate the loneliness, isolation, and desolation of characters, a technique that links his work to those of many other slow cinema masters who were, for him, colleagues, and role models.

SLOW PLACES: HUNGARIAN FILM SPACES, AND TARR'S TRAJECTORY

In his important study of Hungarian film, John Cunningham notes four key phases of cinematic development that closely parallel Hungarian historical reality. From the origins of film to 1920, Hungarian cinema parallels that of other European nations. From 1919 to 1948, Hungarian films go through a dry spell due to the successive political intervention of the Kun, and later Horthy governments. The period 1948–1989 was of state-controlled cinema, which eased somewhat from 1960 onward. Post-1989, there was a decrease in reliance on state subsidies and greater importance given to innovation and market forces (2004, 190). Cunningham's study encompasses the early years of Tarr's career, emphasizing that the filmmaker places himself outside the Hungarian mainstream. He sees already in his early work "classic Budapest school" trademarks: black-and-white photography, handheld camera, a deliberate lack of smoothness in editing, large degree of improvisation and the use of amateur actors (2004, 136).

Situating Tarr within the arch of Hungarian cinema will help establish his place among both his contemporaries and his predecessors. Hungary's national cinema has often been seen as a reflection of the nation's concern with the intersection of geography and political realities that shape national and personal identities. Invaded for centuries with great land lost to the Turks at the Battle of Mohács in 1526, carved up in 1920 by the Trianon Treaty, and again occupied by foreign forces in World War II, the depiction of land, borders, and geographic realities appears regularly in Hungarian cinema. Landscapes may seem inhospitable, the despoliation mirroring a dejected people.

Many Hungarian films and much scholarship of Hungarian cinema focus on time (memory, history, mediation of time, etc.) but land and landscapes, and borders also prove prominent. Some early films were centered in a kind of nostalgic, poor rural setting, but rarely do Hungarian films about village life sentimentalize nature. Many studies of Tarr's films focus on their possible historical or political connections, indeed this is true of scholarly work on Hungarian cinema in general. Given the historical reality in which Hungarian filmmakers had to work, it is no surprise that memorable films tend to have a political or societal message. Several of these films also situate themselves within a particular landscape as a way to highlight the importance of territory to the formation of national identity. In them, the relationships between people bind them, help them overcome adversities. For example, the interwar period the 1942 *People of the Mountains* (*Emberek a havason*, István Szőts) is an overtly religious film, which explores the struggles inherent in an isolated community in the Transylvanian mountains. The poor villagers endure deaths and natural disasters but in the end are saved by the kindness of those around them, equally stalwart individualists who will make a life for themselves in the mountains at all costs. This film has been hailed as a possible precursor and inspiration for Italian neorealism. Given its success at the Venice Biennale, it certainly came to the attention of Roberto Rossellini and other directors. The mountains themselves prove to be an obstacle to the characters as they struggle to survive. Only the cultural and societal bonds among humans can overcome the hostility of geography. The Transylvanian mountains here allude to land lost but also provide a metaphorical backdrop against which to showcase "the people's" resilience, isolated from the surrounding world. The area, annexed to Romania after World War I through the Trianon Treaty and which still contains large Hungarian-language enclaves, became a symbol of Hungary's humiliation after the first war. The film's geographic location provides potential political meaning contextualizing and rendering all the more meaningful the film's central reflection on the importance of human interaction for survival.

Early postwar films such as Géza van Radvány's *Somewhere in Europe* (*Valahol az Europaban* 1947) emphasized finding a place for those affected by war. Reminiscent of Vittorio De Sica's *Shoeshine* (*Sciuscià* 1947) in that it condemns society's disregard for the plight of children displaced by the war, this film continues to link places and political/social/historical realities.

Somewhere in Europe portrays war orphans saved by a kindly musician, Peter Simon, as a way of underscoring the rootlessness of the immediate postwar generation. Abandoned and fatherless after the war, the orphans begin by fending for themselves while creating a makeshift, savage society. The children are seen as ruthless, in the vein of William Golding's *Lord of the Flies*. Upon arriving at the orchestra conductor's castle, they initially try to intimidate him. Yet he manages to subdue them and even teaches them *La Marseillaise*, a symbol of unity. He becomes a benevolent father figure as he recreates society from the ashes for the fatherless children, showing them that unity and order are beneficial. *Somewhere in Europe* is situated in and around the castle at the center of the story. The interiors and exteriors take on subtle metaphorical meanings as markers of the class struggle at the center of the film and the class system in ruins, ready for rebuilding through human solidarity. Perhaps reminiscent of Jean Renoir's interwar French film *La Grande Illusion* (*Grand Illusion* 1937), this Hungarian film shows a life apart from the war—the human side of the war's repercussions. Here, the ruined castle provides a backdrop to showcase the class parameters in which the story will unfold. In both these early Hungarian films, there are prominent indications of places which provide possible metaphorical and political readings of these works. As was the case in Szőts' film, only the intervention of a benevolent human can erase the damage that geography and human violence inflicted on it. In these two films, we see a natural backdrop that presents obstacles, but human beings and their collaborative efforts can lead to renewal. The optimism that human relationships can overcome physical and emotional hardships in the war and immediate postwar period fades in Tarr's films, perhaps as the reality of the damage leveled during the Anthropocene becomes more acute.

Although still firmly under state control, Hungarian cinema of the 1960s and 1970s criticized and at times poked fun at entrenched bureaucracy and totalitarian regimes, films such as *The Witness* (1968 but originally banned; released 1979, *A Tanú*, Péter Bacsó). In this film, a cult classic, the state is seen as a bureaucratic nightmare. Likewise, Szabó began his work exploring the displacement of people and the psychological toll of war in films such as *Father* (*Apa* 1966). In this first compelling drama, a boy, Tako, continues to fantasize about his dead father displaced in the war. In this film centering around the maturing of one emblematic boy, the movement from city to countryside and back again provides a symbolic journey upon which Hungary embarked at the same time the fictional character was growing into a man. The places and spaces of this film provide a context within which the character can claim his birth right, and upon which he can project his fantasies. Places become the staging grounds for the creation of the self as seen in the boy's maturity thus reflecting the human condition. While this film from the

1960s is contemporaneous to Jancsó's films examined previously, Szabó's art style was less dependent on the long take and more so on intricate narrative lines to create an important societal commentary.

Tarr's work resonates within this larger context of Hungarian cinema's attention to land and its effect on people. Tarr's films straddle the pre– and post–Berlin Wall periods. In their complex realities, they often include situations that could be read as critiques of political realities. His feature films include works that explore the stifling conditions of people locked into hopeless towns or families: *Family Nest* (*Családi Tűzfészek* 1977), *The Outsider* (*Szabadgyalog* 1981), *The Prefab People* (*Panelkapcsolat* 1982), *Almanac of Fall* (*Őszi Almanach* 1985), and *Damnation* (1988). These early works include many long takes, but several critics understand them as preludes to Tarr's most distinctive style. The camera in these films often moves tightly into interior spaces as way to make them claustrophobic. Occasional long takes, especially during moments of awkward silence between characters undergoing difficult relationships, give meaning to the technical aspect of the films. Jonathan Rosenbaum's comments on Tarr's career echo those of other critics who divide his films into several thematic phases. For Rosenbaum, Tarr's career includes two parts, films with: (1) an insistence on socialist realism with *Family Nest*, *The Outsider*, and *The Prefab People*; and (2) a movement beyond realism with films that look at moral decay. Between the two was his *Macbeth* (Rosenbaum commentary *The Turin Horse* DVD).

While enrolled in film school, Tarr produced an outlier in his career, the film based on a Shakespeare's canonical text from centuries past that would later become a TV drama in 1982: *Macbeth*, a one-hour production, including only two shots, a short narrative introduction and one long sequence with only ten takes. Sylvie Rollet analyzes this film, which she rightly notes has gotten very little critical attention, and shows that "all the hero's efforts to invent his own destiny" are played out in the first five minutes, with the remainder of the film unveiling the space between the text (Shakespeare's) and cinema, between what is written and therefore predestined and how it will in the end unfold (2016, 132).[14] For György Farkas, *Macbeth*'s non-editing and internal editing within stems from a completely different kind of thinking that can be understood from the movement of the camera ("Zártkörő előadás Tarr Macbethjéről" 2012, 55) for "in this case, the camera is already there, and the characters arrive in a world that is constantly being created by the camera; in other words, they walk into the trap of the camera" ("Zártkörő előadás Tarr Macbethjéről" 2012, 55).[15] Farkas continues that "the series of actions taking place in one space can thus be displayed as a single continuous event, thus creating a sense of continuous present tense, a continuous 'just-happening'" ("Zártkörő előadás Tarr Macbethjéről" 2012, 55).[16]

The end of communism brought Hungarians long-awaited freedom, and attention rightly focused on the positive gains of liberation. Still, it also left many bewildered at how to adapt to new expectations. Following those critics who divide Tarr's films into thematic phases, one could say that his films also changed in tone in his later works, with insistence on long takes becoming a marker of his evolving, and distinctive, style. Following the fall of communism, his masterwork *Satan's Tango* (*Sátántángó* 1994) and the compelling *Werckmeister Harmonies*, for example, present structures of an archetypal, ahistorical past. However, each work centers on somewhat mysterious "foreign" characters who hold quasi-official positions but who in the end become complete disappointments. For Cunningham, the latter shows more a straightforward sense of narrative than the former, but it is still disturbing (2004, 156). Always challenging his audience, *Satan's Tango*—a seven-and-a-half-hour extravaganza—suggests that a village is doomed by the arrival of outside charlatans that the people, out of desperation at the misery around them, feel compelled to follow. *Werckmeister Harmonies* provides a vision of violence vaguely linked to political chaos (the prince who accompanies the circus) and the impossibility of philosophical completion as expressed in the harmonic calculations of Andreas Werckmeister. In the early years of the postcommunist era, then, Tarr often provided images of collapse and betrayal.

His last films, *The Man from London* (*A londoni férfi* 2007) and *The Turin Horse* continue this trend. For Samocki, the former film provides a poetics of capitalism, and "would also be what becomes of this urban poetics in a precocious post-communism. Béla Tarr moves towards film noir codes to give a form to the no man's land that this uncertain political space has become" (2016, 64).[17] Tarr's career is also interspersed with short films and episodes for features produced as collective efforts, briefly introduced in the previous chapter. In 2019, after having declared he would no longer produce films, he worked on art installations and produced a documentary, *Missing People*, for one of them. These post-retirement works are somewhat outside the scope of his purely cinematic language and will be explored in only cursory fashion.

In an interview with Tarr, Jonathan Romney questions the director about the political resonance of this film. Tarr responds: "No, I don't want to speak about the political—I never did. It's not a political question—our problem is much deeper than the political situation. The political situation is just rubbish, shitty things, daily stuff" (2012, 38). While not political per se, Tarr's films explore the difficulties of freedom for a people no longer accustomed to it. While Tarr's films transcend the norm, we can see in some of them a characteristic of Hungarian films. They create atemporal landscapes with tortured citizens looking for a strong eternal presence to lead them, presences that often are revealed as charlatans or violent exploiters. Several Tarr films explore the breakdown of society in which there is a suggestion that political perversions exploit and stoke people's basest tendencies, as well as dense, bleak portraits of stifling families and damned villages.

Tarr has often been asked to discuss his slow cinema techniques. In an interview on February 26, 2019, at the Berlinale, he noted:

> Early on, I noticed that when the camera is rolling, and the whole scene is moving, everyone starts to breathe in the same rhythm: the actors, the crew members, the cinematographer, everyone. You are all "in." And that is very important. It creates a special tension. It gives a special vibration. Somehow you can feel it on the screen too. You become part of it. (Wetherall 2019, n.pg)

In Tarr, geography demands slowness. Through geography and slow cinema combined, he leads us to unthinking, unfeeling man's inevitable downfall, to this geography of indifference. Bálint Kovács discusses "nature" versus artificiality in Tarr's films. In comparing Tarr's work to those of Rainer Werner Fassbinder, Bálint Kovács notes that "both directors depicted the environment naturalistically and theatrically at the same time, their characters were banal, but their impulses, passions, selfishness, and suffering made them extraordinary. Both condensed the dramatic nature of naturalistic situations to the point of unreality." For Bálint Kovács, Tarr almost never lost his interest in a realistic and social depiction of the environment, although he does see some difference in *Almanac of Fall* and *The Man from London* (2008). Although Bálint Kovács reads Tarr's film against the paradigm of realism, his understanding of the tension between artifice and nature begins our journey into Tarr's work from the ecological point of view under consideration here.

Films need to be about relationships that unfold in physical conditions. Lilla Tőke relates Tarr's physical spaces to his understanding of human dignity, for

> human solidarity is a bare, existential need for our survival. Tarr's entire artistic oeuvre in fact testifies to the existence of the outsider in all of us, in our utter isolation and displacement at the mercy of unforgiving social, economic, and even physical conditions. Under these circumstances, it is human dignity as well as a relentless search for intimacy and connection, which demarcate our last, remaining sense of humanity. (2016, 99)

Ultimately it is this sense of the precariousness of human dignity in the face of external forces that Tarr shows us, a damaged world that provides a physical context for incomplete human relationships. Exploration of geography through the activist lens of ecology is enhanced in films that use slow cinema techniques because the absence of movement allows for the reification and magnification of objects. Tarr puts human suffering and the search for human dignity before us, unfolding slowly, within an inhospitable landscape.

Unlike some other critics, who rightly point out shifts in Tarr's career based on techniques more so than themes, I will emphasize the continuity of his work. Tarr addressed this in an interview in 2012 when stating that each film moves a little further, not only stylistically but in a process of deepening. Arriving at *The Turin Horse*, there was no more. Life is finite, the daily routine, getting weaker every day, and that the end will pass in silence (Farkas "Beszélgetésmorzsák: interjú Tarr Bélával," 64–65). Perhaps that is why, as Vincze suggests, his films are filled with people watching. The plots incorporate observations, sometimes hidden, through windows. The protagonist in the films is often some kind of observer (Vincze 15). In the interview we had, and often when he discusses his films, Tarr refers to his manias. Watching rather than acting remains the human condition.

In subsequent chapters, we move to Tarr's exterior and interior spaces to understand how geography, space, and a lingering camera provide an ecology of the human condition. An examination of animals will round out an understanding of Tarr's use of ecological elements to make statements about the human condition. The short films and episodes in collective feature films have been examined in a separate chapter, for even Tarr himself when discussing his production makes a distinction between his feature films, which he insists he will no longer produce, and other types of works. The para-filmic contributions such as more recent art installations will be part of the discussion in chapter 6. Unlike some previous studies of Tarr, I wish to examine his films as a continuum, for films throughout his career provide very similar locations and limited variety of architectural constructions, animals, and natural (presumably not man-made) "wilderness" settings from one film to the other. This will allow us to see the connections in Tarr's filmic production and categorize his overarching vision. In all cases, under consideration here is the effect that the slow camera has on our understanding of how places, spaces, and other creatures influence the human condition.

NOTES

1. Ami az oroszoknál egyfajta vallási színezetű áhítat, az Tarrnál sokkal inkább az elemek, a föld, a víz, a szél tiszteletéből, a tárgyakra és emberi testekre vetett átható tekintet erejéből, és az ezáltal a nézőben gerjesztett már-már hipnotikus állapotból származó lélekállapot: a vallásos áhítattal szemben szekularizált kontempláció.

2. Az Antonioni képviselte analitikus minimalizmust a szikár kompozíciókat kibontó hosszú beállítások, az ezzel együtt járó folyamatosság érzése, a drámai feszültséget egyre csökkentő megfordított drámai konstrukció, illetve a névadó analitikusság jellemzi, mely utóbbit egyrészt a geometrikus kompozíciók kedvelése,

másrészt a különböző dimenziók (háttér vs. szereplők, cselekmény vs. nézői időérzékelés) analitikus elválasztása képezi.

3. Critics often refer to a group of black and white films from Antonioni's fairly early period as a trilogy: *The Adventure* (1960), *Night* (1961), and *The Eclipse* (1962). A fourth, *Red Desert* (*Deserto rosso* 1964) although treating similar themes is in color and not always discussed as part of this group.

4. "Io mi domando perché l'hanno costruito"; "non è un paese, è un cimitero." Translations Clara Orban.

5. A hosszú, folyamatos mozgások sem a metafizikus elvonatkoztatás (mint Tarkovszkijnál), és nem is az emberi viszonyok absztrakt koreográfiáinak érzékeltetése (mint Jancsónál) miatt voltak szükségesek, hanem a néző bevonásához kellettek. Tarr elsődleges célja úgy tűnik, nem a transzcendencia megközelítése, hanem az emberi megtapasztalás, a „benne lét"—sokszor igen nyomasztó—kondícióinak megtapasztaltatása a célja.

6. Tarkovsky produced films during the latter half of his career in the West. In an interview at the Cork Film Festival (2000), Tarr said he preferred the Soviet era Tarkovsky, especially *Andrei Rublev* and *Stalker*.

7. Jonathan Jones's analysis of *Andrei Rublev* states: "Just as Eisenstein asserted the reality of a medieval Russian nation in his 1938 film *Alexander Nevsky*, about a hero who drove back the Teutonic Knights, Tarkovsky asserts the depth and intensity of Russian culture by retelling the life of its first artistic hero. And yet, this life is not made modern, romantic, or contemporary. It is a medieval life, most of all it is a spiritual life" (2004, n.pg.).

8. The film's sections are as follows:
   1. The Jester (summer 1400)
   2. Theophanes the Greek (summer-winter-spring 1405–1406)
   3. The Passion (1406)
   4. The Holiday (1408)
   5. The Last Judgement (summer 1408)
   6. The Raid (autumn 1408)
   7. Silence (winter 1412)
   8. The Bell (spring-summer-winter-spring 1423–1424)

9. A la différence de l'œuvre de d'Andrei Tarkovski où la présence fréquente de ces éléments manifeste une transcendance, la pluie est chez Béla Tarr ce qu'elle est pour les sans-abris : elle rend la vie plus difficile. Le vent est ce qu'il est pour les pauvres : il assèche les puits et rend la progression plus pénible. La boue est ce qu'elle est : le manque de routes asphaltées ralentit la marche. Ces éléments naturels appartiennent indéniablement au contexte réel, mais leur présence est tellement amplifiée que cela en devient surréel.

10. Ce n'est pas le surgissement d'une limbe postapocalyptique, plus ou moins tarkovskienne, qui s'affirme ici. Nous serions davantage en deçà de ce monde-là en deçà, de cette quête commune aux personnages de *Stalker* qui bravent la mort grâce à leur puissance de refus.

11. Jancsó's *Electra My Love* (*Szerelmem, Elektra* 1974) could also be included in this discussion. However it distances itself both chronologically and thematically

from the two films discussed here since it takes as its premise the retelling of the ancient Greek myth. It could be included because it, too, is an example of slow cinema. Constructed of only twelve long takes, Jancsó paces his work in imitation of what we assume to have been performances in antiquity. The crowd functions as the chorus, and their slow chanting and rhythmic movements provide a measured, inexorable drive to death.

12. Les intrigues comme le paysage y sont marqués d'une forte particularité locale (le *puszta*, la steppe de la grande plaine hongroise) et situés dans une époque historique précise. Le monde et les histoires représentés demeuraient pourtant intemporels, anhistoriques, transposables dans n'importe quelle région et à n'importe quelle époque. Tout comme chez Béla Tarr, l'ambiguïté temporelle et géographique, entre universalisme et individualité régionale ou historique, ouvrait la possibilité d'interprétations diverses et permettait à ses films de prendre sens pour un spectateur de n'importe quel coin du monde.

13. "Non capisco." (translation Clara Orban)

14. Tous les efforts du héros pour inventer son destin.

15. Ebben az esetben a kamera már ott van, és a szereplők érkeznek meg a kamera által folyamatosan létesülő világba, vagyis besétálnak a kamera csapdájába.

16. Az egy térben lezajló cselekménysorozatot így egyetlen folyamatos történésként tudja megjeleníteni, ezzel a folyamatos jelenidejűség, a folyamatos „éppentörténés" érzetét keltve.

17. Serait aussi ce que devient cette poétique de la ville dans le post communisme précoce. Béla Tarr se rapproche des codes du film noir pour donner une forme au no man's land qu'est devenu cet espace politique incertain.

Chapter 3

The Claustrophobic Indoors

Indoor spaces with some exceptions are man-made. Perhaps even more so than how humans modify the natural landscape, interiors we create to shield ourselves from the elements represent the footprint humans leave on the Anthropocene. Most of Tarr's indoors are uncomfortable, their shabbiness indicative of neglect of places that mirrors the neglect humans often have for one another. The interiors discussed in this chapter all occupy the landscape but have different functions for the humans that inhabit them permanently or temporarily. Often they can be delineated one from the other in terms of whether they are primarily used as living spaces or rather have a professional function. They can also be distinguished one from the other on a scale of their relative opulence.

Tarr's dwellings include: lower class apartments in block towers, aspiring middle class and faded elite apartments, in both cities and villages. These interiors constitute the overwhelming typology of the filmmaker's indoor universe, the locus of action for the majority of his scenes and his characters. Tarr's locations often include anonymous villages rather than recognizable urban or rural centers. This allows the narratives to unfold in a somewhat mythologized environment, perhaps almost as though in a land of collective myths. Within these larger geographic locations, characters inhabit personal interior spaces, here labeled as dwellings. They often venture out into public spaces that in the hands of another director might provide the possibility of entertainment or camaraderie, places for townspeople to gather, to enjoy each other's company. In Tarr's films, these spaces are fairly limited, the main one being the tavern or more precisely in Hungarian the *kocsma*. I examine these mostly dreary spaces, along with two other types of what I will term "leisure spaces": the hairdresser[1] and the disco. I include them as leisure spaces because, although they are places of employment as well, they each appear in only one Tarr film and when they do, it is the personal interaction within the spaces that are of greatest importance. I include them along with the kocsma in their own subsection because the hairdresser and disco become leisure spaces of alienation. Several interior spaces in Tarr are primarily work related. I will examine offices, hospitals, and factories together, environments where characters confront authority figures. Two unique spaces round out the exploration of interiors: Maloin's signal box in *The Man from London*, and the barns in *Satan's Tango* and *The Turin Horse*, workspaces, observation post, and transparent passageways between inside and outside.

Some of Tarr's films take place exclusively outdoors: *The Last Boat*, and *Prologue*, for example, two short films where the camera never ventures inside, are to be explored along with his other short films in chapter 6. However, the bulk of his films take place indoors, where human interaction can be condensed and studied, and where walls can claustrophobically close in on characters. The interior spaces mapped in this chapter progress from most intimate, where groups of people live together, to those where they interact socially whether for leisure of business (some of the latter being unique to one film), and then to spaces that exist between the human and the animal. Taking *Damnation* as emblematic of Tarr's work, Rancière says that locations produce the characters:

> The real action is the affect that this milieu produces on them. This "milieu" firstly is a historical landscape: the small industrial town which had probably been part of the big industrial and socialist project before being abandoned. We are among the wrecks of the socialist voyage into the future, and this feeling of wreckage is echoed by the neon letters displaying the name of the nightclub, *Titanik*. At the same time, it is a mythological landscape which is emphasized by a horde of dogs. (2016, 246–247)

In Tarr's films, interior spaces are both private and public, with apartments (private rooms in communist spaces, depending on the characters' social class), hotels, public spaces, taverns, and official spaces such as offices, and workplaces such as hospitals, and factories. Tarr's films almost never take place in a location that can be easily identified, in a well-known city or town. Most of the films, in fact, take place in small villages that look the same one film to the next. Essentially every Tarr film contains indoor scenes, which at times may seem strikingly similar to one another. It allows us to trace indoor areas chronologically to see how Tarr uses man-made spaces to tell his stories. In most cases, indoor spaces seem claustrophobic, with the camera panning to highlight either disarray, repetitive objects, or to show characters in some form of either interaction or, more likely, of simultaneous distance:

characters who are assembled in the same indoor space but have allowed themselves to continue to exist separately with only minimal human contact.

As a geographic location, the indoor space contains the characters and defines the scene. Tarr's camera frame tightens and occasionally loosens the physical frame of the room. The camera's proximity to the characters forces the physical space they inhabit at the time to disappear as the close-up of faces overwhelms the screen. The unsettling situations in which characters find themselves, both socially and emotionally, stem from their narrative realities. It also allows Tarr to create spaces that indicate their marginal lives. We have noted that critics often divide Tarr's filmic career into thematic groups but Tarr himself often resists this. With this exploration of space, both indoor and outdoor, in Tarr, I wish to privilege the continuity in his films. We will see that types of interior spaces recur in Tarr (and in the next chapters we will make the claim that his exteriors and his limited animal characters do too).

Among interior spaces I include ruins, such as churches, palaces, or houses destroyed and left abandoned, only to be visited by a character or characters in the film. In his study of organic architecture in Tarr and in Hungary, Thorsen Botz-Bornstein has noted the numerous ruins and decrepit buildings in Tarr's films. Following David Bordwell, he sees walls, especially coming into focus in these destroyed landscapes, through long shots, which bring great attention to the crumbling plaster and pockmarked exteriors (2017, 25). These structures are almost always modern, not historically significant ruins that might point to a layering in time or to a certain moment in national or international history. Westphal describes the intrusion of historical places lifted from their original settings and placed within another context. He would describe it as a deterritorialization, which gives places "a paradoxical continuity by rendering them labile" where you feel "the memory of the place" (Westphal 2007, 143). Tarr's virtual exclusion of recognizable cityscapes, monuments, or ruins is akin to an erasure of sorts, a chronological tabula rasa upon which he can write a new, meaningful history. These ruins show the contemporary setting as being used, or used up, through neglect in much the same way as the characters neglect one another.

A close second in terms of frequency in Tarr's films to the dwelling might be the interior space of a kocsma, Hungarian taverns in cities and towns. These spaces can also include restaurants or hotels (in Tarr's short film *Hotel Magnezit* or in *Werckmeister Harmonies*). Hungary has many different types of locales where eating and drinking take place, indicated with Hungarian words that distinguish them one from the other. The kocsma's primary focus is drinking, and would be best translated as "pub" or "tavern." This is not to be confused with the more known "csárda," a roadside inn or tavern already in the eighteenth to nineteenth century (also of course a dance that was developed in these establishments). The csárda also functioned in previous centuries as a carriage stop because of its location often on isolated stretches of road between towns. Hungarian also distinguishes drinking and sometimes eating establishments with words such as "tavernas," and then at the upper end of the spectrum, the "etterem," the restaurant proper often considered out of reach for ordinary citizen during communism. Perhaps the best-known type of Hungarian eating place is the "kávéház," the famous coffee houses such as the New York Café in Budapest, a Belle Epoque gilded palace popular among writers, editors, and politicians and still in existence today.

Tarr's focus on the kocsma, less folklorically atmospheric than the csárda, is most associated with drinking, and drinking to excess as a way to disconnect, which will be an important element in his films. In an interview in French, Tarr was asked about these spaces, but the interview translates his answers into the French word "café." Tarr notes, "People leave one café to go into another. That is what we call life, after all, and simultaneously time passing . . . if one observes (these humans) one notes that their lives are limited, whether they live in the city or the country" (Maury and Zuchaut 2016, 15).[2] In *The Man from London*, with its northern French setting, certainly the French "café," lace curtains, wooden booths, "zinc" bar, all is appropriate but not in other films. I also hesitate to propose the oft-used translation of "pub" for kocsma because of its English, folksy, rural, connotation to an Anglophone ear. I choose to leave the Hungarian word as the only one that truly reflects the weather-worn, deflated atmosphere of Tarr's public drinking establishments. In Tarr's films, the term "kocsma" as used here captures the essence of this space.

Another meaningful although somewhat less common interior is the "office," official spaces where party functionaries intervene in the lives of the characters. As we shall see, however, characters come into contact in these spaces with the rules, regulations, and by extensions the absurdities of life. Tarr utilizes each of these types of interior spaces as a window into the meaning of characters' lives; they mirror the interior lives of the characters and reflect back at them the hardships of surviving in the system.

Rancière's analysis of Tarr notes that montage takes place at the heart of the sequence as a way to define spaces:

> There is no other means than finding the right rhythm for making the rounds of all the elements composing the scenery of a place, and for giving them their suffocating power or their dream-like virtuality: the bareness of a room or the columns and partitions that punctuate it, the leprosy of the walls or the brilliance of the glasses, the brutality of the neon lights or the dancing flames of the stove, the rain that blinds the windows or the light of a mirror. (2013, 68–69)

The camera moves in a single shot from element to element where "the bistro serves as theater" (Rancière 2013, 69). The sameness of Tarr's interiors and his filmic techniques relate to slow cinema, giving meaning to these spaces and creating slow places.

URBAN VERSUS RURAL

Antonioni's earlier films, we will recall, provide recognizable geographic locations, Italian metropolises, as a backdrop to underscore the isolation of his anguished characters within the context of Italy's post-war modernization. For Tarr, few films take place in recognizable cities: *Family Nest, The Outsider, The Prefab People,* and *The Man from London*. The big city is the first inhospitable location we encounter in Tarr's work. In *Family Nest*, the father talks about how expensive life in Budapest can be to Irén's visiting Roma colleague and friend who is subsequently raped by her husband Laci and Gábor, to definitively show that life in the city is untenable. We do not see any recognizable monuments that could be markers of the city or any indications, but we see city parks and people playing chess, which can reinforce our awareness of the location as Budapest. Otherwise, our only connection to the city remains the father's negative pronouncements, in contrast to the supposedly more welcoming small town. The father notes that it is expensive in the city and that the friend will likely have financial difficulties living there so she should return to the village. The friend notes, however, there are more opportunities in the city and for that reason decides that she is going to remain. In *The Outsider*, characters talk about moving to Budapest, the big city, and contrast it with life in the village. The mise-en-scène definitively visually replicates a small village, the dirt roads, the dusty houses, the empty parking lots, and the long, winding roads in the distance. Here, as different from in *Family Nest*, the city is a place where one might hope to escape.

Portions of *Satan's Tango* and *Werckmeister Harmonies* were filmed in Baja, a town of about 35,000 people (as of 2020) in southern Hungary. The town square features prominently in both films. This town, however, would not be recognizable as would be Budapest, for example, and I therefore do not consider it as a recognizably meaningful location when used in these films. In the interview we had, Tarr mentioned Baja appears only in these two films. He chose the location for its beautiful main square surrounded by buildings representing "a kind of Hungarian classicism" (appendix B). The stateliness of the buildings, with their hint of classical poise, contrasts with the violence that plays out there in *Werckmeister Harmonies*. At the end of that film, we see the square devoid of people as we see it in *Satan's Tango*, the promise of stability and grandeur of this architectural style viewed only at a distance by the two swindlers. While filming in certain sections of Budapest would have provided a similar visual backdrop, Baja's less recognizable location allows the subtle contrast between human actions in the present, violence or neglect, and the implied aspirations of architects of the past who created facades of stability, order, and balance.

Tarr mentions international locations, at least titular, in subsequent films.[3] *The Man from London* only references the English capital in the title but takes place entirely in a French seaside town in the novel. Although Georges Simenon's *L'Homme de Londres* situates the action in the French coastal town of Dieppe, Tarr filmed in Bastia.[4] The man who comes to Dieppe from London is clearly the outsider in this film. In the setting of *The Man from London*, we see the outlines and spaces of a city, a French city. The exotic location and intrigue of the noir motif are both crucial to understanding the film.

In a similar fashion, *The Turin Horse* alludes to a city in which the incident that immediately precedes the film had happened, so presumably the action of the film is somewhere in the countryside on the outskirts. In the *Turin Horse*, however, we do not see any cities or towns. Turin becomes a referent not to a location but rather an apocryphal incident, related in the narrative voiceover at the film's beginning, of Nietzsche's transcendent moment witnessing a coachman whipping his horse. Turin remains far away from the desolation of the film's central house. By the time Tarr composes his last feature film, even his depressing villages have disappeared. All that remains is a house and a barn, locations in the middle of nowhere pared down to the absolute minimum.

Most of the spaces of Tarr's films move around small villages that are hard to place in real landscapes. Small towns and villages provide the setting of *Almanac of Fall*,[5] *Damnation*, *Satan's Tango*, and *Werckmeister Harmonies*. They include houses that could be from centuries ago, or could be fairly contemporary. The element of mise-en-scène that best delineates the action chronologically are the costumes, although there too "peasant garb" seems to have been the overwhelming choice. Men wear felt hats and vests, women shapeless housedresses or faded revealing outfits. The villages usually have few paved roads, long stretches of road moving toward the horizon next to fallow fields, and houses in various states of disrepair. I will explore these outdoor spaces further in the following chapter, but the dusty roads, the endless vistas over muddy, flat fields, makes the landscapes surrounding these villages seem both timeless and deserted, as though they were man-made geographical spaces that human beings had abandoned.

The sameness is accentuated through use of black and white film, Tarr's overwhelming choice. When discussing Tarr's color palette, the distinction and nuance between his blacks, whites, and grays, Samocki states:

A grayish light unveils the muddy essence that defines Béla Tarr's world. It colors the leprous walls, the roads, human skin as well as water, air, and land . . . . The invention of this fading daylight corresponds to a metaphysical and historical political fall. The few dwellings grouped into villages do not even belong to communism anymore: post-communism is already obsolete, faded, or worse, history has retreated from it. *Damnation* still includes industrial activity with its factories that keep running on empty in the outskirts. *Sátántangó* opens with what is left of a collective farm. Whatever the case, the gestures of working are not represented. Community activity exists exclusively as shame, as a shred or a residue. Béla Tarr thus gives the correct, the most tenacious colors for literally representing this specter of Marxism or the Marxist utopia as a dirty ghost. (2016, 60–61)[6]

Samocki's political reading of this sameness also notes the absence of professional activity implicit in these places where, as we shall see, much of the real workday activity characters perform resides in offices where functionaries intervene and mostly exacerbate the difficult lives characters live. This near absence of people doing work implies a helplessness, an acceptance of fate that Samocki links to a postcommunist world. These villages have a sameness to them from film to film, as though it was essential for the director to make them blur into one another. This scarcity of specificity with regard to geographic places allows Tarr's films to seem quasi-mythical.

INTERIORS

From an ecological perspective, Tarr's interior spaces belie a neglect and disharmony in spaces created by man. Houses are at times dilapidated and show disrepair, just as the humans misuse and dismiss one another in the narrative. The walls appear and disappear as the camera zooms slowly in for a facial close-up, as though human neglect overwhelmed even the physical space. Tarr suggests that in the Anthropocene human manipulation of space may have ruined it. When discussing geo-spaces, we begin a map of the types of interiors in Tarr's films. They fall into patterns over the core of each film, and then from one film to the other. In fact, many of the private and public locations are strikingly similar, which creates metatextual webs of references through his oeuvre. Dwellings, taverns, office, and a few other interiors make up Tarr's visual universe, the geography of human misery.

Dwellings

The chronological trajectory of Tarr's work begins by focusing on marginalized individuals, working-class people who do not even have their own place to live, moving then to explore the lives of characters grasping for middle class life while still living in a small apartment. By the time he produced *Almanac of Fall*, Tarr is examining the faded bourgeoisie, depraved, and rotting from within as their carefully preserved objects gather dust. There are also spaces that have been abandoned but that we assume once contained living quarters: houses, castles, or churches, such as both the abandoned house and the abandoned church in *Satan's Tango* and then again in *Journey on the Plain*. Bayon discusses the second part of Tarr's career taking the same position as many critics, dividing it into the first four films and the rest (although as we recall, Tarr himself resists this division). The two phases differ in their spatial expansion. The first films move "from domestic crises playing out in hysterical outbursts, the claustrophobic era of saturation, of the apartment as setting, where bodies bump against one another until they are suffocated" (2016, 47).[7] In the "second phase," when Tarr begins to work with the novelist László Krasnahorkai using his novels as screenplays, these films replaced social realism with "a cosmic formalism, enlarging the frame to the dimensions of the Puszta" (Bayon 2016, 47).[8] From the standpoint of his use of interior versus exterior locations, Tarr's films do "open out" to include more outdoors in his later productions.

Tarr's first films were shot almost exclusively indoors. *Family Nest* presents a grim vision of Hungarian life under communism, based on historical reality. Corinne Maury reminds us: already in October 1958, the Socialist Central Committee focused on the lack of housing in Hungary, and wanted to mobilize industrial production to mitigate it. At the making of Tarr's first film, nineteen years later, the situation remained just as bad as before, which is something Tarr highlights (Maury 2016, 35). The family in question, father, mother, adults, and children, share a small flat in a working-class neighborhood. Rancière emphasizes the way this film focuses on the daily routine, the workday in the sausage factory, taking the bus to work, coming home, and in all of it the weary faces and the close-up of the father's face as the family begins to quarrel (2013, 11). Irén is obsessed with getting her own apartment, and if only she, her husband, and her child could, life would be better we are made to understand. However, one after the other, we discover the deeply flawed, even criminal nature of the people in the household. The mother spews racist comments, and the father is verbally and physically abusive. The friend from work, denigrated partly because she is a Roma and new to town from a rural town, is raped by Laci and his brother Gábor when they escort her down the stairs.

The apartment's interior has few decorations, some plants against the window, curtains, and furniture crammed to make do for more people than the apartment was meant to hold (e.g., fold out couches that turn into beds). The plants constitute a moment of the natural world intruding into the man-made, an instance of greenery in this film, which has very few exterior scenes. Shots of characters' close-up often exclude the apartment's interior from the frame, with the characters thus dominating the geography as though crowding out other creatures as suggested by the Anthropocene. While not yet indicative of Tarr's best-known style, filled with long takes, this film's use of close-ups creates a claustrophobic mood to trap the viewer within the stifling universe of this problematic family.[9]

The TV set blares news of construction of atomic power and plays the music announcing daily broadcasts in Hungary at the time (figure 3.1).

This moment of geopolitical reality is rare in Tarr's films and situates the action within a specific time and place. The paranoia of the atomic age could therefore be a referent for the difficult family, or it could be another suggestion that the family is merely a product of its time, with the threat of violence ever-present. The family could just be a harbinger of things to come in an increasingly confrontational moment.

In this film, action is minimal, with even the violent scenes playing as though in slow motion. Characters verbally berate one another all the while movement is hindered by overcrowding. The dialogue is sparse and only at times becomes heated. The family members seem to sleepwalk most of the time, punching in and punching out. They come home, go out, come back, with only minimal attention to those who live with them. The scenes in the factory highlight how their life, tethered to the machines, has made them into robots. The salami factory's redundant mechanized work environment stultifies Irén and her colleagues, brutalized and subjugated.

Figure 3.1   The Television in *Family Nest*. Screen capture October 7, 2020. *Family Nest* DVD.

The isolation of characters one from the other is highlighted by the use of extreme close-ups throughout the film. Maury observes:

> The filmmaker prominently features faces and makes himself the architect of the word: he structures persistent verbal exchanges and thus lets us see the experience of bodies subjugated by skimpy geometries. Walls and rooms emerge not as simply functional and architectural elements, but act as psychic knots that paralyze life. Oppressed and crowded bodies in *Family Nest* are deprived of all spatial grounding, and in these conditions of impossible *territorialization* family communities break up, are lost, and end up divided. (2016, 36)[10]

This technique also allows the viewer to experience the claustrophobia of the small apartment. The characters seem trapped by their existence as the audience is by the limited camera perspective. As Roland Végső describes it, *Family Nest*'s title "simultaneously evokes the image of the 'family nest' (*családi fészek*) and the catastrophe that a fire can unleash on a family nest (the word *tűzfészek* names a fire hazard)" (2018, 316). While most of the scenes take place in the apartment, the "family nest," the tight camera angles and close-ups continue in scenes from the housing office where Irén goes to see about finding another apartment, an official space I will discuss later. There is no escape, no wide-open space for these people. Only the confines of the "nest."

The Outsider modifies and brings forward the apartment interior that was almost absent in *Family Nest*, although in this film of bohemians, artists, and drifters, there are still few shots of apartments. The main character is dislocated, moving from one house or apartment to another between gigs playing in a band in public kocsmas, or in the parking lot in front of the empty road. In András' apartment, besides the sparse furnishings hang two wall rugs. The visual interest of these pieces that take up much of the background, especially within this otherwise crumbling apartment interior, is in contrast to the majority of the decors in this film. We see it because the camera zooms out slowly as he leaves his apartment, somewhat of a departure from most of the scenes in this film and in Tarr's previous one. As was the case previously, there are many scenes of people in extreme close-ups with characters inhabiting public spaces, or other people's spaces when visiting other people's houses. The clash of generations that was the central aspect of *Family Nest* has become almost irrelevant in *The Outsider*.

One new type of interior location in this film is Balász, the artist's, chaotically furnished apartment; he is the entrepreneur who encourages András to take his music more seriously (figure 3.2).

He has his own beautiful paintings, vases, richly appointed furniture, all piled helter skelter around the fading artist's studio. The randomness of the

Figure 3.2 **The Cluttered Apartment in the Background.** Screen capture October 7, 2020. *The Outsider* DVD.

objects in this space, however, downplays and erases their aesthetic function. These paintings and objects become more junk, clutter in a life that has the financial means to afford non-essential elements. This small gesture toward luxury, to an alternative from the dreary dead ends of many of the characters, disappears because we cannot appreciate the beauty of this pile of objects. He is the first character we encounter who represents another way of living, another possibility in this bleak human landscape.

One other new type of interior location is the completely bare apartment where András, dressed in formalwear, "air conducts" Beethoven's symphony as it plays on the phonograph record. He is on a higher ground, and the only things on the floor are the photograph and record jacket. He is enveloped by the sound and that is all that matters in this rendition of a classical composer gone mad. This sequence again distances us from the dreary reality of the character's lives for the most part and shows us the possibilities afforded by a life of music and the wasted potential that is André's life. Music cannot provide an escape, however; it exists in a vacuum with only bare walls and floors as audience.

The Prefab People continues the arc of furnished flats but this time, the film itself centers on the flat and its inability to become a home. Both the translation and the original Hungarian title refer to a type of rather flimsy, quick, impermanent dwelling, and the prefab home constructions popular after World War II. The Hungarian "panelkapcsolat" indicates a precast, concrete panel house used in the Soviet Union and satellite countries as a way to create affordable mass housing. This family inhabits a corner of one of these sterile, concrete blocks. The wife Judit and husband Robi, parents of two children, fight constantly about the traditional household roles. The mother insists she is trying to make the house a home, but when the breadwinner stays away, her efforts at domestication serve no purpose. The father instead emphasizes that she would not have all the material things with which he surrounds her if not for his hard work. For Carr, *The Prefab People* is "Tarr's most explicit examination of consumerist culture" (Carr 2017, n. pg.). Along with *Family Nest* and *The Outsider*, he considers this part of a "proletarian trilogy" (Carr 2017, n. pg.). In this apartment, the location and texture of material objects is a key to understanding the tension in the characters' lives (figure 3.3).

There is a small fridge, a TV, a bed that folds out in the living room, many decorative objects such as doilies, lamps and lampshades, knickknacks, tablecloths, and a cabinet for good glassware and dinnerware. The first two films were about the lower classes, both in Budapest and outside, while here, characters strive to reach the middle class.

The Prefab People makes explicit reference to political realities. The husband explains a television program to his young son, where the evolution from primitive man to communism is explained. The father remarks that socialism and capitalism are coexisting, although capitalism is a bit stronger economically. He interprets his own life clearly through this lens of what capitalistic possibilities he might access. While *The Prefab People* presents a pre-capitalist vision of people trapped in totalitarian realities, the

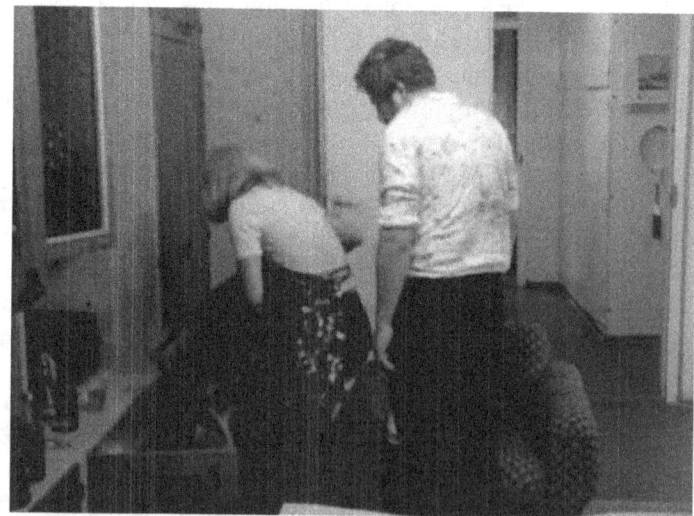

Figure 3.3 The Pullout Couch, Tennis Racket, and Objects. Screen capture October 7, 2020. *The Prefab People* DVD.

main tension between husband and wife is the desire for more things, for an increased standing in life, and the desire for a "normal" family life. Although it would increase their well-being, when the husband tells his wife that he had been chosen for a job that would bring him to live outside of Hungary for a year or two, his wife becomes irate, stating that is no way for a family to live. For Rancière, the unfolding of the narrative already points to the great distance between official planning—of production and of conducts—and the reality of lived time, the expectations, aspirations, and disenchantments of the men and women of the young generation (2013, 3) The pressures of the material world weigh heavily on their relationship as they try to understand one another and their shared situation within a political context they barely understand.

Although neither a dwelling, a tavern nor an office, this film has one of the few stores in Tarr's movies as a way to emphasize that the race for material objects is the only link keeping this couple together. The quasi-final scene brings the couple to an appliance store where they buy a washing machine to cement their fatalistic surrender to capitalism. Symbol of the tidiness expected of a well-run house, the machine cannot satisfy the ill-matched people within it. The husband remains at the side of the screen while the wife and the salesman discuss the various washing options of machines on display.

In the final scene, we see the defeated, exhausted husband and wife in the back of an open-bed truck, forlornly cradling the cardboard box with their washing machine inside, as we see the empty apartment blocks and virtually deserted streets passing by (figure 3.4).

No closer to one another than they were, at least they have material goods. Their facial expressions, vacant and defeated, show the joylessness of having achieved this materialistic status. They are together but alone, thus bringing the viewer full circle to the beginning of the film where a band plays lively music in the courtyard of the cinderblock apartment complex, without the viewer really understanding for what reasons. There are virtually no people or cars in the vicinity, only a few people watching the band from their windows in the complex. Each family lives in isolation, together but apart, in this prefab existence. These deserted landscapes which suggest instead locations teeming with people in their apartment blocks show the emptiness of the material search that will go nowhere.

Within this constraint, the washing machine becomes a lifeline that saves neither one of them. It is an inanimate object that sits beside them as they stare into the distance. When the husband had announced that he was going to accept a job abroad so that they could improve their financial prospects and the wife had objected that would leave her as the sole family member responsible for the children, it becomes clear that providing material goods is the only thing that will keep this family together. Throughout the film, the

Figure 3.4 **The Washing Machine Ride.** Screen capture October 7, 2020. *Prefab People* DVD.

wife covets others' goods, travel, and other exterior signs of material comfort. In contrast, the husband appears as a broken-down grunt, going about his daily existence, trying to better himself but hampered by the responsibilities of home and children. On the job, he plays soccer with colleagues sitting in their office chairs, just going through the motions of making a living. The flat becomes a prison from where the wife insists they escape so they can have things as good as others around them seem to, while the husband tries to shut her out but cannot do so, brought back by his role as breadwinner. The other characters in the film—colleagues, singers in a restaurant, and neighbors—become impediments to the good life, not something to augment it. Like the cookie cutter apartments in this prefab world, this couple and their children aspire to something else but cannot affect the true emotions to move toward their goals. The washing machine shows the emptiness of their search to clean their lives without success. This film shows us an evolution of the living spaces in Tarr's films as he continues to explore the various degrading situations in which Hungarians found themselves.

Somewhat of an interlude in his career, Tarr directed Shakespeare's *Macbeth* (1982) for Hungarian television although it was made during his student days.[11] In the interview he granted me, he explains in detail the genesis of this film. Born as a student work for a final exam of sorts, Tarr's twenty-five-minute classical adaptation came to the attention of Hungarian TV through his film school professor, who encouraged him to complete a longer, one-hour version for television. Tarr seemed to indicate a tense relationship with the school and its faculty and the choice of adapting a classical play was not his in the end. He suggests that his career even from its earliest moments centered on depicting what he often calls his manias. In the interview, he allowed a glimpse of some of them: an open window, a horse stall. Interestingly, they are liminal images, places that allow passage between one reality and another (as Tarr insists that films are about reality, not constructed on literary of rhetorical conventions). In this instance, he was forced to work on a classical play.

For his literary exam, he had just read all of Shakespeare and, according to him, *Macbeth* was the last play he read and the one that came to mind when mandated to provide an adaptation of a classical work for the exam. However, it became clear in our interview that *Macbeth* was selected more than just because it was the only play he could think of at the time. In many of his films—two of which he mentions in the interview, *Macbeth* and *The Man from London*—Tarr is intrigued by intimate groups of people and how they interact. In Macbeth, it is the relationship between Macbeth and his wife, which intrigues him, and which therefore takes center stage. In both these adaptations from foreign literary texts, he "forgot" the play or the novel, respectively, to distill the play into an examination of human relationships. For *Macbeth*, it was the couple and their dynamic. For *The Man from London*, the family and then the life of the lonely signal box worker.

Given that he was interpreting such a well-known text, the spaces, both indoors and outdoors, were dictated by it. He situates his interpretation in Buda castle, with exterior shots along the castle walls and courtyards, while interior shots are of castle passageways and rooms (figure 3.5).

The scenery provides little furniture or other interior decorations to focus instead on the stone of which the castle is build. In this film, Tarr continues to use close-ups and medium shots to signal the suffocation and impending doom of the characters. The frequent close-up of the stone facades is a way for Tarr to emphasize the claustrophobia of the location. In the interview I conducted, I thought I was asking a factual question to confirm the play was filmed in Buda Castle. His answer, factual as well, mentioned that there is a kind of labyrinth under the castle and that is where filming took place. This word, labyrinth, can reinforce the importance of this particular location to film a classical adaptation about power and revenge. The twisting and turning of the man and wife weaving from one tight corridor to the other provides a visualization of the struggle for control that constitutes the foundation of their relationship. Farkas points out that in the final scene, the actors move out of the castle but are shot one after the other from the castle; there is no other way out of the system than through destruction ("Zártkörű előadás Tarr Macbethjéről" 58).

A film that exposes the estrangement of the middle class rather than the working classes, *Almanac of Fall* replicates much of the spatial dynamics

Figure 3.5 The Stone Walls behind the Unhappy Couple. Screen capture October 7, 2020. *Macbeth* in *Satantango* DVD special features.

of *Family Nest*. The endemic corruption of the characters remains as well. The son, János, fights with his mother Hédi and the violence escalates. The housekeeper/nurse Anna is exposed as an interloper. János rapes her in the kitchen as she goes from man to man in the household. By the time Hédi realizes the damage Anna has done she cannot get rid of her. The entire house is poisoned, but from within. In the chronology of Tarr's films, this is probably the first one with extremely detailed interiors scenes, made all the more crucial because there are no exterior shots. The title itself indicates an exteriority, with the suggestion of fall landscapes, but there is nothing visually in the film to bring us indications of the seasons.

Inside the deranged household, there are numerous signs of the upscale lifestyle. The main character is a professional and the son is able to live off the mother. In fact, several of the characters seem to survive because they take advantage of living in the opulent house, or of the food and other provisions the mother provides. The house is filled with beautiful furniture, china, crystal decanters for beverages, and delicate curtains (figure 3.6).

Tarr emphasizes these objects in extreme close-up, almost a tactile rendition of their physicality. Their delicacy contrasts with the unseemly behavior of the house's inhabitants. We see kitchen scenes in which characters drink from fine china cups. The film is bathed in colors, for which Tarr used colored lamps, making the film somewhat reminiscent of Antonioni's in *Red Desert*, although the Italian director applied color to the film.[12] The suggestive blue, red, and green casting to the scenes seems to render the interior even more

Figure 3.6 Objects in the Bourgeois Apartment. Screen capture October 7, 2020. *Almanac of Fall* DVD.

artificial than it would otherwise have been. The interior of the house in this film where there are no exterior scenes, becomes a symbol of bourgeois decay and decadence that is the family and the interlopers in this film, when corruption seems to come from material decay.

Like in *The Outsider*, the wedding scene in *Almanac of Fall* is bleak. The celebration of Anna and Janós's wedding takes place at the same dining table that had been the center of many of the family's controversies, but this time the couple mournfully dances to the song "Che sarà," a fatalistic tune, on the phonograph. The only guests at the wedding are the family members, making it seem as though the ceremony itself is a celebration of the destructive relationships. Tarr again shows us an insular world where exchanges with the outside are few and claustrophobic interiors contain damaged human relationships.

The films that follow *Almanac of Fall* begin to provide greater variation between interior and exterior scenes, but they remain as bleak as those Tarr's had already produced. *Damnation* presents the story of another damaged group of people in an equally blighted town. Karrer, the engineer of the town's coal pits, begins an affair and, obsessed with maintaining his relationship, he tries to involve his lover's husband in an intricate smuggling plot that he hopes will land his lover's husband in jail. The apartment interior becomes almost emblematic as well, when the camera pans from room to empty room lingering on objects that have no apparent significance. The bedroom, furnished simply, provides a space for intimacy where the camera at times pans across the room zooming in and out slowly from the couple making love.

The close-ups show their blank, loveless expressions, while when the camera takes in the room and its furnishings the couple seems dehumanized, as merely a static part of the décor. The squeaking bed echoes the noise the coal buckets make, as though the ruined landscape mirrored this joyless existence.

Various places within the film show the faded interior that has become commonplace by now in Tarr's village universe. Botz-Bornstein mentions the sequence of walls in *Damnation* alternating walls and people staring out at the rain, and scenes in *Satan's Tango* where the doctor spies walls vertically through binoculars. Borrowing from Frank Lloyd Wright, he notes that the camera's slow, horizontal movements alongside walls can also be seen as cinematic exemplification of the "'principle of plasticity working as continuity.' Those slow shots along the ruined walls in *Damnation* and *Satantango* present people not directly but through wall openings" (Botz-Bornstein 2017, 25). Karrer watches out the window of his small dining area day after day, staring at the coal buckets as they pass by. In *Damnation*, there are several dwellings, but the town is shadowed by the incessant rumble and clatter of the coal buckets on an overhead line making their way to and from the pit. From the interior of the house among other spaces, we see the buckets move, always with the same rhythm, although in the final outdoor scene in the pit itself the buckets are suspended but have stopped moving.

In *Satan's Tango*, despite its length, there are only a few different types of dwellings; the village and the surrounding area contain similar broken down houses, which seem to mirror the town structures toward the end of the film when the villagers scatter to different parts of the country. We see the interior of the doctor's apartment, where he finally walls himself up in the last scene. He sits at the window with lace curtains and watches the square where so much of the action takes place, the stack of books all to the side of the frame showing us his learning. The doctor's apartment constitutes the one dwelling of significance in the film, the place from which the destructive activities of the townspeople and the menace of intruders from without (real and imagined) can be spied. This is a film of public places, of communities where people's private fears coalesce into public alarm. The one exception is the empty ruin, the Álmos manor to which the villagers go as Irimiás escorts them to their new location. The almost uninhabitable interior echoes the ruined lives as Irimiás prepares to conclude his swindle.

In *Werckmeister Harmonies*, there are the ordinary dwellings of inhabitants of the village, with their wooden furniture, the beds, curtains, and fairly spare furniture, contrasted to Mr. Eszter's bourgeois apartment, with its rich furnishings, tapestries, elaborate glassware, and other markers of his social status. *Werckmeister Harmonies* shows how the unknown, the magical, can spark philosophical discourse (implied in the title) but also bring chaos within an archetypal, ahistorical context. The film, which lacks what Bálint Kovács calls "historical or geographical coordinates," is also Tarr's film that makes most references to military power and social unrest (2013, 131). The viewer is therefore led to extrapolate to the historical context in which the film was produced. Bálint Kovács notes that in this film, more so than in other Tarr films, the feeling of "no way out" is related to a subjective feeling, and the process of destruction so common in his films is here linked directly to the illusion of a superior spirit (2008). He notes that Tarr's films from this more recent period offer a complex vision of the historical situation in the Eastern European region thus underscoring that, despite an absence of diegetic historical elements, this film could be read as an allegory of historical events (n.pg.)

Werckmeister Harmonies takes place in a village made timeless because neither the buildings nor the costumes can be attributed to a specific period. The only real indicator that the film takes place in the twentieth or twenty-first century is the presence of machines such as tanks, stoves, and tractors. There are no allusions to specific, recognizable historical personages or events. The title involves the most important philosophical musing of the film, a philosophical treatise on music. Mr. Eszter, an intellectual, withdrawn from the political upheaval around him, tapes a lecture on musical harmony. He notes that the Greeks accepted the imperfection of their instruments and thus only utilized a few notes—perfect harmony was the province of the gods. Instead Andreas Werckmeister falsified the system to include all-natural harmonies—but by doing so, he sacrificed some higher tones. Music and harmony, therefore, are based on deceptive foundations.

The main character, János Valuska, the town everyman, wanders throughout the village on his mail route as the viewer is introduced to a growing sense of unease. He stages a total eclipse in a bar with the help of patrons showing them how darkness can overtake light. Meanwhile "Aunt" Tünde, Eszter's ex-wife, and her lover the police chief talk of restoring order through a political takeover. The prince, a shadowy figure, comes to town in a seedy circus, which also features a dead whale. Both the prince and the whale prove unsettling as the sense of dread grows. The dead whale arrives in a corrugated crate and lies in the center of town where patrons pay to enter the stinking container. At one point, Valuska suggests the whale is a sign of God's omnipotence. The whale thus evokes the creature in Moby Dick or the beached sea animal at the end of Fellini's *La dolce vita*, both allegorical figures suggesting the presence of God.

We learn that the prince has been rousing the populace to violence in other towns. The prince's followers ransack the town's hospital, stopping only when confronted by an old naked man in a tub, a sort of filmic *memento mori*. After attempting to escape and being captured, Valuska goes to an asylum with caged beds. Only Mr. Eszter survives intact, going to contemplate the whale in the town square as fog closes in to engulf the film's final scene. The central image of the film suggests that universal harmonies are out of tune. We search for perfection but, as musical principles show, slight disharmony is all we can achieve. Disharmony is linked in this film also to authority. The arrival of a political figure, the prince, brings random violence and unrest, his disembodied voice urging his followers to violence.

The whale suggests contemplation of a higher philosophical meaning. Its presence in town excites but seems always out of place: characters express their fear of it. The film's end leaves open the fate of the town and characters. Mr. Eszter leaves Valuska in the institution to examine the whale, now out of its container, in the town square. The film dissociates plot and character from identifiable historical moments in a failed search for an ideal, made impossible because of human imperfection that leads to Valuska's ultimate madness. The postman's optimism, perhaps childlike wonderment, led him to organize his neighbors into staging the planets and their orbits, predictable, logical, soothing, yet invisible realities. Instead, these harmonious orbits cannot be sustained in the face of chaos, and the result is madness. Tarr's film suggests that the impulse for political unrest is always with us because perfect harmony in unattainable.

Unique to *Werckmeister Harmonies* is the interior of the trailer carrying the whale, the central tragic, dead figure of the film. Like many of the scenes of the interior of the hut in *The Turin Horse*, there is virtually no light in the trailer. This is the one interior space in Tarr's films that is completely destroyed. Even the hospital survives the mob attack. In the final scenes, we see the sides of the trailer taken down, presumably by the mob, and the dead whale lying in the streets. Botz-Bornstein considers the trailer another form of prefab housing, the type that was the focus of the dismal family life in *The Prefab People*. He notes that this structure travels through the town in the middle of the night, lands in the center to become a curiosity as townspeople pay to enter and see the whale despite the unilluminated interior, and then is completely destroyed after the rampage, with the whale exposed and lying half in the square itself (Botz-Bornstein 2017, 26). The impermanence of this structure comments on the otherwise other-worldly nature of the whale itself in the middle of this landlocked town. The dead creature's worth is merely that: a lifeless object of observation. The postman goes into the trailer to see the whale and comes eye to eye with it. This scene is replicated at the end when, the mob having destroyed the trailer, the whale lies listing in the town square. This time the professor can come eye to eye with the beast and looks at the monster's blank stare. This unrecognizable creature provides an almost metaphysical connection with the characters, which goes nowhere and Tarr rejects a reading that provides solace for the characters who cannot connect with their own world.[13]

The indoors spaces become quite varied in this film if compared to previous ones because the main character is a postman. Valuska goes from door to door, introducing himself into interiors and the people that live in them. Among the spaces most often visited are his own modest dwelling and that of the professor. He also lingers in Tünde's bedroom when she entertains the commander. As was the case with Mr. Eszter's house, decorated in faded elegance, replete with books, a piano, rugs and other luxuries, Tünde's house also clearly situates her in the middle class of this town. Her furnishings and multiple rooms contrast with Valuska's small room as well as with the dwellings of multiple other inhabitants he sees on his route. *Werckmeister Harmonies* brings together rustic and elegant interiors of previous films to highlight class distinctions, which accentuate the political, moral, and philosophical differences in the community under siege. Valuska also visits a canteen, the post office, and a small hotel, along with a few other modest individual dwellings. He remains at the entrance, the threshold, a visitor to these places, leaving behind the mail as a trace of the world outside.

In *The Man from London*, there is one central dwelling that provides the alternate space for the main character after he has finished working in the signal box. In Maloin's house, the French decor is indicated in the bookshelves, the light, white kitchen with many implements in it, the tile floors, and the lighter-colored furniture. The bedroom has a dresser and a bed that show a sort of modern veneer, more so than the Hungarian interior decors of most of Tarr's works. Tables where food is shared hold a special significance in Tarr's last two films, the stages where family dramas play out. Kitchen tables appear in many of his films, from *Family Nest* onward, but they rarely provide meeting places for convivial exchanges. Meals are often sullen affairs, with arguments, screaming children, or taciturn adults. While we will see that drinking alcohol seems to provide a constant escape in Tarr's universe, little food is consumed. In one important scene from *The Man from London*, the husband and wife fight bitterly in front of the daughter as they sit across from one another at the table. This scene will return even bleaker in *The Turin Horse*, when father and daughter sit across from one another at the table with no food on it. The table embodies the last possibility of human communication but in these last two films, there remain only recriminations and silence.

Phillip Roberts reads poverty in *Werckmeister Harmonies* and *The Turin Horse* arguing that the two films

> focus on the conflicting currents of deterritorialization and reterritorialization that are essential to the functioning of the control society. One film demonstrates the emergence of other virtual worlds, while the other demonstrates their negation and the reduction of all possibility to a wretched world of immediate poverty. (2017, 71)

We could add that the poverty extends to a lack of communication between family members. *The Turin Horse* explicitly announces its kinship with, and inspiration from Friedrich Nietzsche, exploring the life of the horse reputed to have driven the philosopher mad when he witnessed it being whipped in a Turin street. It reintroduces many themes and techniques Tarr used throughout his career. At 146 minutes, it contains only thirty shots. In *The Turin Horse*, the dwelling has taken over for all the other locations since there are no taverns, no official locations, and no houses of neighbors or friends. The entire human experience in this film is from the confines of the hut. In the documentary *I Used to Be a Filmmaker*, we see how Tarr constructed the set of *The Turin Horse*. Great attention is paid to the roof, for example, and to the solid stone walls. The horse barn, too, is precisely constructed for the film in an area where the hill and the tree are of primary importance. The buildings and their structure are constructed with a specific atmosphere in mind.

The driver, his daughter, and the horse, as Tarr imagines them, live in extremely primitive conditions, all dependent on one another to survive, while nature itself seems to be conspiring against them. The final day at the end of the film shows only the two peasants, huddled at the table, unable to eat or talk, waiting presumably for the end. In an interview with Matt Levine and Jeremey Meckler, Tarr says,

> Somehow this is an anti-Creation story. Somehow, it's attempting to show a very simple—"okay, we are doing our daily life." The same routine, but every day is different, and every day just becomes bleaker, bleaker, and by the end is just suffocating. That's all—in a very quiet and very silent way. No apocalypse .... Nothing. Just the simple pain of living. (2012, n.pg.)

In another interview for *Sight and Sound Magazine*, Tarr notes that the characters show no emotions, they all just need each other, including the horse. He also said that "Kundera talks about 'the unbearable lightness of being' I wanted to talk about the heaviness of being" (Romney 2012, n.pg.). In this film, besides the dwelling where the two main characters eke out their existence, there is the important semi-ruined interior of the barn, which houses the eponymous horse. The two spaces are intertwined as the couple moves inexorably toward the absence of light in the film's last scene.

As is often the case in Tarr's films, it is difficult to precisely situate the timeframe, a timelessness both infinite and infinitesimal. In an audio commentary, critic Rosenbaum has noted that the costumes may indicate the late nineteenth century, which would coincide with the incident between the philosopher and the carriage driver. In the film, a cyclical temporality is emphasized through repetition of daily activities (Rosenbaum *The Turin Horse* DVD, n.pg.). The viewer comes to recognize that a day has begun by the characters' actions in the bleak interior. The girl gets up first, helps her infirm father dress, they have a shot of brandy, and begin the day. She fetches water from a bucket that appears in most scenes, either as she carries it, or in the kitchen. In a press conference during the Berlin Film Festival (2011), Tarr singled out a few objects in his films as of particular importance: the bucket, the wind, and the lonely tree. These three, according to him, were part of a constituent system, of a pathological clinging to life, where characters seem to exclaim "I can't go on like this, but then they do" (*The Turin Horse* DVD n.pg.) The repetition of these three elements on screen helps emphasize the temporal cyclicity.

There are only two breaks from the daily routine involving the intrusion of other characters, the one we will discuss here being the only entirely indoor interruption. Bernhardt, their neighbor, arrives to buy a bottle of Hungarian spirits (pálinka). Here, the bleak interior of the house is important as a backdrop to discuss the death and destruction of "the town" that has just been ransacked according to Bernhardt (reminding us of the mob action in *Werckmeister Harmonies*). This is the first of two scenes where characters from the outside intrude in the father-daughter's lives, the second being when a group of Roma arrive and leave (we will discuss the entry of these characters in the next chapter because the arrival of the Roma not only is situated entirely outside the house, it also spurs the father and daughter to try to escape). When the father asks why Bernhardt has not gone to the village, the visitor notes that the village has disappeared. This remarkable occurrence elicits little surprise.

Although activities repeat themselves throughout the six days, every day is not exactly like the next. Rosenbaum explain that one of the ways in which repetition is saved from boredom is through camera angles (Commentary n.pg.). In this film, the camera does not simply follow the action but is doing something in counterpoint to the action. The viewer therefore sees the actions in new ways. Both characters, for example, find themselves at the window staring out. The camera picks up subtle differences in the characters' stances as it shows them primarily from behind. Also, every morning we see the daughter dress the father, but the camera notes new aspects of the scene: once, we see the daughter put the nightclothes on a hook, another time, the camera is positioned behind the girl rather than between the two. These nuances of camera angle allow the viewer to focus on new objects or gestures that come into view, in a way pinpointing moments within the overarching temporal frame. Reminiscent, for example, of the squashed bug viewed from multiple perspective in Alain Robbe-Grillet's *La Jalousie* (1957), Tarr may be suggesting that only through multiple retellings and the multiplicity of voices can the dominance of a single narrative voice take place, emphasizing our fragmented perception of reality.

Notions of time in this film are infinite, with cyclical time manifest through repetitions and wide-angle shots emphasizing the horizon. They are also infinitesimal. We see each movement in excruciating detail. These moments, which force us to focus on individual gestures, are caught between a doomed cyclical timeframe to heighten the characters' desperation. Just as was the case for temporal boundaries, the film abounds with spatial barriers that set the father and daughter apart from the landscape.

The physical divisions of this world of limited possibilities are also emphasized through use of interior divisions, reminiscent of Antonioni's architectural features as frames within the frame. Tarr uses furniture or interior walls as frames, for example, the pillars in the horses' stall, which provide a semblance of functionality in the second building of the farm. In one long scene, even the horse itself divides the frame as it stares blankly in close-up at the viewer. Although the farmhouse is minimalist, there are columns dividing interior spaces, which function somewhat as walls in the house. Furniture and other objects of daily life become the equivalent of spatial barriers, dividing the people from one another (figure 3.7).

The lamp, viewed in close-up at the film's beginning and then set as a barrier between father and daughter, could also be an allusion to the philosopher's light and a nod to Nietzsche. The table is a barrier between the father and daughter. The camera emphasizes this division by often being positioned at the head of the table, looking right down the middle. The lack

Figure 3.7 Washing in the Hut. Screen capture October 7, 2020. *The Turin Horse* DVD.

of dialogue, the hopelessness of their lives that not even human interaction can mitigate, comes most in view during these dinner scenes. Another divider to the room is the clothesline, which comes out when there is washing to do. It is a moment when their meager possessions are on display, as though they are at once extravagant and threadbare. In terms of both time and space, this film provides multiple divisions to reinforce the isolation of the characters.

Among the objects in this space, the book proves a fairly unusual inclusion. Most books in Tarr's films remain on shelves, more symbols of a certain luxury than intellectually meaningful items. The meager existence of Ohlsdorfer and his daughter gives the book the Roma leave behind, the only item in the character's lives that is not necessary for survival, added meaning in this film divided into six days: the entire film is subdivided by intertitles indicating the day with the words "the fourth day," "the fifth day," and so forth. In an interview during the Berlin Film Festival (2011), Tarr has described the book as an "anti-Bible" (n.pg.). When the daughter haltingly reads from it, the text seems devoid of meaning. The text includes passages which allude to retributions for transgressions, where "The Lord WAS with you," indicators that reinforce temporal boundaries that seem limitless. Tarr himself, who was often loath to admit to symbolism in his films, admitted in the Berlin Film Festival interview that there is no seventh day in *The Turin Horse*, because "On the seventh day, God rested after his poorly-done work" (n.pg.). For A. O. Scott, in this film "The Nietzsche story is like an absurd punch line placed ahead of an extended joke, and what follows—seven days in the life of the horse, his owner, and the owner's daughter—is a kind of Genesis story in reverse" (2012, n.pg.). The book, along with the film's divisions, could suggest that human lives remain powerless.

Dwellings represent human beings carving a space for themselves in the natural landscape, erecting barriers to shield them from the outside. The assumption that these functional spaces created during the Anthropocene, which represent humanities' imposition of itself upon the environment would also become places of human interaction is negated in many of Tarr's dwellings. Interactions become hostile, coupling accentuates emotional distance, and objects lose their aesthetic value through neglect.

Kocsmas/Taverns, a Hairdresser, and a Disco: Urban Leisure Spaces

The Hungarian tavern plays a critical role in most of the films, especially as on numerous occasions characters' flaws revolve around drunkenness—or rather alcohol becomes an excuse for a more profound and disturbing lack of emotional connection between characters. In a few films, the tavern appears more elaborate when characters find themselves in a restaurant of a more elegant nature, usually for a formal occasion. This happens in *The Outsider* when András gets married and at the end when he meets the group of Serbians and Hungarians having a business lunch. It also occurs in *The Prefab People* when the couple goes to an office party, but the suggestive lounge singer and the husband's inattentive behavior brings the couple to the brink of dissolution. A further evolution of this type of space could be the flophouse in *Hotel Magnezit*, a run-down hostel for the down and out (to be discussed along with other short films in chapter 6).

In Tarr's films, there is a striking similarity in the establishments where people go to drown their sorrow, whether they be in the big city, in the villages, or in a supposedly foreign country. In villages, the taverns tend to be quite simple, with rough wooden tables and chairs, a bar, a stove that comes prominently into view occasionally, coat hooks or a coat rack somewhere, a few odd plants, and very few decorations. In a few there are maps or some sort of folk art. Many of these taverns are in the center of the village, part of the regular activities of the inhabitants, providing a central location for gathering, exchanging ideas if there are any, and in general creating a community. However, these places very rarely provide any kind of festive atmosphere. They are dark, dank, with dirty floors and walls, often with drunks in a stupor or, alternately, expounding on quasi—or actually—philosophical idea.

Despite their very Hungarian origin and ambiance, these spaces can also be clever allusions to an outside, largely materialistic world of which Hungary was not yet part but to which it aspired. In several of the kocsmas, signs in English, or touting American product—such as Coca-Cola, for example, in *The Outsider*, and the sign that says "Hungary" on the tavern wall in *Family Nest*—come clearly into view on camera, usually behind the actors in a particular scene. This intrusion of the capitalist sign is surely a sly reference to the arrival or capitalism even during the still communist Hungary. *Family Nest* also contains another indexical object pointing to the nation, broken and in need of repair. The mother- and father-in-law find themselves trying to glue a glass-covered crest of Hungary that the children had broken in school. They are expected to replace it but cannot afford to have it remade, so they attempt to repair it, but their attempt leaves obvious marks on the wall hanging. These sly political references to the nation in these early Tarr films, and its conflictual relationships to capitalistic societies, especially the United States, allows for another example of how these films explore relationships of humans toward their environment as well as toward each other in both personal and political contexts.

Some of the taverns are more elegantly furnished, for example, in *Damnation*, where the tables and chairs seem less worn, and the floor artfully patterned, probably since the locale is also the dance hall. In fact, in this kocsma and others in Tarr's films, dance scenes appear prominently. Once again, however, all elegance and social grace remains absent from this world, where the dancers for the most part ignore their partners, hanging on their arm, listlessly, and (quite literally), going through the motions of showing affection or closeness.

In almost every kocsma glasses, mainly beer steins, appear, often heaped in piles after cleaning, awaiting to be filled. Tarr's camera pans or freezes over these piles in close-up, almost making them into abstract objects with emphasis on the glassware a subtle allusion to pervasive drunkenness, a sub-theme in some of these films. In corollary to this, the one rather elegant restaurant in *The Prefab People* provides the setting for a work celebration. By the end of the evening, however, there are piles of dirty glasses on the table as the guests get more and more drunk and morose. These functional objects throughout his films are a way for Tarr to emphasize this non-salubrious function of the kocsma: it is not only a meeting place but also the place where humans go to lose themselves. And that may indeed be one of the things Tarr is trying to tell us about the drunkenness through is films. Characters remark that they acted a certain way because they were drunk, or one family member belittles another because they were drunk, they lose their jobs because they are drunk, or drank too much. In many ways, drunkenness is an excuse, in Tarr's world, for the inhumanity that is innate in characters. Their brutish lives lead them to close themselves off from others, especially their own family members leading to tragic ends. In *The Outsider*, András's real interest is playing the violin, but having failed the concert hall he contents himself with playing in the kocsma, a flawed location for failed talent. In one of the more festive scenes, András's wedding, we see this interior bravely decked out to revitalize the atmosphere, but to little effect. As the guests drink more, many of them become ever more morose. That, too, is one of the characteristics of many Tarr films, the heaviness that excessive drinking brings to peoples' features that mirrors the damaging lives they live. More often than not, the glasses remain or are already empty, useless or used up, like the kocsma patrons.

The tavern has a redeeming feature besides being where humans interact with each other fairly freely. It is also overwhelmingly where diegetic music is heard. Bands play for weekend dances; small traditional orchestras play for weddings or for other occasions. A rare instance where music provides a major component of the plot appears in *The Outsider*, for example, when András air conducts Beethoven to a phonograph record in an empty apartment, or when he plays the violin in the interior of a tavern where a sad group of partygoers listen. As will often be the case with Tarr's public restaurant scenes, the interior decorations are mostly warn out and haggard, the floors are often dirty or have needed straightening up after a night of revelry. Tables and chairs appear rustic, broken, or misplaced, the tableware shows signs of age. These interiors mirror the run-down nature of the way people lived during these years, the impossibility of leading an adult life for characters who have been infantilized by the regime.

The kocsma also provides the public space to face disappointment. In *Family Nest*, rapists and victim share a drink in a crowded kocsma as though the incident were over. Completely anesthetized to their grinding life, the members of the family become brutes. In this film, the close-ups of victim and rapists takes over the entire screen so that it is not possible to see much of the bar in which the action is happening, although we know it is a bar because of the sound of clinking glasses and the ambient noise of conversation. And yet the tavern's reality is dwarfed by the close-up of the faces of the individuals whose lives are being held in the balance by this tenuous family nest of lies, racism, violence, cowardice, and hopelessness generated by institutional ineptitude and cruelty. Also in this film, the father meets up with his lover who rejects him in the kocsma. This space for failed people, where human contact is dehumanized, provides a bleak counterpoint and continuation of the dreary apartment they all share. We suspect that this innate brutishness would preclude their improving their lot even if the new apartment they desperately try but fail to obtain were available.

In *The Prefab People*, besides a traditional kocsma where the character goes to drown his sorrows, we also see a restaurant with tablecloths where a large crowd of employees is watching a lounge singer perform with a teasing dance. The wife, who had been waiting for this day to go out, dress well, get her hair done, and go to the dance and dinner regrets it when the lounge singer involves her husband in one of the acts and when she sees him dance with his coworkers. She had remarked to the other patrons at the hairdresser that as a young girl she loved to dance, thus preparing the viewer for her bitter disappointment at not being asked to dance here. As he gets more involved in the evening's festivities, she gets more sullen and depressed. In the final part of this scene, as the husband drunkenly sings traditional songs with the last people to leave the establishment, she begins to cry softly to herself at the table.

In *Damnation*, the lounge singer's act in the kocsma leads her to Karrer who introduces her and her husband to the scheme at the core of the film. This establishment is a bit more polished than some of the others, with a tile floor, probably because it also serves as a dancehall. Most important in terms of symbolism for this film, the outside of the bar is often featured, the façade glowering under a large neon sign in script, Titanik Bár. The reference to the highly anticipated but doomed ship could imply get-rich-quick schemes that ultimately lead to the police station at the end of the film. The Titanik Bar is poised to sink and the characters in the bar will sink with it as soon as they begin this ill-fated relationship and this ill-advised scheme. The façade's sign provides one of the rare moments of light, artificial though it may be, in the raining, bleak village with omnipresent coal buckets. The sign's allusion to a great disaster caused by human collision with nature reinforces the despair inherent in the failed loveless relationships mirrored in the bleak interiors.

In *Satan's Tango*, the village tavern represents the center of life for the characters, the one place where they meet, where plots are hatched, and where villagers gossip about the mysterious people that seem to be coming into their lives, and, at the end, about the doom that is presumed to await them all and from which the main character boards up his house and closes our vision for the film. The very long sequence in which Estike watches outside the kocsma at dancing inside the bar places the camera at Estike's view. The reprise of that scene in a separate section instead positions the camera watching her at the window from several different angles. This is Tarr's way of making this universe of suspicions, doubt, intrigue, plots, scandals, criminals, petty thieves, and dishonest villagers center around the village meeting place.

The bar also functions as a morgue when Estike's body is found after she poisons herself. The most vulnerable person in the film takes her own life after she herself takes the life of the cat, the only creature that had paid her any attention. Her betrayal of an object of comfort is more than she can handle, and she takes her own life with the same means with which she took the cat's. Her terrible burden then becomes the villagers' burden as they see her body before them. Irimiás is able to use her death and their almost criminal indifference to the smallest child in their lives to guilt them into giving him money for the scheme he says they obviously now need in order to move beyond the horror they have caused. The kocsma here, transformed into a funeral parlor, becomes the bait for the final swindle, the one that makes the villagers leave their homes and thus uproots them. The irony of using a pool table as a casket highlights the swindle, the subterfuge of the slick gamblers Irimiás and Petrina who will hustle the town as they stoke and take advantage of their fears. The kocsma cannot remain a place of empathy, of grief, of genuine emotion for very long, only long enough to provide the basis for the final shakedown. The camera zooms into a close-up of the money the villagers leave at the ersatz funeral home in preparation for their final downfall. The function of interiors becomes interchangeable in this ecosystem of mistrust and human manipulation. Interiors change and mutate to provide cover, more so than shelter.

In *Werckmeister Harmonies*, the kocsma is again more than just a meeting place as it is the location of the guiding philosophical principal that keeps the film together (figure 3.8).

The Harmonies referenced in the title are discussed in the bar and in Eszter's home, so that we have two poles of knowledge in the film. For those less initiated, the bar is the locus of a discussion on the wonders of the universe. For those who can see and understand the professor, his lecture

Figure 3.8 Eclipse in the Kocsma. Screen capture October 7, 2020. *Werckmeister Harmonies* DVD.

provides more ample evidence of that knowledge. In one sense, then, in this film, we have two different classes against one another, two group that are diametrically opposed. In the case of the bar and the professor's house, we have two spaces for knowledge-based discourse. In the case of Tünde, Valuska, and the professor, we again have two distinct political worlds, one that is trying to overtake the other with the help of the mysterious prince to whom the characters allude. The divisions of the bar also become the divisions of the political realities underpinning this film. The kocsma unites patrons of different social classes and presents an orderly façade and interior as the postman expounds about the alignment of the planets. Tarr emphasizes the lines on the tavern floor and their pattern as we hear about the harmonies of the universe and how they are slightly out of alignment.[14]

There are no taverns in *Almanac of Fall* nor in *The Turin Horse*. Both these films, as we have been able to explore, provide an extremely closed universe for their characters, where they are trapped within the house in the case of the former film, and in a countryside without any apparent neighbors with only a cottage and a barn in the latter. In these two cases, the absence of a public place where the characters can meet others and have some semblance of human interaction is absent, which makes the remaining spaces particularly claustrophobic for the viewer. With the destruction of civilization alluded to in *The Turin Horse*, the hut becomes a kocsma as Bernhardt consumes some of the pálinka he secures from Ohlsdorfer, as though that is the last bastion of civilization where humans can interact.

In only one film does Tarr takes us to a unique indoor "feminine" location to explore the discourse and feelings of the female characters. The hairdresser in *The Prefab People* is a liminal location where the wife goes to get her hair done before the big dinner dance. She sits with other women under one of the hairdryers placed in a row against the wall and is initially extremely upbeat as she gets ready to mix in society. But the discussion soon sours her, as the women talk about the trips they have taken abroad, sure that she must have gone as well. She demurs, saying they intend to go in the future, but the children have kept them busy. This unfortunately does not satisfy the other women as they tell her they had gone on trips with their children in their day and it had worked out very well. This is one of the instances when the wife feels trapped by the pressure to move into the bourgeois class in this changing communist society. Tarr is clearly critical and warns of the aftermath of capitalist culture, mirrored in a location where the good life can be purchased, as was the case in the appliance store. Tally and Battista remind us that mapping geographies and equating places to their ecological reality can indicate a critique of capitalism. For Robi and Judit, happiness does not result from this capitalist exchange.

The disco in *The Outsider* represents another unusual public space in Tarr's interiors geographies. We have explored singing in the context of the kocsma in the vast majority of cases, but in this film, there are scenes of a 1970s Western-style disco, an ironic comment on the nature of art and of the appreciation of it in this brutish environment. András tells of his failure to maintain his standing in the classical music program where he had enrolled, thus leaving him to a life of itinerate playing despite his great talent. At the end of the film, he opens the disco with money borrowed from Balász, and it is in this disco that he ends up breaking up with his wife. They yell at one another near the stage but the deafening sounds of two U.S. megahits, The Animal's "The House of the Rising Sun" and Chubby Checker's "The Twist," does not allow them to hear one another, again an intrusion of capitalistic ways of being into a flawed Hungarian milieu.

The final scenes in the disco present both a moving forward and back for András. Instead of his small band and his own violin playing, he becomes a manager and no longer plays his instrument. The violin had been portrayed in the film as his one avenue for escape. While we do not see his dismissal from the music conservatory on screen—it is meant to be a prelude to his firing from the mental institution—we see that his lack of personal responsibility leads to his no longer being able to function in society. The disco band, playing American pop music to a packed crowd of young people, seems artificial, but it represents the one great success of András' life. Material success has erased aesthetic considerations in this world where capitalist culture, specifically American-inspired, triumphs. The disco becomes the modern equivalent of the kocsma. The dreary kocsma becomes in Tarr the central meeting place for exchanging of ideas, plotting actions, and meeting others, but the mood shows us that in Tarr's world of human relationships gone adrift, there can be no real connection, no real exchange, only time passing.

Workspaces: Offices, Hospitals, and Factories

In a few films, characters come up against the regime in an official space, usually an office where a functionary will interact with them as they try to improve their lives. In *Family Nest*, as the couple tries to get an apartment, a central scene shows the wife asking the official once again to allow the family to rent a flat so they can escape her tyrannical father-in-law. In *The Outsider*, András' first job is in a mental institution where two official spaces exist within this one locale: the ward where patients are housed in communal rooms and the office where he is brought up on disciplinary charges resulting from fighting with a patient as he tries to give him an injection. In *Satan's Tango*, the office represents the "reality" outside the village central to the narrative. We see the functionaries discuss what is happening in the village with its eventual intruders Irimiás and Petrina. We wonder until the end if this office is one of the spaces of the narrative, or if it is the metadiegetic space where the story is being created or refashioned to go into a report. Also under this heading, we could consider the workplace, mostly the factories such as the salami factory in *Family Nest* and the gear factory in *The Outsider*. Discussions of places of employment provides an opportunity to examine labor in Tarr's films, and Christina Stojanova notes that in works such as *Satan's Tango*, filmed shortly after the fall of communism, Tarr found a new "aversion for the nascent free market economy with its strictly monetary incentives and dehumanizing potential" (2013, 180). She traces a thread of symbolic exploration of the "postcommunist transition to liberal democracy and market economy effectuated by God and under competing types of power" in several films from *Satan's Tango* onward (2013, 180).

The downfall of the family happens in the housing office in *Family Nest*. Irén and Laci are forced to live with the abusive father and the racist mother throughout the film. They dream of better circumstances if only they had an apartment of their own. They have been on the list for a flat for years, and the wife continues to apply, waiting in seemingly endless lines to ask about their chances, only to be told that there is nothing available and that they don't know when there will be. Close-ups of the official who insists there is nothing to do for them because she does not have enough points for an apartment emphasize his expressionless face. Even when Irén pleads for him to come see their desperation he remains unmoved, reminding her of the interminable lines of people in her situations outside his door. Living space and its scarcity frustrates and forces the family to coexist to the breaking point.

In *Werckmeister Harmonies*, Valuska moves through several official interior spaces in his role as town postman. While he goes to many homes, throughout the film as he delivers his mail, he also has occasion to move inside official and public buildings such as the post office, and the local hotel. In one of these, we see the inside of a canteen kitchen where lunch pails are being prepared. The post office is an important hub of information as the sorters report what they have heard, and as the radio blares out information about the impending unrest. In each case, Valuska wanders, enters briefly, and leaves, as though leaving only a trace, a letter, behind. His almost invisible presence makes him a catalyst of the actions—moving in and out of events, both their witness and their chronicler from his vantage point in the institution where he ends up in the final scenes.

In contrast to the potentially convivial but in reality bleak public interiors such as the kocsma, the hairdresser or the disco, the office is a public space with a particular operative function. In Tarr films, we usually see the office occupied by functionaries who in some way can influence the lives of the people in the films. *Satan's Tango* includes a police office, which, like the housing office in *Family Nest*, brings the official communist structure to influence spatial constructions. In those two films, the official space was where the families tried to negotiate a better living arrangement. The housing office had an almost metaphysical dimension, where life decisions can be made. In *Satan's Tango*, in the police office, the charlatans are coerced into spying on the village. In the end, the police rewrite their report to make it seem more professional by eliminating rough language. This office controls the characters and controls the narration and these official spaces provide a regimental imprimatur to the schemes in each film, but provide no help to those who need it most.

Continuing with this dynamic of interior spaces that highlight characters' loneliness and desperation, the institution in *The Outsider* from where András is evicted resonates significance. András supports himself by day working as an orderly in an institution for psychiatric patients but in the first scenes, he is let go for dereliction of duty. Tarr's camera lingers in close-ups on the faces of the inmates, and then in reverse shot to András (figure 3.9).

A disciplinary board gets rid of him and the camera pans from one judge to the next a way to show that his fate is sealed. The hospital provides a warehouse for the infirmed but little opportunity for recovery. As with other aspects of Tarr's geographies, characters cannot affect change nor hope for improvement in their surroundings. The proximity of the infirmed to one another seems to close the walls in around them, echoing the impossibility of

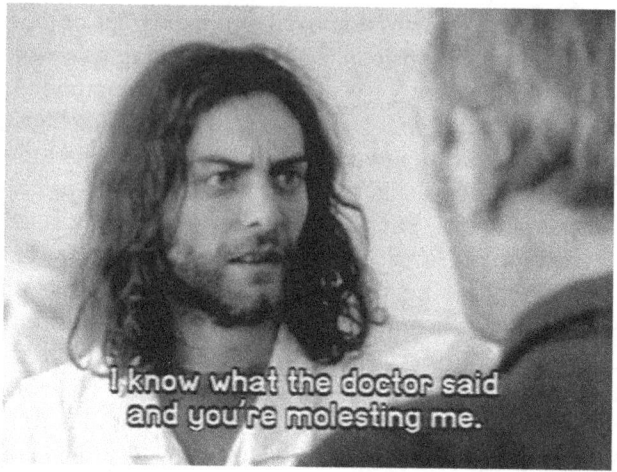

Figure 3.9   The Asylum. Screen capture October 7, 2020. *The Outsider* DVD.

escape. Just as leisure spaces do not bring people together, hospitals do not allow for healing.

The hospital reappears in the final scenes of *Werckmeister Harmonies*, one of two nightmarish interior spaces that through mob action are appropriated by the public: the destroyed hospital and the appliance store. By the time the mob arrives at the hospital, it appears vacant of staff. Only the infirmed, those who cannot escape, the most vulnerable, are left behind and the mob takes out its hatred on them. They are only stopped when they see an old, weakened man, naked and standing in a shower stall, waiting for them, powerless. The mob begins to retreat, perhaps sensing they have reached total domination in their destruction. This scene reminds the viewer of Estike's killing of the cat and her subsequent suicide with rat poison in *Satan's Tango*. The most vulnerable members of the society come to extreme measures when there is no one left in their world to take care of them. In *Werckmeister Harmonies*, after the hospital's destruction the scene cuts to a looted appliance store. Unlike in *The Prefab People*, we do not see the appliance store with people buying goods, only after it has been raided and there is nothing unbroken. The store is reduced to a pile of useless items, the aftermath of a mob riot. Valuska sits reading an account of the mob activity to emphasize its senselessness. A second hospital, an asylum, appears in the quasi-final segment of *Werckmeister Harmonies* as Valuska sits on a bed in a psychiatric facility where he has been taken after he tried to escape from the town under the new regime. They catch him in a thrilling helicopter chase. He is next seen in hospital gown on a sterile bed, limp as he accepts his fate.

Family Nest and *The Outsider* have another important indoor space: the factory. In *Family Nest*, the first scene shows the wife tiredly riding on the bus, unable to find a seat and forced to stand. She gets off to go to her job at a salami factory, where we see thousands of the products handing from the ceiling. It is payday and at the end of her shift she and a line of equally tired colleagues goes to pick up their pay. As a final indignity, they are frisked as the leave the plant to make sure they are not carrying any salamis home. It may be that the choice of workplace again provides a subtle nod to a sociopolitical context as salami, a Hungarian culinary specialty continued to provide one of the few gastronomic exports. This grounds the film's story in the most destitute of situations, and this destitution continues into the film itself. In *The Outsider*, unable to make a living from his violin, András goes to work in a factory that one of his friends helps him get. In the gear factory, the faces of the characters are often hidden behind the gears in close-up as they move about the floor. At the end of the film, we see a meeting at the plant where management tells workers that foreign machines have so increased productivity that it has disrupted their overtime expectations. The workplace's promise to potentially lift the character's misery is all a pose and ends up going nowhere. The foreign element again subtly intrudes into the working life of these characters who are merely getting by. The social fabric that underpinned communism, that all workers would be taken care of, is exposed in this film.

Interestingly, in *The Turin Horse*, there are no officials or official buildings; the action centers entirely on the house and barn, as though the characters lived in a bubble outside the world. Or perhaps that is the point: this is a post-apocalyptic world already, without the intrusion of any buildings, whether public places to eat and drink, or places where officials come into contact and try to control the people's lives. The official working spaces in Tarr's film are either where the government oppresses the people or where the people try to get ahead, but barely get by. In neither case, sadly, does any real connection or assistance take place.

Signal Boxes and Barns

Tarr's most recent films include unusual spaces that fit into the narrative: the signal box in *The Man from London* and the barns in *Satan's Tango* and *The Turin Horse*. In both these instances, these spatial typologies play pivotal roles and Tarr uses them to great effect. They need to be considered separately since they are more transitional spaces than permanent human dwellings.

The Man from London feels like a departure for Tarr. It is a film noir with the look and feel of 1940s thrillers. The interior is a signal box for most of the film (see figure 1.1), with its technical but timeless gear fully on display. There are also scenes in the café with the billiard table, clearly a middle class eating establishment as well as the interior of a small apartment where Tarr's camera lingers on the tight spaces. The signal box provides both a public and a private world for Maloin and his colleague where they perform a role as constant witness, as voyeur over the horizon, making the space an extension, in geographic terms, of the condition of not only the humans in the film but also of the film's audience. The signal boxes' walls are almost completely glass to allow Maloin and his colleagues to keep watch. They are tasked with aiding trains arriving at the waterfront, but this transparent space also allows them to become the ultimate witness. The temptation this affords leads to Maloin's downfall when he retrieves the briefcase filled with money. His seemingly impenetrable foolproof plan proves itself vulnerable, too transparent to succeed. The signal box, perched above the town, becomes the location of perdition, the transparent walls close in on Maloin and on the greed that tempted him. The signal box remains almost always dark, as are many of the spaces of this film, filled with shadows, one of the key elements that builds the suspense of the film noir atmosphere of the film. In the interview we had, Tarr insisted on the importance of the loneliness of this space, which mirrors the loneliness of Maloin within his society and his family. Of crucial importance to Tarr, as it was in *Macbeth*, is the relationship of the two women and the two men, of their attempt to create a connection to pierce the loneliness. This seemingly open space allows Maloin to hide and to observe.

Barns also serve a practical function that takes them out of the realm of the human but which also by necessity must remain interlocked with human activity. The barn in *Satan's Tango* seems to serve little purpose except perhaps to store hay and grain from the fields that remain barren through the course of the film. There are no farm animals housed there, and the cat's role is probably to catch mice and keep the barn clean. Its sacrifice therefore appears even more evil and random because this animal is the one creature that seems to have a place and a purpose in this liminal environment. Estike's brutality can exist in this marginal space, neither inside nor outside, which serves as a desperate last refuge for this suffering. Barns provide the possibility of both inside and outside locations in one, a sort of ruin showing traces of its former usefulness.

Although the barn appears centrally located in *Satan's Tango* and is the setting for a pivotal scene leading to Estike's suicide, the barn in *The Turin Horse* is of much more consequence because the film's settings are so sparse and elemental. The title character is housed in a location, which appears on screen as equally small, dilapidated, and dismal as the environment of the cottage. Here, the barn shows us that the horse and the people are almost interchangeable, and there is little meaningful dominance by one toward the other. When the horse decides not to eat, it is exercising its will in a way that the humans in this film rarely do. Inside the barn, Ohlsdorfer and his daughter provide rare moments of human caring as they coax the horse to eat and drink. Being unable to do, they close the barn doors for the last time as the camera shows an extreme close-up of the horses' face. Just as the whale in *Werckmeister Harmonies* provided a final reckoning of human misery, here too the horses' blank stare presages the end.

The interior space of Tarr's films brings us to understand how he views the lives of the character: bleak and unforgiving, timeless and eternal, since these space do not include items that could tie the context to a particular time and place. Interiors are often cramped, and the tight camera angles accentuate this reality. The sparse furniture and décor in most of the films indicates the socioeconomic reality of the characters and the political overtones in many of the films lead us to think that perhaps some of this reality is due to the fact that these characters live in a time of political repression that may have had an effect on their lives.

These interior spaces define where communities form and therefore where people can potentially build relationships. But in Tarr's films so often these constructions are in ruins; when interaction happens people remain separated. Guillaume Sibertin-Blanc sees in Tarr the ways "of the sensitive existence of a community, and these films never cease to put into question the community's consistency, all the while not erasing all communitarian concerns but on the contrary giving them a singular insistence" (2016, 151).[15] These spaces should have been built to house a community and also foster community instead stand crumbling as testimonials to the decay of its human inhabitants. As we have seen, Tarr rarely provides us with a recognizable space such as big cities or monuments. Most films are situated in rural or quasi rural areas with indistinct habitats. The city and country become one in such films. György Kalmár has explained *The Prefab People*'s first scene, a band playing in an empty garden pathway as the camera pans and its numerous claustrophobic interiors as a reflection of the sense of entrapment Hungarians may have felt under the waning years of socialism. He uses the figure of the labyrinth to describe these enclosed spaces and organizes certain aspects of the films he discusses related to camerawork "types of shots, building up scenes, the combination of different shots," including body language and acting (2017, 8). The spaces mirror the human inhabitants, created by them but then neglected or abandoned as the human relationships tattered.

Human beings usually create dwellings to house groups of people, to shelter them. In our interview, Tarr mentions his interest in exploring couples and their relationships, for example, Macbeth and Lady Macbeth, or Maloin and his wife. Even in films that include large groups, Tarr's lens often zeros in on couples: Laci and Irén, András and Katie, Judit and Robi, Hédi and

János, Irimiás and Petrina, Valuska and Eszter, and father and daughter in *The Turin Horse*. The dwelling becomes the setting for confrontations between two people that increases their isolation within the nuclear group. Loneliness becomes a pattern of human existence throughout his films, beginning with two people in conflict with one another and extending to larger groups of people either extended family at the dinner table, or townspeople in the kocsma. Tarr's interior spaces reflect the claustrophobia of lives lived without emotion for the most part, the stultifying hold of a society that limits humans and closes walls around them. The village houses have traditional elements, but often faded or run down. Characters socialize largely in environments where they try to numb their feelings over bottles of pálinka while expounding either on truly lofty philosophical ideas, or spouting nonsense. Officialdom intrudes in many films in the form of offices, factories, and workplaces that force characters to confront the limitations of their lives. Here exists a claustrophobia of indifference, where interior walls come closing in on characters as they move along their fated trajectories, and the Anthropocene where the human footprint has already begun to erase.

NOTES

1. I purposely use the term most often heard in the 1960s and 1970s for a hair salon, given the dating of the film *The Prefab People*.
2. Les gens sortent d'un café pour entrer dans un autre. C'est ce qu'on appelle la vie humaine après tout, et simultanément le temps s'écoule . . . si on les observe bien (les humains), on constate que ce sont des vies très limitées, qu'il s'agisse de vies en ville ou à la campagne.
3. I will not here take into consideration *Macbeth* since the location is dictated by the text. Tarr chose to film in Buda Castle but his camera remains in close-up through most of the film. Without panoramic views of the castle, it is difficult to identify.
4. Jeremy Carr reminds us that this novel has twice been adapted to the screen before Tarr: in Henri Decoin's 1943 *The London Man*, and in Lance Comfort's 1947 *Temptation Harbor* (2017, n.pg.).
5. Although here, too, the location of the town is meaningless since all the action takes place indoors.
6. Une lumière grisâtre dévoile l'essence fangeuse qui définit le monde parcouru par Béla Tarr. Elle colore les murs lépreux, les routes, les chairs ainsi que l'eau, l'air et la terre . . . L'invention de cette lumière de jour effondré correspond à une pensée à la fois métaphysique et historique d'un échec politique. Les quelques bâtiments qui se regroupent en village n'appartiennent même plus au communisme : le postcommunisme est déjà obsolète, couleur de ruine, ou, pire, l'histoire s'est définitivement retirée. Une activité industrielle persiste dans *Damnation*, avec ces périphériques d'usine qui tournent à vide. *Sátántangó* s'ouvre sur ce qui peut subsister d'une exploitation agricole collective. Quoi qu'il en soit, les gestes du travail se soustraient à toute

représentation. L'activité communautaire existe sous la forme exclusive de la hantise, comme un lambeau ou un résidu. Béla Tarr donne ainsi le coloris le plus juste, le plus tenace pour représenter littéralement le spectre du marxisme ou l'utopie marxiste comme une saleté spectrale.

7. De la crise domestique éprouvée jusqu'à l'hystérie, ère claustrophobe de la saturation, celle du logement comme du cadre, où les corps butent les uns contre les autres pour dire l'étouffement.

8. Un formalisme cosmique, élargissant le cadre aux dimensions de la Puszta.

9. Carr reminds us that Tarr directed *The Outsider* and *The Prefab People* during his stay at the Hungarian School of Theatrical and Cinematic Arts (Carr 2017, n. pg.). This film features some elements that are more rarely used in Tarr's later works such as overlapping dialogue, and fewer long takes, which instead begin in earnest in *Damnation*. They also feature quasi-documentary monologues, the camera fixed on the speaker, without establishing shots, so we do not know to whom they are speaking: only to us.

10. Le cinéaste offre une prééminence aux visages et se fait architecte du verbe : il structure de persistants échanges verbaux et donne ainsi à voir une expérience des corps soumis à des géométries étriquées. Murs et pièces ne surgissent pas comme de simples éléments architecturaux et fonctionnels, mais y agissent comme autant de nœuds psychiques qui paralysent la vie. Les corps entassés et oppressés du *Nid familial* sont privés ainsi de tout ancrage spatial et, dans ces conditions d'une impossible *territorialisation*, les communautés familiales se désagrègent, se perdent et finissent par se diviser.

11. I will be discussing Tarr's *Macbeth* as a feature film. Since it eventually became a TV presentation in Hungary, it has less similarity to a short film than to a feature film, therefore, discussing it within the pages of the central chapters seems appropriate.

12. Maury talks about the color palette in *Almanac of Fall* as a basin of humors, as though the colors represent the character's mood, a sign of cinematic formalism for her (2016, 40).

13. With a human staring into the eye of a dead sea creature, this scene is reminiscent of the final scene in Fellini's *La dolce vita*, where Marcello (Marcello Mastroianni), having given up any hope of becoming a serious writer and instead launching a career in public relations and advertising, has ended a night of orgies at the Roman seaside and goes for a walk on the beach, hungover, with the other revelers. Fishermen bring up a fish, somewhat of a ray but difficult to identify, which has died in the net. The others are disgusted, but Marcello approaches and listlessly stares into its eyes. He wonders what it is looking at. Nothing. In a move that reminds us of the central idea in Beckett's *Waiting for Godot*, where Godot never comes, this moment forces Marcello to realize there will be no assistance from outside. Only nothing, no answers.

14. In *The Man from London* Tarr recreates a French café, with white lace curtains and a cleaner environment than most of Tarr's Hungarian kocsmas. The atmosphere, however, is similar to that in the Hungarian locations. There is a pool table, and patrons tend to be often isolated from one another, not really interacting at the same

table or in the same rooms. Only when there is a potential confrontation is there animated dialogue. In this way, although we are in a French seaside town, we could still be in a Hungarian tavern. As mentioned, given the non-Hungarian setting, this public establishment is correctly labeled a café rather than a kocsma and will therefore not be examined in detail here.

15. D'existence sensible d'une communauté dont ses films ne cessent de mettre en cause la consistance même, non pourtant en effaçant toute question communautaire, mais en lui donnant au contraire une insistance singulière.

Chapter 4

The Empty Outdoors

As a matter of course, Tarr's films take place primarily indoors, with spaces reflecting the human inhabitants and the mood that the film conveys. The psychological dramas that families, neighbors, and friends live through reflect off the walls, and reflect their living arrangements. Interiors show us the desperation of the people and their predicaments. In contrast, outdoor spaces allow for the possibility of seeing Tarr's conception of nature and of the natural world. Even man-made outdoor spaces such as parks, gardens, and town squares open up ecologically possible geographies. Tarr, however, rarely indulges in showing us lush natural landscapes, naturally occurring vegetation or neat, sunlit public urban areas. His outdoor spaces continue to reflect a disheveled, desert-like, desolate terrain that seems inhospitable to humans. Even the few public squares in his films often seem shrouded in fog or gloom, with films from the beginning of his career and more recent ones maintaining the same type of exteriors. When discussing *Satan's Tango*, Bayon comments on exteriors in Tarr in a way that resonates with his other films. She notes the postcommunist, infertile tracts, incessant rain, and vegetating inhabitants of a collective farm susceptible to a charlatan's sway (2016, 50). She notes the doctor who cures no one, but also does not leave the village to follow the charlatan's scheme (2016, 51). Karl Sierek sees "vast Hungarian landscapes, travelling shots among factory ruins and collective farms, glances through openings in crumbling dwellings . . . emptiness, desolation . . . these images suspended between the landscape and creatures, between abandonment and obstinacy, come back in all Béla Tarr's films" (2016, 113).[1] These bleak exteriors often hide and mask unsavory deeds, while continuing to emphasize the hopelessness of the characters' lives.

We might be tempted to think of a discussion of the outdoors as revolving around "nature." Many ecocritical essays focus on this theme. One of the early books to explore cinema through an ecocritical lens, Ingram's *Green Screen* defines environmental films as works "in which an environmental issue is raised explicitly and is central to the narrative" (vii). Not only does an exploration of nature but also nature's appropriation by humans become a central theme when looking at films. Ingram's study is useful in that it provides a mechanism for ecocritically examining Hollywood cinema, against which all other national cinemas contrast themselves. He rightly notes that in much of Hollywood's film industry, environmental sensibilities are "always likely to be moderated by its vested interest in promoting commodity consumption as a social good" (Ingram 181). Ingram's descriptions of Hollywood may be useful as a contrast to Tarr's use of "nature" in his films. Rarely are natural settings indicative of commodity consumption; most of his parks and town squares are devoid of commercial activity and even largely of people. We cannot really speak of "wildness" in Tarr's films because often his open spaces are adjacent to human habitations. As we shall see in chapter 5, animals, too, are not wild but domesticated. Finally while much outdoor space in Tarr includes fields plowed by human hands, they remain empty, sleeping through winter. In his use of nature, then, as in his use of slow camera, Tarr provides a counterpoint to the Hollywood cinematic production. By deliberately excluding a representation of natural spaces untouched or unobserved by humans, Tarr's outdoors reflects human influences. As in the Anthropocene, humans have altered the surroundings not only by establishing indoor spaces to inhabit thus carving up natural space, but also by modifying, and in the case of Tarr's landscapes, subsequently ruining, the natural world.

We will examine external spatial elements that can be considered domesticated outdoor spaces, that is, locations that have been shaped by human beings to serve a purpose. These include public squares, lots (in Tarr, rarely parking lots, for, as we have seen, the trappings of modern life are absent in many of his works), public parks, and an amusement park in *Family Nest* and a pool in *The Prefab People*. We will also explore "wilderness," although Tarr rarely indulges in scenes or backdrops of untouched, pristine natural settings. He does, however, very often include open fields and forests. In a few films, he alludes to or shows scenes of open ocean.[2] An interesting, and unique in Tarr, landscape in *Damnation* is the ever-present coal pit, and the relentless squeak of coal buckets moving on an aerial conveyor, which becomes a kind of surreal soundtrack. As a final note, we look at rain and wind, unusually frequently present in Tarr, as a way to establish the dreary mood. As was the case for indoor spaces, we move from those outdoor spaces that offer the most potential for human interaction to those are most desolate, ending with the overarching conditions that might make those landscapes and geographic locations even more uninhabitable.

Although in interviews Tarr often denies metaphorical readings of his work, Peter Hames notes that Tarr meditates on the power of nature and the search for perfection (n.pg.). Rosenbaum suggests some of Tarr's films present a "demonology," which can be gleaned from titles such as "Satantango" and "Damnation" (1996, n.pg.) In these films, Tarr explores "grubby human behavior" as though the universe were out of joint. Cunningham says that Tarr places himself completely outside the mainstream. He describes Tarr's "trademark mise-en-scène" where "everything is grim, isolated, dilapidated and bare, using extremely long takes (often the full reel), with the camera only moving very slowly and often remaining static" (2004, 154). *Werckmeister Harmonies* explores authority, violence, and worlds out of kilter in a timeless village, exploiting this technique to create a metadiegetic meaning.[3] Botz-Bornstein had discussed materiality and the shot in connection with his exploration of organic cinema where the long take and the landscape are conceptually linked:

> The main tool for obtaining an organic space in cinema is the long take, which can transform space into a coherent and respectable entity, similar to the stable entity of a face. Tarr is the modern master of the single shot . . . in those long takes, time is not a liquid and abstract but rather obtains the more tactile, organic and "sticky" fluency of a paste . . . each moment is a microcosm. Each sequence shot (plan-séquence) has a duty to the time of the world, to the time in which the world is reflected in intensities felt by bodies. (2017, 179)

The world thus rendered unfolds before us with enriched meaning.

For Bálint Kovács, there is a political dimension to Tarr's choice of rural landscapes, which he sees as a cause for Tarr's cool reception at home while garnering accolades abroad. Tarr's films clearly show the Hungarian countryside, but in a dark, negative way, with stifling villages and dismal fields. This vision could be interpreted as that of the postcommunist Hungary, although Tarr's political vision is implicit rather than explicit (Bálint Kovács 2016, 29). Much of the grubby, desolate, and dilapidated element and feeling appear, as we have seen, in interior spaces constructed to emphasize disarray. The selection of outdoor locations and the shape and construction of outdoor shots continue this trajectory of a reflection on human misery.

Before delving into the outdoors, I must mention that Tarr created two films that have no outdoor scenes, an important consideration when discussing and analyzing those films. Both from the relatively early period of his work, these two films concentrate on claustrophobic interior spaces to explore how human interactions can be heated to the breaking point in a claustrophobically tight crucible. One is *Hotel Magnezit*, a short to be discussed in a chapter 6. The other, *Almanac of Fall* contains essentially no outdoor spaces, locking the violent family within itself for the duration of the film. The interior of this middle-class house is created to emphasize the desperate condition of the people that live within its walls. The outdoors does not matter because it will not influence their behavior or the outcome of the narrative.

There is one small allusion to the outdoors in *Almanac of Fall*, which becomes especially poignant because we can sense the good weather, in contrast to the psychedelic interior colors. As the film begins, we see the delicate lace curtains, indications of the family's status and wealth, flutter in the breeze with the window open behind them. The extra-diegetic sounds bring us chirping birds, and light streams through the window, indicating a glorious day. This might seem inconsequential, but we will see later in this chapter to what extent Tarr's films contain increasingly inclement weather creating a somber mood, with many of these mid-career and later films essentially bathed in rain, wind, dust storms, and other extreme climactic conditions. The beautiful fall day indicated by this open window is instead showing us that these characters are deprived of the beauty that might be waiting for them outside the walls of the house, thus rendering their living situation even more depraved and desperate. The film's characters rarely seem to want to go outside, although some of them come from outside back into the house. They are trapped in the stifling confines, just as their animosity, violence, and control over one other dooms them to live in an eternal nightmare which plays itself out in the bleak, joyless wedding scene at the end of the film. The fluttering window curtains represent almost an intrusion of the outdoors into this hermetically sealed environment, just as Anna the nurse has intruded into the family's disfunction and exacerbated it. The only "outdoors" in this film, which bring some joy, remains a breath of air through an open window.

The title itself, with reference to the seasons, provides an ironic comment on the fact that these characters do not venture outside to experience fall. The seasons have no effect on those who remain trapped indoors, closed off. The film also suggests a kind of inbreeding of the characters, who leach off one another as they try to satisfy their base desires and control one another for the sake of power and dominance, although that, too, leads to nothing. It would be tempting to think of this title, "Fall," as a play on words. The "Fall" here is indeed reference to the season and not a play on words between a biblical fall and the seasons. The Hungarian word "öszi" firmly roots the title in the seasons and therefore to a situation where the outdoors would presumably be enacted in the film. Perhaps the allusion is really to the somber, reflective, and somewhat twilight character of fall. In the only film to make specific reference to seasons, the humans cut themselves entirely off from nature.

There is one work with only minimal outdoors scenes, and those are determined by the source material. Tarr's *Macbeth*, as we saw, provides a rather traditional setting and scenery for the Shakespeare play, but continues to use tight camera angles to heighten anxiety. Outdoor scenes, while all still in the castle's courtyard, emphasize the weight and size of the stones with which the castle is constructed. The castle's impenetrability traps the characters within the space and provides a backdrop for the inevitable tragic conclusion. The castle walls represent essentially the entire outdoor area of the film and the characters are often seen hugging the walls, cornered against the walls, and in many ways trapped within the walls as the dramatic moments of the tragic story unfold. Macbeth's fall is inevitable as the walls almost literally close in around him before his head is paraded around the courtyard in a page's hands, the final downfall of man's greed. All these elements indicate a film, which, while extremely faithful to the original text, still uses the outdoors to great effect. As was the case with interior spaces, as we explore outdoor spaces in Tarr's films, we can create a map of spaces that recur. Just as his interiors project the hopelessness of the human imprint on the landscape of the Anthropocene, Tarr's nature shows similar neglect and bleakness.

PUBLIC SPACES

Domesticated Outdoor Spaces

We can divide Tarr's outdoor universe into spaces created and shaped by humans for their own consumption, to wild spaces that humans have tamed (for example as agricultural lands), and spaces that continue to be wild. Tarr examines and exploits all these geographies and looks at the ways they have been changed and otherwise manipulated, which can point us toward a kind of reading for these spaces. As was the case when discussing his indoors, Tarr's outdoors recur from film to film and within the same film. I have grouped the outdoor spaces thematically and will explore them so as to expose the ways in which geography and, in the case of outdoors especially, ecology shape the character's lives in Tarr's films.

The Public Square

From the most ancient theatrical representations, the public squares, the *agora*, the *piazza*, the *plaza*, have been locations where the citizenry congregates. Here, humans share convivial moments, gossip, exchange information, listen to the discourse of their officials and leader, rise up and reclaim their land and their lives from tyrants, and rebuild their *polis* from the ruins created by the destruction of power. In this way, the public square holds tremendous meaning when on display in film. Tarr uses public squares to great advantage in several of his films but they are rarely the neat, clean, busy thoroughfare for idea exchange. They occasionally seem menacing, often dirty, and sometimes very empty where lone characters migrate and in so doing highlight for the viewer their loneliness and isolation from their fellow humans. This, then, for Tarr is the point. If the humans that inhabit the city have become dehumanized, the spaces they have created for idea exchange no longer have value and can only be empty, like a wilderness that has been inhabited and then abandoned.

In *Damnation*, we begin to see the importance of the square but here it is still the equivalent of an empty location devoid of people. Karrer often lurks outside buildings, spying on his lover's husband leaving in their VW Beetle. At times he just looks into the houses from the outside. The village has a central square, but it is difficult to identify as an important city location due to its neglected nature, unpaved, with little if any vegetation, with debris all around. Karrer sidles against dilapidated walls that overlook a muddy field that has been soaked by the almost incessant rain that dominates the film (more on that later). This open area between houses could be a cross between an actual square and a parking lot that has not been paved over. Except for Karrer, this square is essentially always empty except for the occasional glimpse of the person he is watching. Maury sees *Damnation* as the beginning of an outdoors aesthetic, where Tarr

> exposes buildings, streets, squares, as dynamic of closed spaces : alleys, sidewalks, walls, are understood as ordinary materialities that reinforce the impression of being *nowhere*, and give off the sensation of heaviness, of stasis. Human habitats and their muddy outdoors suggest an air of abandonment that overtakes the desire for order and conservation. (2016, 44)[4]

We could say the same about *Damnation* as Botz-Bornstein says of *Satan's Tango*, citing the scene in this film in which the camera pans over an exterior wall, and, occasionally, the wall gives way to a window at which dancehall patrons watch, motionless, as the rain pours. Botz-Bornstein cites László Krasznahorkai's novel *Sátántangó*, in which the Hungarian author "describes walls as canvases on which reality is projected . . . . The walls do not have an identity spelled out in terms of ornaments, function, or anything *on* them. Rather, they speak the silent language of emptiness" (2017, 25). We will examine animals in Tarr's films more closely in the next chapter, but the film includes numerous dogs who roam around this plaza, scavenging for food. The only other place we see these dogs is in the dramatic final scene when Karrer goes to the coal pit, finds the dogs rooting around, and challenges one of them, barking and snarling on all fours as the canine does the same to him. Ultimately, he starts to stand and the dog, intimidated, goes away. These dogs, as we shall see, represent the abandonment of the outdoors to return to its wilder previous form.

This film does contain one other square, this time neat and with some vegetation, outside the dance hall/bar that we examined in the previous chapter. Here, the camera moves to a solitary man dancing in this square while the dancehall is filled with people doing the jitterbug. This space could have been inviting enough to be filled with people or otherwise full of life. Instead, it, too, is practically deserted. The man dancing on his own is within earshot of the merriment but outside, in his own world, a kind of liminal space between empty spaces.

Satan's Tango is centered in a desolate village, far from the city, far from other habitations, and the isolation of its citizens leads to the central swindle in the story. The center, one could say, of this village is the square, really a muddy space between the village's few houses. The main character, the doctor who ventures out only, it seems, in search of pálinka, has his writing table laden with books overlooking the muddy space leading to a few of the other dwellings in the film. From there he can watch the comings and goings of the characters and also hear about, and prepare for, the final destruction alluded to and which leads him to begin barricading himself in his house and thus also closing us all off from light in the film.

The doctor has an important encounter in this square, with Estike, the little girl who commits suicide. She runs out asking for help as he is stumbling toward the kocsma looking to replenish his pálinka. She runs up to him, he falls from the impact, and as he struggles to get up in the muddy, rain filled pavement, he curses her. This scene recurs in the story and is seen from different angles, the film's structure moving in repeated patterns just like the black and white tiled floors of Buenos Aires's "baldosas" where tango dancers meet, or even of the way the dancers themselves mirror each other's intricate tango moves.[5] In some ways, this is the decisive moment for Estike. She cries for help in a bumbling way, and is rebuffed. She is the outcast of the village, put out by her mother as the latter prostitutes herself to the village. The barn becomes Estike's refuge. The cat's vulnerability leads her to kill it, the only thing over which Estike can have power, and she shows that power as do the adults around her, through violence and cruelty. The squares of this film could provide a place for conviviality, but the town has descended so far into deceit and subterfuge, neighbors pitted against one another trying to cheat one another, that the open space languishes or provides only moments of collision that lead to greater isolation and desperation.

More so, really, than a square, this village has two public open spaces, in front of the doctor's house and outside the kocsma. The former, never-dry mud pit provides an open area on one side overlooking the fields and beyond them, other towns, the railway station, and other signs that this village is connected to other communities of human beings. The latter seems more like a recognizable "piazza," but with no monument, church or cathedral, benches for leisurely lingering, or other humanizing elements. The tavern and its drunken desolation represents the center of this village's universe, from where inebriated patrons will debate the arrival of the menacing "other" that leads the doctor to entomb himself and thus to cut off the viewer from all life as the film ends. The public square encloses the inhabitants outside as effectively separating them from one another as their suspicions of each other provoked by the swindle do.

Werckmeister Harmonies brings Tarr's camera back to an urban setting (we know he filmed in Baja, a town near Hungary's southern border as discussed in chapter 3), a town somewhere near a hostile foreign power. Exterior spaces in this film lose all their potential to sooth or comfort and any aspect of bucolic potential. The town square, the center of the village, is either empty or teeming with menacing crowds, a harbinger of the danger inherent in the upcoming political overthrow. Tünde greets the leaders of the uprising in a secluded alleyway from where the postman Valuska spies her, half hidden by the trees, as she works through details of the invasion. And the postman goes from house to house with his mail as though he were sewing together the inhabitants of this town but to no avail. He is truly the one tie that binds them all. His occupation as mail carrier also provides the villagers with some of the only contact they may have with realities outside their world through the letters he brings.

In this film, the square is absolutely essential for the development of the narrative since the subtext includes dark political forces from the outside coming to overthrow the town (figure 4.1).

Unlike in *Damnation* or *Satan's Tango*, here, we have a genteel, paved, beautiful square flanked by outwardly elegant buildings, for the most part in still excellent condition. The square contains large paving stones, period streetlamps, and a wide vista, made even larger by Tarr's camera panning from one section to the next. It becomes the central location of the unrest that will engulf the village and doom Valuska to the asylum. The square attracts people, almost exclusively men, who mill about aimlessly. In the first scenes, the crowds are scarce, but as the unrest intensifies before the mob scene, the crowd grows larger and more restless. The agitation of the crowd is an indication of the activities in which it will engage, and Valuska, who has gone to see the whale, becomes buffeted by the groups as they prepare to riot.

The whale and the trailer that carries it are the central focus of the square once they arrive in town in the dead of night, witnessed only by Valuska as he makes the beginnings of his postal rounds. The trailer sets up in the center of the square and initially opens itself for viewing so villagers can pay to see the dead whale. The trailer is destroyed in the riot and the whale stands exposed in the center of the square, surrounded by the period beauty of the buildings, barely visible through the fog that has engulfed the village and

Figure 4.1 **An Elegant Square and a Whale Trailer.** Screen capture October 7, 2020. *Werckmeister Harmonies* DVD.

made it virtually disappear. This creature takes up the space that convivial human contact should have taken but that has, instead, been relegated to the margins of the scene. The silent, still whale in the center of the square contrasts with the unrest and destruction that are to come, as announcements of the prince can be heard on the radio emanating from the trailer compartment. The suggestion is that the whale itself and the mysterious prince who is leading the riots from afar, are linked in some way, and that they are also linked to Tünde's collaboration with the militia that gathers on the outskirts of town, which only Valuska noticed. These public areas are in a sense taken over before the entire town is destroyed, as though the harmonies of the title have all gone out of tune and have been perverted by the new system and by the inattention of the old system to the importance of fighting to maintain freedom.

Filmed in Bastia, *The Man from London* provides the viewer with "foreign" spaces (that is foreign to Hungary) by definition and the importance of these spaces comes to play in the mysterious intrigue of the films. The main character remains in his house and can look out on the central square lined with beautiful, full trees, complete with park benches and streetlamps. Here, too, the spaces remain empty as the characters negotiate their unsatisfactory existences. One important liminal area of the public square is right outside the main character's window. As requisite in a film noir, a man with his identity concealed stands under a period lamppost outside the window to show us that the main character is being watched; the subtheme of intrigue, identity, shadows, and illicit money in the person of the mysterious man from London is encapsulated in that scene. The lamppost near the main square becomes not a beacon but rather a mysterious light that throws only shadows on the characters and their motives.

The film script is Krasznahorkai's reworking of Simenon's novel by the same name. Rancière compares the novel and film:

> From this story, Béla Tarr has essentially retained one situation: that of the solitary man in his tower of glass, the man whose work, every night for twenty-five years, has consisted in watching the passengers disembark from the ferry, and in pulling the levers that release the train's rails: a man fashioned by routine, isolated by his work, humiliated by his condition, and for whom the spectacle entering through the window offers the pure temptation of change. (2013, 75–76)

The empty town squares mirror the loneliness of Maloin's situation and in Tarr's insistence in the final sequence through close-up on the only true victim of this murder mystery, Brown's widow. Her lonely face exemplifies how the characters' actions leave them isolated from one another. She cannot even take the envelope of money, the "recompense" for having lost her husband. She stares in the distance as the camera shuts out all the space around her. Only the tears of her grief remain. Simenon's novel ends with Maloin incarcerated, and the fatalism ultimately inherent in his character is reinforced when, upon his sentence, Maloin leaves: "He followed the guards quietly/in a docile manner" (189).[6] He looks around, presumably for Brown's wife, but not seeing her he accepts his fate. In the novel, there are also several more moments when Maloin encounters coworkers, while Tarr focuses tightly on a smaller group of characters. Rancière states that "the story borrowed from Simenon ends like one of Krasznahorkai's novels: with a return to the point of departure. But Béla Tarr's film ends differently: with a miniscule tracking shot slowly rising mere centimeters up the unshakable face of Brown's widow" (2013, 78). As the camera excludes all external elements from the frame, the empty landscapes of the film give way to the only thing left: loneliness. The empty public squares in Tarr's films expose these spaces as the antithesis of the agora and show how the characters in the films continue in their isolation and doubt.

(Parking) Lots

Many vacant lots in Tarr are simply empty spaces surrounded by dwellings. In some films, they include parked cars, but these are not parking lots, ordered, and marked spaces where vehicles are parked before and after use. Any cars in these spaces in Tarr almost always seem randomly placed. The lots, therefore, maintain their wild characteristics. An extension of public spaces, the lots are like graveyards for human activity. Filled with cars or empty, they elicit the idea of rest rather than movement. Cars also are, by definitions, markers of a particular time and place and ground the film that includes them in a modern and technologically advanced setting, as well as indicating a level of economic well-being of at least some of the inhabitants. As we have seen, in many of Tarr's films, the ambiance exudes timelessness rather than being grounded in a particular time frame. So in films that include cars and parking lots, the effect is to modernize and make the action and narrative a part of more modern concerns. It also paradoxically "dates" the films as Hungary has moved from communism to capitalism. Initially sprinkled with Trabants, the East German utilitarian vehicles ubiquitous in satellite countries and commonly and almost satirically called "Trabis," films such as *The Man from London* "show its age" with the more modern Western vehicles parked in the town.

In one film, the parking lot is almost an extension of the dusty public square and the cars and trucks that fill that run-down space are rickety, just as the habitations in the film tend to be. As we have seen in the previous chapter, in *The Outsider*, spaces begin to open up to allow the drifter to move indoors and then outdoors. A liminal character, András inhabits many world—psychiatric orderly, classically-trained musician, folk music band member—but is equally ill at ease in all of them. His real interest is playing the violin which he does in the kocsma and in the village. Tarr shows us a dusty parking lot where he plays for the villagers with his violin case open for tips. Although the film does open out somewhat with occasional natural scenes, the world these characters inhabit is barren, dry, and frail, just as the characters themselves. In this parking lot, Csotesz, András' brother, and Kati escape to begin their relationship. They leave on his motorcycle, both a symbol of his rebellion and of his standing in life. To have a car or a motorcycle indicates the character has begun to possess the trappings of capitalist society that are difficult to afford and thus a sign of luxury in Hungary during the communist era. The motorcycle speeds past the horse-drawn carriages, the old trucks, and the cars parked as their owners listen to András and the others in this street band. They leave behind these scenes of village life and instead make their way to the open road, perhaps going toward Budapest, the location that calls to them but that is always outside their reach. The orderly rows of planted trees lining the road frame this "wild" escape and both tame and contain it within a more claustrophobic, less open frame. Even this one joy ride closes the characters up. The parking lot, therefore, is the place that is to be left behind, the place that must be abandoned.

In a short extension of the parking lot in that film, the roller-skating scene shows András carefree and almost recklessly skating around an elderly drunk who is trying to cross a street. He dominates the space trying perhaps to emulate Csotesz and the motorcycle. But as is the case with almost everything András does, it is a poor substitute. He is shown to be an impostor, someone who had aspiration but who allowed himself to self-destruct and to become just a shell of his former self. The film does not provide a sense of hope for him. Roller skating through town, András has difficulty growing up and acting like an adult, developing his talent, holding on to a job, no matter how unsatisfying (such as in the gear factory). The final scene in the restaurant where the Serbian dignitaries come to the town for an official visit, a scene filled with music (Liszt's "Second Hungarian Rhapsody," another subtle indexical element to indicate the historical and cultural context) that a band other than András' is playing, excludes him. Having been given the nickname "Beethoven" during his failed stay at the conservatory, music provides the anchor to the past through the sounds of classical Hungarian compositions, and lives on, despite life's difficulties. He, however, no longer participates, marginal now to events and possibilities for new encounters, managing a disco where he pedals foreign culture to make it big.

Damnation's primary scenes of intrigue involve parked cars. The very few vehicles we see in this film are parked in a muddy, deserted square, which may indeed be a parking lot. Karrer spies on his lover's husband's VW Beetle that reappears in several scenes, parked near their dilapidated house. He watches as people get into the vehicle and then we see it again parked in front of the Titanik bar. The places where we see this automobile become those which might provide an escape in the plot. But we only see the car parked, and then take off, with the camera stationary in front of the vehicle in the middle of the screen, signaling the impossible promise of escape. We know, however, that it leaves the village to retrieve a mysterious package at the center of the illicit activities, the get-rich-quick scheme. Cars are linked to unsavory activities, as another car in the film is parked outside the Titanik bar when it is used for a sexual encounter. But these two cars are dwarfed by the empty lots and the few objects they contain, as Karrer watches. We, too, become voyeurs of this desolate, muddy landscape of empty lots.

The Public Park

The public park remains distinct from the public square. The latter alludes to classic, even classical, theatrical spaces. Ancient Greek, Renaissance, and many Enlightenment play often situate their action in the public square, also as a way to facilitate unity of action. The public park, instead, is a place for the flaneur, for children to play, at times shown as a long expanse of manicured natural vegetation with benches that connect two roads, two sides of a housing complex, and so forth. Given their potential for convivial encounters and controlled contact with nature, public parks are rare in Tarr, and at times their emptiness further reinforces the character's loneliness.

As we have seen, *Family Nest* provides very few outdoor scenes. One important outdoor area with plants and trees appears in the simply manicured landscape created to surround the housing complex where the family lives. The allusion to a pleasant, bucolic element such as a nest indicated in the title becomes an ironic statement on the suffocation of the ill-suited family. The father and son play chess in another public park near the housing complex, and the father takes advantage of this rare moment of what could be congenial distraction to infiltrate his son's mind with ideas that his wife had been unfaithful while he was in the military. Offering no proof, the father keeps providing hints until Laci turns on his wife, accusing her of infidelity, which leads to their separation. The public park, the suggestion of a cerebral game of chess, is a marker of pretense rather than closeness.

As mentioned in the previous chapter, in *The Prefab People*, the opening scene takes us to a tended public walkway/garden where a band plays jaunty tunes while residents watch from inside their apartments. Here, the appealing grounds are empty. The band plays in the center, with a few inhabitants looking out their windows at the scene, the camera moving from one window to the other while families listen. This in itself creates a sense of emptiness and loneliness, of a community with no sense of togetherness. The reception in the banquet hall, the hairdresser, and all the places where people gather convivially in this film become instead sites of anxious exchanges, worried glances, and jealous interactions, showing the moral bankruptcy of this community.

In two scenes in Tarr's films, we see some happiness in a public park, an amusement park where Laci and Irén take their daughter in *Family Nest*, and a public pool outing in *The Prefab People*. This scene in *Family Nest* is one of the few moments when the camera opens up and shows a landscape behind the people. This manufactured "happy space" provides a glimpse of what could have been for this family falling apart. The outing represents a moment of escape from the claustrophobia of the shared apartment, and the only time parents and daughter are alone. They seem to enjoy the rides, as the camera accompanies them, or shows them from below, in medium shot or zoomed out. It does not end well, however, as the father vomits after the ride before they continue. Even alone they cannot create moments of pure happiness, indicating that even if they were allowed an apartment of their own, the tensions inherent in this relationship would not be resolved.

Even though the amusement park outing in *Family Nest* hints at unhappiness, that episode cannot compare with the bitter events at the public pool in *The Prefab People*. It is there that the couple experiences one of its most violent arguments, attracting attention from the other patrons. The refrain remains the same: the wife accuses the husband of having abandoned her to see his friend while she is stuck with the children who may have come to harm without both parents present. The pool, which should have provided recreation and a way for the children to enjoy the outdoors, becomes a battleground for a very public fight between the two married people in front of their children. They are all at one another's throats and even this soothing location cannot bring them to family harmony.

Before the tense family moments at the pool, the father shared a rare pleasant moment at the friend's tavern on the river, an important setting precisely because it is located on a river with its suggestion of timeless flow. In close-up scenes, the two friends reminisce as they drink beers with the river floating in the background. There are no habitations on this bend in the river, only beautiful wild forests, and meadows. It is during this scene that the friend notes he wants to leave Hungary. The husband asks why, since the location is so beautiful. This particular scene encapsulates the estrangement of the "prefab people," those who are seduced by capitalist dictates but are already seeing the desolation that a life of consumption can bring. As they drink their beers, the two friends share their disillusionment with the system that provides them only prefabricated dreams.

THE WILDERNESS, MAN-MADE AND OTHERWISE

Up to now we have explored outdoor scenes constructed or confined by humans for their utility or enjoyment, usually in areas where those humans live and congregate. Tarr's films include areas outside villages—open fields and forests—which provide contrasts to areas where human must attempt to interact in a civil manner. The coal pit in *Damnation*, unique to that film, is a man-made location, which has to some extent reverted to a wild space. There are perhaps, however, less frequent outdoor locations in Tarr's films than the completely open field. With *Satan's Tango* open fields dominate the "wild" outdoors. We shall explore the open field and other wild locations to see that Tarr shows the difficulty of taming those spaces.

The Open Field

Open fields start to materialize and expand in Tarr's later films, iconic spaces of emptiness. Almost always, they are fields in late fall and winter, when the crops have already been gathered, when the land is cold and barren. And, in Tarr's films, because they are often bathed in rain, the landscape appears muddy rather than potentially fertile, growing food for human sustenance. The land itself resists human contact and has become unwelcoming, without yielding any fruits. In this way, the fields themselves become the kinds of desolate landscapes that mirror the human lives in the films.[7]

In *Damnation*, vistas of open fields beyond the houses appear, but the emphasis is on the village itself and its houses and public areas. This film closely follows the exterior of the houses as Karrer spies on the people inside them, although fields cast their shadow at the edge of the screen. When he follows the singer to her house when she returns from shopping, we can see some open areas behind them in the distance, but it is only part of the alluring possibility beyond the town. There is no escape for them there as the swindle and Karrer's betrayal to the police closes around the doomed relationship.

It is with Tarr's great extravaganza that the open field begins to overtake the outdoor spaces and become the symbol of the desolation of human existence. *Satan's Tango* provides ample exterior open spaces, which replicate the pattern that Tarr has already established in his earlier films. The barn's existence as both interior and exterior, as liminal space, provides one possible example. The outdoor scenes of this film emphasize the bleak fields of winter. Tarr includes several moments when character leave the village to go out on the open road, and these trackings show a straight dirt road going seemingly nowhere through muddy winter fields. There are fallow rows of a field that seems to have been planted once with a few trees, often without leaves, interspersed. The misery and desolation of the people is mirrored in the incessant rain and mud, which abound in the countryside. Tarr has de-emphasized any bucolic elements of the rural setting and instead provided a bleak world of dirt.

After the mob attack in *Werckmeister Harmonies*, Valuska is chased out of the village through an open field very reminiscent of the landscapes in *Satan's Tango*.[8] The fields are fallow and seem to be in an interminable winter, with no grass and only a few trees to see as the horizon looms low at the end of the straight mud road that the postman runs on to escape. He runs as the helicopter chases him presumably to imprison him for "resisting" as the authorities wrested control after the rioters helped them gain power. In the end, the postman is taken to an asylum where only Mr. Eszter, left somewhat unscathed, comes to visit him. He completes his final journey, the film's final scene, when he goes to the square and meets the whale eye to eye.

The Forest

Locus of evil, of spirits, and of confusion throughout human literature, the forest in Tarr continues at times with this sense of wonder and of mystery. While many forests seem to be made up of artificially planted trees in rows, constructed just as the rest of the outdoors and indoor spaces, some seem more natural, and the difference between these two can be important for understanding these films.⁹ In *Damnation*, the first Tarr film that presents a glimpse of forest, it appears at the edge of the town, next to the fields, always on the outskirts but never really in view. They are places the characters do not inhabit but that remain as a possibility just outside the screen.

The first important use of forests arrives with *Satan's Tango* where it links the towns. Just outside the small village at the center of the narrative, characters continually reference "the town" in the distance where escape is possible. A train will presumably be able to take them outside the constricting confines of this village and lead them a more productive, less insular life. The forest lies just beyond the muddy field immediately outside the village and one must cross it to get to the town. It provides the location of the secret burial place for the money Estike gives her brother, and where she realizes he betrayed her. He tells her to bury the money so it will grow like a tree; the brother swindles the little sister in a miniature version of the larger swindle that Irimiás is perpetrating on the inhabitants. Estike's fate is foretold in this initial lie and the forest hides the deed from others' eyes.

Irimiás and Petrina leave the town after the swindle to arrive at the next town in search of a train (figure 4.2).

They travel through a forest to escape the village after Estike's death when they take the villagers' money. They end up walking through a denser forest and come upon a ruined church outlined against the sky beyond the trees.

Figure 4.2 Irimiás and Petrina in the Forest. Screen capture February 7, 2021. *Satantango* DVD.

Irimiás stops and kneels at the site until Petrina mocks him to continue their escape. This moment shows the forest as a location for escape, where the civilized world has come to a halt and could be seen as a quasi-mystical moment, almost a sarcastic repentance by the two swindlers, although they continue their journey after this brief moment. When discussing indoors scenes, we noted that ruins constitute a fairly rare but important subgenre of indoor spaces, once useful and perhaps beautiful but now meaningless and perhaps in some ways grown back into nature to become a kind of bridge between man's presence and his absence. Here, the ruin takes on a mystical purpose. It is where Estike goes to die after poisoning herself and where the voiceover tells us "the angels" will come. Irimiás senses this perhaps and by falling on his knees in the forest creates a moment of emotional connection, only to be shattered by Petrina's sarcasm. Tarr does not allow these moments of revelation to last, and shows us the hypocrisy of these gestures.

The first scene of *The Turin Horse* is a lengthy close-up of the horse straining under the bridle to bring a buckboard back to the stable with a strong wind and blowing leaves against it. This scene creates the initial tension of the film and we understand and feel the elemental struggle of this horse, and of this man, against nature and the elements. The horse and carriage are moving through a forest, with dense trees framing the back of the screen behind the horse's hide glistening with sweat. The horse is framed close-up in a low-angle shot, so that it dominates the frame. This film is filled with outdoor scenes, but the forests are limited to this initial sequence. The horse is going toward the house, the last place it will go. In Jean-Marc Lamoure's documentary about the making of this film, *I Used to Be a Filmmaker*, Tarr narrates a voiceover where he explains his connection to the landscape that became the scenario of this film.

> The landscape, the films, sets, all have a face. They have as much character and meaning as a human face. There is a kind of eternal malediction around this place, something immutable, something unalterable. The people who live here also die here. With little chance to leave this place, it is a bit like living on an island. In a certain way, these places are at the end of the road where you can't go any further. When you reach the end of the road you feel a sense of peace. You are left facing nature and you become one with the place. You do not think of going further, projecting yourself forward or doing anything, desiring anything. No, you are there, and you look around and you understand that it will never change. And in a strange way you do not struggle against this. But maybe that is how I feel because I can leave. (starting minute 7.38)

Framed up on the hill is a lone tree that remains in zoom out shots above the house. Like the lone tree in the scene directions of Samuel Beckett's *Waiting for Godot*, it remains as a stark symbol of the devastation and all that is left in the time after. In *I Used to Be a Filmmaker*, Tarr carefully selects the exact location of the hut he will be built for the movie so as to be below this lone tree on a hillside. The tree in this film is also, as are all others, buffeted by the wind and surrounded by the blowing leaves, in an eternal whirlwind that leads to nothing.

The Coal Pit

Damnation presents us with perhaps the starkest outdoor space of all, the coal pit. In this film, as bleak as the interiors can be, the exteriors are truly infernal. Tarr focuses his static camera on the line of coal bucket swinging in the breeze as they make their way to and from the mine, with incessant noise and movement outside Karrer's window (figure 4.3).

The camera focuses initially on the long line of coal buckets stretching toward the horizon but zooms out excruciatingly slowly until it reveals the window frame, and the man watching the scene as we see him from behind. This is our first introduction to Karrer, the protagonist. For Rancière, the initial sequence shot is "like the signature of Béla Tarr's style: a movement in one direction and the camera moving in the opposite direction; a spectacle and the slow displacement that leads us to the one who watches it; a vague, black mass, which is revealed to be a person seen from behind" (2013, 27). We see the outsides of some of the buildings in the town, but the streets, too, are deserted as he walks from one building to the next. Tarr's camera shows

Figure 4.3 Coal Buckets Out the Window. Screen capture October 7, 2020. *Damnation* DVD.

us in detail the "leprous walls" as Rancière called them with their peeling paint, the chipped bricks, and the littered streets.

The last scene brings this hellish exterior to its climax as Karrer walks among the coal-pocked landscape and finds dogs rummaging for scraps. Like Cerberus, they guard the gate of this underground hell. They howl as he nears, not necessarily to warn him, rather almost as though they were calling. And indeed, in the final scene, he gets on his hands and knees and begins to howl along with them, having become the animal that the film had alluded would be his destiny. The coal pit was a natural area, decimated by humans to provide fuel, and subsequently abandoned, a principal example of man's influence in the Anthropocene. Similar to Ginn's analysis of the lamp's role in *The Turin Horse*, a reminder of the fossil fuel humans extract and in so doing scar the earth, the coal pit pockmarks the land as the peeling paint leaves behind defaced walls. All these natural, geographic, and physical elements appear as the visual side-effects of human mismanagement.

The Ocean

Not surprisingly for a filmmaker who situates most of his films in the countryside of a landlocked country, oceans, and large bodies of water do not figure greatly in Tarr's films. They provide important spatial referents when they do, and we can briefly examine some of them. I will limit discussion in this chapter to the ocean, which appears only in one film. Tarr produced a short film, *The Last Boat*, which takes places on the Danube, but I will discuss that film more in depth in chapter 6.

The Man from London provides occasional scenes of coastline when the characters go to the abandoned hut, perhaps the only natural setting in his feature-length films. It also provides for outdoor scenes as characters walk along the harbor walls, with massive stones lining them bracing the cliffs, reminiscent of Buda castle in Tarr's *Macbeth*. The harbor appears in two different manifestations in the film. First, we see the ship's bow as Maloin watches the illicit exchange from his signal box. The camera focuses on the gangplank and departing passengers, with a small boat transporting goods to the dock. In other scenes, we see a harbor with small crafts as Maloin makes his way around the harbor area. As he rounds the curve, in the far-off distance, we see the lighthouse beacon and open ocean. The port provides the aquatic focus of this film, so we see only glimpses of it shining in the foreground. Usually at night, the water simply becomes an extension of the dock and provides a context for understanding the location and the setting. There are a few scenes, however, of the open ocean beyond the beaches when the characters go to the hut by the beachhead where the murder takes place. Here, the water in the distance alludes to an escape that will not be possible.

It is where the man from London will come, and from where he should return home once his job is complete, an almost ominous backdrop as the waves move energetically toward the shore.

RAIN AND WIND

Rancière takes rain as a central constructing element in Tarr's films. He notes:

> The threat of animality, the threat of the non-human, and possibly the inhuman, is present almost everywhere in Tarr's films, running alongside these stories of swindle and betrayal. Now the mythological and the historical merge into the same element, the rain. The rain is, at the same time, an entirely material element, and the condensation of the whole situation. In a way, it is the zero degree of history; it is that which falls, only falls, always falls, and ceaselessly penetrates the bodies and the souls. (2016, 247)

With *Damnation*, Tarr expands his meaningful atmospheres to include weather and other natural phenomena. Most of his films are situated in late fall or winter and the weather and climate are central to setting the mood. In *Family Nest*, *The Outsider*, and *Almanac of Fall*, the weather was not a factor in the narrative, but with *Damnation*, the setting and rain is clearly intended as a way to indicate the misery of the human lives portrayed.

Satan's Tango includes mostly scenes where characters are trying to fend off a driving rain. We see it trickle off windowpanes, and in the distance as swindlers are trying to make their way from one location to another. We see the rain as it washes over the animals in the film, usually the only ones who are forced to stay continually in water. The rain pervades everything and often characters cannot get dry. In many scenes, the kocsma stove is also used as a way to get dry after coming in from the rain. Characters even remark about the rain, and the effect it will have on the dark forces that are arriving in the city.

Werckmeister Harmonies continues this use of rain for the setting but also complicates it by having period after the rains have ceased when the town, and especially the town square, is enveloped with fog. This atmospheric component is clearly also an allusion to the fog and confusion surrounding the people as they await the prince and as the mob that is following him gears up to riot in the town. The last scene of the film shows the empty square, glistening just after the rain, with the destroyed trailer open on the side to expose the whale. Mr. Eszter moves closer to see the dead eye, staring back at him. This scene shows us the blank expression of nature as it witnesses the self-destruction of humans.

In *The Turin Horse*, the constant wind provides a setting for the characters, buffeted by fate as they try to survive with little food, and in the end, no water (figure 4.4).

The dryness of the ground presages the well's drying up, the crucial factor that makes the man and his daughter attempt to escape, only to return shortly after and close themselves in the house, waiting for the end. The absence of water is critical for all living creatures. The only liquid besides water for drinking, washing, and cooking during the first few days is the pálinka the men drink and that will not sustain life, only bring oblivion. The wind and swirling leaves suddenly stop on the last day and this unexplained absence seems even more terrifying. The viewer now knows that father and daughter are doomed, and the extinguished lights at the end only punctuate this finality. Jaffe provides an important analysis of *The Turin Horse*, *Werckmeister Harmonies*, as well as Corneliu Porumboiu's *12:08 East of Bucharest* in his discussion of slow cinema. He alludes to how the long take works alongside the atmospheric landscape elements such as when, upon their return to the house, "Fred Keleman's camera, which remains stationary almost until the shot ends, displays the front of the house in long shot as dust and debris fly across the windswept space" (2014, 154). Ohlsdorfer leads the horse to the barn outside the frame then continues to help his daughter with the belongings. Jaffe notes landscapes filled with fog, the importance of the hill in the distance, the almost total lack of vegetation or crops in the landscape, all elements that heighten the characters' desolation. Emphasized by the long take, these natural elements create an excruciating environment where rebellion is impossible.

Figure 4.4 Wind and a Well. Screen capture October 7, 2020. *The Turin Horse* DVD.

In the previous chapter, we explored the first intrusion into Ohlsdorfer and his daughter's existence with Bernhardt's arrival. That event, as we saw, took place entirely indoors and the bleakness of the interior highlighted the desolation of the discussion about the meaning of the extermination of the village. Reminiscent of the town's destructions in *Werckmeister Harmonies*, here however we never see the town nor the acts that destroyed it. *The Turin Horse* begins once the destruction has ended. The second intrusion is the arrival of a band of Roma who come from the horizon as though out of nowhere, out of the dust itself, in a carriage driven by two white horses (in contrast to the skeletal, dapple gray horse the father and daughter own). They leave after unsuccessfully trying to get the daughter to come with them as they shout, "the water is ours; the earth is ours." The new characters arrive and depart without leaving permanent traces except for the "anti-Bible" they give the daughter. The Roma's disappearance, however, brings with it the most elemental moment for the father and daughter. The next morning their well is dry, the last means of survival. The Roma, the outside world that beckoned them but that went unheeded, now necessitates their escape. The father and daughter load a cart and try to leave the cottage, only to return when nothing awaits them on the outside (perhaps in reference to Bernhardt's declaration that nothing of the village remains). Physical and temporal cyclicity coincide. Further emphasis on timelessness is helped through absence of temporal markers: there are no indications of time, no clocks, not even sunsets or sunrises, only night and day and indications marking the beginning of each day.

Just as was the case for temporal boundaries and interior boundary divisions, the film contains exterior spatial barriers that set the father and daughter apart from the landscape. In this most elemental framework, inside and outside the house divide the apocalyptic outdoors, with its endless wind, from the relative calm, interior of the house. The house's walls are often framed against the landscape; rarely does the house fill the frame except to emphasize other frames such as the window. The endless horizon, the lone tree, and the hill dwarf it. The horse stall walls and the well in front of the house are really the only man-made divisions in this landscape. Spatial infinity is somewhat narrowed by the camera angle through many of the beginning sequences. To emphasize the difficulty of the labors, a low-angle close-up uses a camera positioned looking upward from the bottom of the hill on which they must go each day to reach their cottage. In this way, the film emphasizes the hardships by limiting the horizon, as when the daughter gets water from the well. The physical divisions of this world of limited possibilities are also emphasized through use of interior divisions, reminiscent of Antonioni's architectural features as frames within the frame.

In terms of both time and space, *The Turin Horse* provides multiple divisions to reinforce the isolation of the characters. With scenes that emphasize the horizon interspersed with claustrophobic shots of frames within the frame, Tarr provides us with spatial barriers that both open out and close out the film's visual universe. From the outset, the film explicitly references Nietzsche and many studies of Tarr's work explore possible connections between the filmmaker and the philosopher. In the Berlin Film Festival press conference, Tarr was asked about the relationship between Nietzsche's work and this film. His answer was evasive, but he admitted that the German philosopher's work has been influential to him throughout his career. Echoes can be found in the film's only notable verbal exchange of any kind. Bernhardt launches into a monologue denouncing two unspecified groups, "they," who have fought over the remainders of the world and have in the process destroyed it. He says there is neither good nor bad in what he portrays as a confrontation between two forces that debase and acquire. There is no hope of return, for Bernhardt notes "the change has taken place." If we are to take his words as truth, then these three characters are all that is left, underscored at the conclusion of Bernhardt's monologue when Ohlsdorfer ridicules his neighbor's rant. While none of the characters can be considered mad, the dogged determination of the father and daughter constitutes a kind of insanity. They attempt to regain their footing by escaping toward the uphill horizon and lone tree, perhaps to the village Bernhardt has noted no longer exists, but only find themselves caught back in the cycle from which they were trying to flee. The characters cannot escape; they show that they are the perpetually subjugated because the forces around them do not allow them to break free.

The Turin Horse has little moralizing. Ohlsdorfer trivializes Bernhardt's monologue, essentially rejecting a framework that would contextualize their predicament in terms germane to Western religion. And Bernhardt does not fight to defend his position. After being rebuked, he leaves money for the pálinka and retreats back up the hill toward the unnamed, unseen, place where he resides. We cannot attribute the hardships of the characters, their fate, that of the village, or that of the horse, to any lack of faith, or outside metaphysical force acting for or against them. In the end, then, the framework within which these characters exist is nature and all its forces. The wind is a constant reminder of nature's indifference as each character, including the horse, must work intensely to accomplish all activities. Even when other humans arrive, Bernhardt and the Roma, they appear through the swirling dust as though brought by, and carried away, by the wind.

Zsuzsa Selyem has noted that there is an absent horse in this film. The harness was made for two horses, but only one drags the cart. This makes the initial minutes of the film even harder to watch since the horse is pulling against itself. There are no partners with whom to share the burden, she concludes. The wind, the lonely tree, the blowing leaves, and the well are life sources and death knells. By constructing both time and space in this film with explicit, obvious, and underscored barriers, Tarr has shaped a relentless landscape beyond morality. In the end, only the wind matters.

Neither interior nor exterior space, an important ecological and geographically real object in this film remains: the exterior well, the lifeline for the characters. When it runs dry, their fate is sealed. It stands against the landscape for the entire film, often the one thing besides the tree that the characters see outside the window. Created by human hands, it provides a transitional point between the human and the natural. As was the case with ruins, and ruined walls, the dry well represents perhaps the moment when the manmade will revert back to nature, when man's attempt to dominate the landscape will have proven itself a failure, introducing whatever will replace the Anthropocene.

ECOLOGY AND OUTDOOR SPACES

We have seen that we must qualify the idea of nature in Tarr's film, for much of the open space is in reality man-made. The use of extreme close-ups in many of his films calls us to see very little in the frame outside the character's faces, the lines therein, their expressions, their bloodshot eyes, and their glances and evasive stares at their fellow humans. The man-made spaces are almost always empty, even if they would, in other contexts, be filled with life. Tarr's universe is an ecology gone awry. We can perhaps even see in Tarr a filmmaker who fills his spaces with artificial landscapes to show that ultimately "taming" nature will not help humans to arrive at a satisfactory existence.

"Natural" spaces therefore take over an ecology of the human as though they were in fact man-made. Truly wild spaces exist just over the ridge, just across the screen, in the distance, and are allusive. Would they provide a kind of harbor or is that too an illusion that humans have manufactured to make their existence more meaningful? Ultimately the wilderness becomes another stifling environment from which the man-made catastrophe can happen.

The elements provide a quasi-apocalyptic universe from which the humans themselves cannot escape. Jaffe discusses Tarr's landscapes (especially in *The Turin Horse*) and tells us:

> The importance Tarr attaches to climate and environment as well as the notion that these factors simultaneously oppress and mirror his human characters has been asserted by Tarr himself as well as by commentators. Asked by Vladan Petkovic how he starts to make a film, Tarr replied "When you're doing a movie, you don't do theories. I just look for locations. A location has a face. It's one of the main characters. So I found this little valley in Hungary and the

lonely tree." Since he dislikes artificial sets, Tarr and his crew built the house, stable and well. Then, during filming, they simulated the all-important windstorm by activating a wind machine, much as a rain machine had been deployed in *Satantango*. (2014, 160)

Jaffe continues that Tarr's belief in the near equivalence of location, face, and character, remains constant, for "the face is a landscape" (2014, 160). Any hint of optimism in landscapes must disappear. Tarr mostly films in spring and autumn, but he dilutes the bright green spring colors very often by making the film black and white suggesting more a fall or winter backdrop, showing the importance of outdoor spaces in this world of claustrophobic interiors that mirror the bleak lives of the characters. In the same way, outdoor spaces are deprived of joy and both create and mirror the emptiness of human lives. In outdoor locations, characters are often alone—Estike in the forest, or Valuska or Eszter alone in the square—unlike indoors where confrontations take place. Even when accompanied, characters usually walk in silence. This solitude of outdoor spaces is not a respite, but a continuation of the social isolation of characters from one another.

The Turin Horse is a film about human life arriving at its end. For that reason, the fields in Tarr's films, with at least the potential to nurture and sustain, have become merely meadows and wildly growing uncultivated land. The meadows provide little comfort or aesthetic respite since they are constantly blown with wind and leaves. There is no place to rest here, and they provide no food for the horses or the people. The land is as barren as the well will become, all which point toward the ultimate blackout that ends the film. Perhaps as Tarr completes his last feature film, man's influence on the earth, incomplete and unsatisfactory in previous films, disappears. Perhaps the end is also the end of the Anthropocene, time and space annihilated together.

NOTES

1. De vastes paysages de Hongrie, des travellings parmi les ruines d'usines et de fermes collectives, des regards échappés par les ouvertures d'habitations délabrées . . . le vide, la désolation . . . de telles images tendues entre le paysage et la créature, entre l'abandon et l'obstination, reviennent dans tous les films de Béla Tarr.

2. *The Last Boat*, filmed almost entirely on the Danube, will be discussed along withTarr's other short films in chapter 6.

3. There is one film that is almost exclusively outdoors, *Prologue*, a short that will be discussed in chapter 6.

4. Expose des bâtisses, des rues, des places, comme les lieux de dynamiques renfermées : ruelles, chaussées, murs, sont saisis comme des matérialités ordinaires qui renforcent l'impression *d'un nulle part*, et répandent la sensation d'un engourdissement,

d'un arrêt. L'habitat des hommes et leurs dehors boueux témoignent d'un climat d'abandon qui domine toute volonté d'entretien et de conservation.

5. In the Cork Film Festival interview, Tarr indicated his film is faithful to the novel, structured like a tango in twelve parts, six forward and six backward.

6. Il suit docilement les gendarmes. Translation Clara Orban.

7. In *The Outsider*, we have discussed the motorcycle ride where characters ride out into the fields with the wind blowing as they experience what they think is the freedom of the open countryside. They cannot escape because they are trapped from within. The fields themselves only yield a temporary diversion.

8. As we have seen, both films also share the location of Baja in Southern Hungary.

9. In *Family Nest*, we noted the absence of any real natural spaces. *The Outsider* had only a short moment with a forest as background. In films such as *The Prefab People*, we have noted few forests as well, only the trees on the riverbank as the two friends discuss their lives.

Chapter 5

Animals

In December 2018, the editors of *Scientific American* wrote that the Anthropocene itself has come under scrutiny precisely as humanists embrace the term that was first coined in the social sciences and that has great implications for the scientific community. Philosophers and sociologist, to name only a few, have begun to question this term (2018, 10). Why, for example, should all humans be under the same umbrella and be implicated in the natural destruction implicit in the Anthropocene when only industrial societies have ravaged natural resources? Also, why should the entire period be under scrutiny when in fact the destruction implicit in the Anthropocene began during the Industrial Revolution when the capitalist model became operative? The Anthropocene implicates humans in the modifications of the natural world and its nonhuman inhabitants given humanity's overwhelming capacity for environmental influence. The indoors humans create to shelter themselves from nature modify the landscape and ostensibly protect the people. In Tarr, humans in these indoor spaces remain isolated, the dilapidated structure mirroring the neglect. Tarr's outdoor spaces show the influence of humans but here, too, instead of flourishing landscapes we encounter mud, rain, and wind. If we are in the Anthropocene, man's relationship to animals matters also in this study to round out an understanding of humanity's imprint on our geography.

Animals in Tarr's films live both indoors and outdoors, liminal creatures like some of the humans. They represent the objects of the Anthropocene, those most affected by humanity's dominance of this period of time. Tarr includes animals in key films and at important moments as a way to highlight the plight of humans, and as a way to show how humans' largely destructive tendencies can filter from themselves to encompass the world. It is precisely also through the use of animals that Tarr's films show us the effects of the Anthropocene.

For Rancière,

> Ever since *Damnation* the animal inhabits Béla Tarr's universe as the figure in which the human experiences its limit: dogs drinking from puddles, which Karrer barked with in the end; cows liquidated by the community, horses escaped from abattoirs, and a cat martyred by Estike in *Satantango*. (2013, 79)

Almost all the animals in Tarr's films are domestic, living around the humans who at times abuse them and whom they mimic (and in some cases who mimic them). There are no wild animals, even caged, to be seen, only naturally occurring birds, for example. The domestic animals include barnyard animals and household pets/service animals such as dogs and cats. Interestingly, rarely if ever do his films include animals humans tend to shun such as rats, or insects. It might seem that these animals could foreshadow and duplicate the insignificant, even unhuman lives that many of Tarr's characters live, but they are essentially absent. The humans in his films provide all the indications of their own degradation already. In some rare instances, sea animals appear that do not belong to any categories previously studied. These animals stand out among the others for their way of bringing to the surface the exotic, the foreign.

Not only are the animal species limited but Tarr does not fill his films with animal. They are sparsely used and when they are, it brings an added element to the mise-en-scène. Even here, however, Tarr does not emphasize the human-animal connection, good or bad, that is implicit in animals that humans have domesticated for work, for food, or more lately for companionship. Dogs are almost always roaming in the streets when they do appear, not belonging to anyone nor seemingly cared for by anyone. Cats, too, remain essentially outdoor inhabitants of barns. Cows, pigs, or horses appear in barns or barnyards that contain them, but they also spend much time in the streets or in the muddy field traversed by the humans in the film. In this way, they become part of human lives rather than being subservient to them. This does not mean, however, that we see loving animal-human connections. Domestic animals are left mostly to fend for themselves, cut off from human contact, or at times exploited or killed by them in almost random negligence or cruelty. The humans in his films fare the same fate. This chapter will be organized according to the animals' level of domesticity because they appear in Tarr's films as a way to highlight human behaviors that were at least implicit when humans interact with one another. They are subjected to some of the same difficulties as their human counterparts and often suffer the consequences. Together these animals provide a way to read, or perhaps reread, the scenarios of human failures and thus round out the menagerie in Tarr's filmic landscape.

DOMESTIC ANIMALS IN THE TOWN AND ON THE (COLLECTIVE) FARM

Dogs, Cats, Pigs, Cows, and Horses

Creatures of all types lose control in Tarr's films. For Sierek, "Béla Tarr's *iconic contingencies* show the painful truth that for some time the ability to control events has abandoned domestic creatures and is anchored in a future of pure duration" (2016, 124–125).[1] Dogs and cats in Tarr's films tend to behave like wild animals in some ways, bridging the gap between the city and the wilderness. Dogs are seen roaming the streets, fighting, or scrounging for scraps. Cats wander through houses but are almost never cuddled or treated as members of the family. The humans' inability to incorporate these domestic animals into their households per se shows us another aspect of their distance from any nurturing feelings. In the case of each individual film, animals appear to serve functions and interact with the characters, and we can trace a map of their existence as we did for spaces.

Especially for a European/American audience in the twenty-first century, domestic animals in films hold the promise of showing the viewer another side of the humans on screen. In decades before the new millennium, while prevalent, films that centered around animals were often taken from novels, such as *Old Yeller* (1957), or concerned current events, such as *Free Willy* (1993), which revealed the exploitation of large marine mammals in aquarium shows. Films such as *Babe* (1995) about a lovable anthropomorphized pig started a trend that proliferated in the new millennium. Films about people's attachment to pets, especially, and pets' importance in people's lives, is showcased. Several extremely successful Hollywood films have animals who soften their stressed and dysfunctional humans, films such as *Beverly Hills Chihuahua* (2008), *Marley and Me* (2008), and *A Dog's Purpose* (2017), are all centered on dogs and their "crazy antics" in formulaic Hollywood narratives, character and plot driven, and created in many cases as vehicles for superstars such as Jennifer Aniston (*Marley and Me*). There are also many films where anthropomorphized, digitally pixeled animals appear to mimic and lovingly mock human behavior, almost all of them animated comedy films. In commercial feature films, stray domestic animals usually signal that the humans in the film are derelict, or from a social strata unable to properly care for animals. These animals, then, signal to the viewer that the humans are "deficient," but the film itself may contain within it the rehabilitation of the humans as they care for their animals. Dogs and cats are often interchangeable in these features, but both are the overwhelming choice when focusing on domestic animals in Hollywood films (very few domesticated birds or reptiles, for example, are present, unless they are part of the filmic setting for extravagant or extraordinarily bizarre humans). Given pets' increasing importance, both in number and in monetary value, to industrialized societies, it is no wonder that dogs and cats in films become surrogate humans and that they demonstrate both human failings and human redemptive potential.

In Tarr's films, too, we can trace a kind of portrait of dogs and cats in each film and see their relationship to the human characters. Tarr's animals almost always roam outside without human guidance nor real human interaction, in the undefinable village, or a small town that is hard to locate. It may be that the randomness of domestic animals in these films mirrors the places, belonging to a kind of distant, indistinct past, when the idea of keeping animals indoors was less frequently held. Or it could be that these animals roam without being taken care because, like the humans, they do not belong, they are isolated. Fending for oneself out of necessity because of being closed off or isolated from others is a theme in Tarr's works and we see again when discussing the animals in his films that they belong to this world where there are no ties that bind.

Several of Tarr's films include dogs within the frame, and only rarely do we hear dogs barking off screen, a fairly common occurrence in films when some sort of warning is being given or a dangerous situation is being revealed. In Tarr, instead, the dogs are part of life in the town and villages, and we often do not know who owns them, if they are even owned, or how or when they can survive by themselves. One of the most striking encounters between dogs and humans appears in *Damnation*. Dogs are the only animals in this film, everywhere roaming around the city scrounging for food. We never see them in the house or being taken care of by anyone. They appear under the rain as well as under the sun. They move around cars parked in the empty lot, which creates this abandoned "outdoors" discussed in the previous chapter. Dogs also cross in front of key landmarks of the film such as the Titanik bar, as though they were part of the action within the walls. The presence of dogs in this film, with their heads down in the mud presumably searching for food, points to the neglect that living beings have for one another in this film where trickery, blackmail, and prostitution are the primary ways in which humans interact with one another. Suspicion abounds among the characters and the dogs constantly searching for something underscores the randomness of the humans' existence, also searching for connections through lifeless intercourse or financial schemes.

In the final scene in the coal pit, dogs roam the heaps presumably looking for food. They seem by this point to have formed a pack, returned to their wild state, in the hellish landscape of the pit. Karrer goes to the pit in the final scene, gets on his hands and knees and begins barking along with the dogs, in a beastly chorus howl. The dogs in fact stop momentarily, surprised to be joined by this human. They do not approach, nor is there any physical contact. Dogs and human continue to communicate using a kind of surrogate canine language. This scene bears witness to the transformation of the human into an animal, which was alluded to in so many other Tarr films where humans have debased themselves.

As he approaches the pit, Karrer walks through the driving rain with his raincoat held close on his hands and knees because of the difficult terrain. But this posture becomes his default position as he finds himself in the pack and adapts instantly to it. Without missing a beat, as one of the more aggressive dogs begins to growl, he growls back. Karrer's is a dangerous position—on his hands and knees with a pack of dogs around him (figure 5.1).

Yet, the rest of the pack has already moved away, accepting this new "alpha dog." In a natural-occurring pack of canids, leadership dominance is established through fighting and other dominance behavior. Once established, the dominant dog protects the pack in exchange for subservience from the pack members. The snarling dog backs off, and Karrer has become the leader. Here, Karrer, who initially tried through trickery to infiltrate the couple (his lover and her husband) and thwart their future, now becomes the alpha of this pack. Perhaps Karrer has regressed to a "lower" form of mammal by becoming one of the dogs, unable to dominate and swindle the humans. Or it could be that the animals themselves have taken the place of humans in the destroyed landscapes so perhaps Karrer, having debased himself, intuits this change and "becomes one" with the new social order. Furthermore, the coal pit itself represents human destruction on the landscape and Karrer, the new dog leader, may already be preparing to survive after the apocalypse and integrate into a new social structure and world.

Figure 5.1 **The Coal Pit Pack.** Screen capture October 7, 2020. *Damnation* DVD.

His status after having fought off the other dogs could have grave consequences for the animals, who would now not be able to fend for themselves. He has in essence ruined the ecology of these former domestic animals gone wild. They would need the protection of the alpha dog within their society, and yet they now have no leader except a failed human who does not seem to have any intention of caring for them. The role here is reversed in an ecological evolution going backward. This is tantamount to the regression of human society in the village, where human emotions have been supplanted almost entirely by greed and deceit. This may then indicate why the film's title, *Damnation*, resonates as it does in the totality of Tarr's work.

William S. Allen notes:

> The final scene where Karrer encounters the dog is clearly a point of realization or discovery, but it is not entirely clear what this point is or how it has been reached. We could say that, having lost his connections to human society, Karrer has been swallowed up by the landscape, but it is perhaps not until the camera finally comes to rest on a black mass of overturned earth that we recall the same silhouette that was the putative subject of the opening shot and the displacement that this implies, which has been present throughout. (2015, n.pg.)

The final mound of dirt serves as a visual reminder of the erasure of humans from this small place.

Satan's Tango offers a veritable menagerie of animals compared to others Tarr created, as might be expected given the rural setting and the length of the film. The central role is reserved for the cat, which will be discussed further. A word about dogs in this film: they appear often in the courtyard of buildings barking at Irimiás and Petrina as they come to or exit the village. Less central to the film's thematic thrust than in *Damnation*, dogs in *Satan's Tango* still roam about the village aimlessly, unprotected or cared for by humans, in another sign of a society where humans no longer care for one another and do not provide shelter, food, or warmth for other creatures either. Moritz Pfeifer explain that *Satan's Tango* has the same types of roaming wild dogs that we saw in *Damnation*, although they are not as much a part of the film's meaning. They add to the general atmosphere of randomness of the existence of the humans that care for them but that fundamentally neglect them. For example, dogs appear outside the kocsma, and as people are leaving the village, living on the margins of this marginal society. They appear as they often do in *Damnation*, rooting around for scraps. Dogs in *Satan's Tango* do not, however, go as far as they do in *Damnation*, because in this village, there is no equivalent of the coal pit, an already ruined world from where an alternative society may rise up after the apocalypse (Pfeifer 2013, n.pg.)

The cat at the center of *Satan's Tango* plays an important role as well within this examination of animals in Tarr's films. We should note that Tarr still often gets queried on the scene involving Estike's killing the cat, which then leads to her own suicide using the same rat poison. In a February 2019 interview, he addressed once again the recurring critique of the cat murder and mentions lengthy rehearsals with the cat and the girl, and a sleeping injection to mimic death that Tarr's vet administered (Weatherall). In this interview, Tarr made a point of saying he himself had two cats at home, as a way to counter those who would consider him unfeeling. Directors being questioned on the use, or potential abuse, of animals in their films reaches back to the early years of filmmaking. Tarkovsky, for example, was criticized for killing a horse during filming of *Andrei Rublev*. The horse was purchased at a slaughterhouse and used in a scene built around the Tartar destruction. It was intentionally injured, stumbled, and fell down the stairs, then was stabbed. The horse was shot off camera after filming. Tarkovsky's crew brought the horse carcass back to the slaughterhouse and the animal was subsequently sold for meat, as it had been originally intended. In more recent times, however, films will often have a preface in the credits noting that no animals were harmed in the filming as a way to assuage audience sensibilities. Recent advances in digital and animation make the use of live animals less necessary.

Given the placement of the episode of the cat in this film it plays an important role in understanding and decoding the meaning of this lengthy masterpiece. For Pfeifer, the cat stands in metaphysically for Estike, similar in their helplessness in the face of cruelty. Pfeifer concludes from this, however, that

> this psychologically explain(s) the motivations for the girl to torture her cat, but it doesn't disquiet the violence of the scene .... For (some), the essential part of the scene is not the torture but the suicide. There's a sacrificial side to the story. (2013, n.pg.)

In *Satan's Tango*, then, Pfeifer sees the incident of the cat's torture and death as symbolic of the tragic human relationships in the film, which lead to the suicide at the center. It is only when faced with Estike's suicide that the villagers rally and decide they are going to act, once they see their youngest and most vulnerable member driven to despair and to violence. They may hope that by leaving the village, they will also leave behind the paths that led to their estrangement from one another. Irimiás promises them a new utopian reality, although those who leave with Irimiás abandon the doctor and a few other characters, at once embracing a new social community and rejecting their old one. The death before them spurs the otherwise cautious villagers to act, perhaps indicating that the suicide brought about at least a partial reckoning.

The cat roams around before coming to the barn with Estike. It mainly stays out of the way of humans, which seems to be moving about freely in a way that the characters notably cannot. It does not appear overly suspicious of Estike or of other characters, probably used to coming and going freely in this rural setting where cats served an important purposed in rodent control. This useful, practical side never appears in the movie, in some ways negating the utilitarian side of the animals. Just as other farm animals are lifted from the roles they usual play, either emotionally or pragmatically, the cat in this film (one of the rare cats in Tarr's works) appears to mirror the emotions of the humans around it, coming close without being overbearing. In that way, the "betrayal" of the animal becomes synonymous with the adult's betrayal of the smallest child of the community.

Hopelessly, however, we see that the characters cannot overcome the desperation, deception, and greed that had been the cornerstone of their lives together. They are trapped by their own existence and it may seem that Estike's ultimate desperate attempt is the only one that can give any meaning. Despite their prevalence in human society, dogs and cats play limited roles in Tarr's films, and when they do appear they are the antithesis of "pets" in our current sense. They return to their wilder state and live on the periphery of human society, and when they do interact, it is often at the animal's expense. The scared humans do not know how to react with empathy to other beings. In this way, they are, as Ginn might have declared, already post-apocalyptic beings, showing what the world will be like without humans.

Farm animals, those both used for work and for human consumption, play roles in several Tarr films from different periods. Already in his earliest films we see farm animals in urban setting as props in the mise-en-scène. Barnyard animals play important roles to show the indifference of nature in several Tarr films. We first consider pigs, because they play a role in only one film, which might be somewhat surprising considering how important they are for the Hungarian diet. In *Family Nest*, Irén works in a salami factory, so some allusion is made to the importance of this animal and its meat, highlighted when the workers are frisked after their shift for fear they will leave with stolen sausage. Still, pigs appear in Tarr films in the same way dogs do—roaming around the streets foraging for food, not in pens, slaughterhouses, or barns.

Satan's Tango, with its multiple animal "roles," has pigs rooting around the town from time to time, often close to the houses. This might be consonant with the rural setting, but it also underscores the idea of scavenging human beings. Pigs in fact reappear at crucial moments, always roaming about in the streets rather than in a barn or near humans. A huge pig eats placidly outside the bar where the townspeople listen to the accounts of the strangers who are making their way to the village. The drunken patrons recount, over again, the story of how they were seen, who they might be, what their arrival might mean, harbingers of doom. The pig continues to search for food outside the building, food which he needs to find for himself, a kind of self-reliance that the humans in the film do not seem to have. They remain paralyzed from fear of what these new arrival might mean, whether their lives will continue or not. The pig continues to eat as though time were standing still.

Cows, too, appear in only one film, which also might seem somewhat strange given that so many Tarr films are ambient in rural settings (figure 5.2).

Critics have variously interpreted their appearance. Rancière notes:

> Cows are animals endowed with a weak symbolic power It is, therefore, as an actual herd, and not as an image of herd mentality, that they must appear to us. Their inaugural presence is certainly given without explanation, but we can justify it *a posteriori*: with the departure of these cows, the last stock of a collective farm is being liquidated. And it is the money from this sale that will be at the center of the intrigue. (2013, 39)

Famously, *Satan's Tango* begins with an almost ten-minute shot of cows walking in an empty, muddy field next to the village at the center of the film, a scene often highlighted to show Tarr's slow cinema style and his extensive use of fixed camera at crucial moments. The parade of cows munching on

Figure 5.2 Cows. Screen capture October 7, 2020. *Satantango* DVD.

grass becomes uncomfortable for the viewer waiting for some form of action to take place. The real-time existence of the cows signals the continuity, and the indifference perhaps of nature and any supernatural entities to the human's plight in the film. They simply exist and the tragedies that will befall the humans in the film will have no consequence.

This herd is also no longer part of the economy of the village; we do not see them milked, nor do we see their meat on display. Almost all the consumption in this film is of alcoholic beverages, notably either beer or pálinka. The cows of this village could be considered simply part of the mise-en-scène. Their appearance marks another indicator of the futility of the human existence. In essence, they, like the pigs and the dogs, are left to roam without human care, without a purpose, They are neglected, as are the humans in the films, left to their own devices because humans do not know how to connect with one another or with other living beings. We come to learn that the cows are now left on their own because this last herd will be sold as the failed collective farm disbands and the villagers scatter, all before the arrival of the swindlers. The villager's gullibility, then, is contrasted with their previous pragmatism as seen by the arrival, and displacement of the herd.

Horses have the reputation of being noble creatures, associated with work, leisure, or noble activities, but they are used in Tarr's films for work, although an allusion is made to horses used as human food at least once. These animals never take on the noble characteristics of the racehorse or show horse. Equines in Tarr's films are often straggly, run down, emaciated, and overworked, as are the characters in is films, living in difficult circumstances. Horse-drawn carriages appear already in *The Outsider* when András plays his fiddle in the dirt lot. A few other instances of horse-drawn carriages appear in this film, representing the past and transportation that has already been bypassed in the big city that many of the characters long to inhabit. They are a way of life that is timeless but also stultifying, like the factory floor where András churns out gears, only to be told at the end of the film that the factory jobs will offer no overtime. In the same way, the violin he plays is replaced by the disco at the end of the film, whose loud, mechanical music deafens him, and he cannot talk to his wife even though they are standing only a few feet from one another. The contrast between modern life in the big city and provincial life is a central part of this film of talents wasted and promises unfulfilled. Similarly, in *Macbeth*, there are horses in the courtyard used for transportation but given the medieval setting, they are part of the expected staging. Even more so than in *The Outsider*, the horses in *Macbeth* are part of the fairly faithful recreation for period ambiance.

Given the importance of cows and cats in *Satan's Tango*, it is easy to overlook an important, rather surreal moment in the film. Irimiás and Petrina arrive in the town square as they come from the ruined almost abandoned village to let the police know they have arrived. As they get off the train and walk toward the hotel, a herd of horses without saddles runs through the misty square, coming from behind the camera, galloping in a circle, and taking off in two directions on either side of the central fountain. The two remain fairly mystified about this event, just watching it unfold, backs to the camera, until the last horse trots out. They surmise that the horses escaped from a local slaughterhouse and were running for their lives. Tarr may well resist metaphorical meanings to his films, but there is no doubt that this moment can be read as a *memento mori* directed at the characters of the village that has been taken over by the two swindlers.

Tarr's last film is of course named for, and centered on, a horse. In *The Turin Horse*, Ricsi the horse—the only animal in the film—signals the end when she stops eating. Ohlsdorfer and his daughter simply close the stall and walk back into the house. They take her with during their only attempt at fleeing their impending doom when the well runs dry, but after that failed voyage, she shuts down. The horse becomes the barometer for the end. This film does suggest a kind of metaphysical dimension to this end in its structure: six days of existence for this father and daughter, and then, darkness. In a Berlin Film Festival interview, Tarr said that perhaps we would also want to embrace the horse. Konstanty Kuzma also notes that when the horse stops eating:

> The father starts whipping the horse repeatedly to get it to pull the cab. Again, flogging a dead horse. But the whipping is not an act of viciousness, but rather one of desperation. The father—although being the culprit—is finally a victim. His acts of violence are nothing but an attempt to fight the obstructions created by the environment and to prove his authority, and herein lies the profound tragedy of his character, which goes deeper than a shallow pity for his age or his injured arm. (2011, n.pg.)

He sees *The Turin Horse* as a film that evolves through emotion rather than through a series of actions that lead to emotions, as the purest cinema should be. The horse's fate will befall the last humans as well. Pfeifer provides us with a detailed analysis of the horse and its people linked in their fate: "The animals reflect the people. Father and daughter lose their will to live, like the horse that stopped eating in the beginning of the film. They can also no longer perform their daily labor, and seem (to) have already retreated from life" (n.pg.).

Ricsi is not the only horse in the film. Although of secondary importance, the Roma who appear from the horizon arrive in a carriage driven by white horses. The contrast between the gleaming beauty of these animals and the gray, tired horse that has worked and now refuses bring to the fore the difference between the mysterious and the profane as it is viewed in this film. The contrast between the two entities exists on many levels. Ricsi's gray against the two white horses in *The Turin Horse*, the dilapidated wooden buckboard Ohlsdorfer uses versus the more sturdy Roma carriage, and the number: Ohlsdorfer has only one horse. As we saw in the previous chapter, Selyem has noted the absence of the second horse: Ohlsdorfer's buckboard was constructed for two horses. The absence of a horse already exacerbates the difficulty of pulling it, thus increasing the effort of the entire family to try to survive. It also creates a ghost presence in this landscape where want and apocalypse will lead to destruction. Ricsi must bear all the burden, just as Ohlsdorfer and his daughter ultimately die alone. In *I Used to Be a Filmmaker*, we see Tarr shooting the initial scene of this film at times with a second horse. The second horse disappears from the final film, leaving behind a trace, which could stand for the normalcy, the survival, the subsistence, that will never be.

This particular film was also the subject of Ginn's article on the Anthropocene. He looks at fantasies of the apocalypse that are both a product and a producer of the Anthropocene. He is proposing a hopeful reading of the contemporary apocalypse, and for Ginn, films offer us "a way of measuring our sensitivity to the Earth (rather than measuring the Earth's sensitivity to human activities)" (2015, 352). He wishes to "connect geographical debates about socioecological futures to those taking place in the interdisciplinary field of the environmental humanities" (2015, 353). Bringing in Ivakhiv, Ginn notes that films have internal ecologies and that this "makes cinema different from other cultural forms" with their motility and openness. Each film's internal ecology can be read a different way (2015, 353). Taking his cues from *The Turin Horse*, he notes:

> The apocalyptic differs from other ecofilms, which might aim to shock the viewer, or to prompt an emotional reaction to suffering, or to mourn, to bear witness, or to inspire. Although apocalyptic film can do those things, its more important function is to prompt a yearning for something different, a transformation—the beginning of a new world, not the end of an old one—as well as prompt the question of how to respond to an uncertain future. Apocalyptic cinema is not, of course, preprogrammed to do this; rather, a desire for the new emerges out of the ecological relationship among film, viewer, and world. (2015, 354)

In his analysis of the elements of the wind, the horse's refusal to eat or to live, the humans' attempted escape only to end in their destruction and the extinguishing of all light and the connection of these elements to the

Anthropocene, Ginn notes this film contains the possibilities of a new human at its edges. It is the horse that struggles against the wind at the beginning, Ginn notes, and the horse "signals how humans are made through the biological" (2015, 355). As Ginn sees it, the horse betrays the man and his daughter because it is when the horse's instinct to eat is gone that the humans are doomed: The final terror here is not any historical calamity, it is that the father and daughter are deserted by their nonhuman ally (2015, 356). Ginn concludes from this that:

> Anthropocene apocalypse does not therefore demand action or politics in the traditional sense. Instead, apocalypse undercuts the familiar modern narrative of progress . . . . Anthropocene apocalypse might not be exactly hopeful, but it demands a kind of depressing redemption: realizing that the question is not how to continue present ways of life, but the deeper challenge of crafting new ways to respond with honor and dignity to unruly earth forces. (2015, 357)

In the end, for Ginn, this is not a hopeful film: "It shows the destruction of a version of the human that has been elevated into a planetary agent as the anthropos of the Anthropocene. The film enjoins us to imagine the characters doing things differently, breaking out of the law of rain and misery, seeking alternatives to their repeated daily routines" (2015, 357). As we think about *The Turin Horse* in the series of films Tarr produced, we note its special places, not only because it is the last feature film he professes to make but also because he shows us the limits of the roles that humans can play on the planet. As we are arguing, this has been one of the motifs Tarr explored throughout his career, without producing "nature films" or "ecology films." He has nonetheless brought the dimensions of human activity and the destruction it can wreak to bear on humans' relationships with one another as well as their relationship to nature and to other creatures that inhabit it with us.

Birds

Birds appear in virtually every Tarr film, either chickens (domestic farm animals) or birds flying seemingly free in the rural or urban landscape. Birds might seem to be only part of the mise-en-scène, but the scarcity of animals in general in his films as we have seen signals something about what Tarr tells us of our relationship to the universe and to the environment. Birds, therefore, almost exclusively flying free in nature could take a central place in this reading of animals rather than indicating a kind of documentary reality.

Chickens appear in courtyards and open spaces in villages featured in several Tarr film. They are more part of the location, a marker of rural life, than intrusions into the narrative and therefore serve a less striking purpose than pigs rooting in the city, dogs barking in a coal pit, or even than a cat trying to ingratiate itself with a human who will betray it. Given the rural setting, *Satan's Tango* also contains chickens that spend much time pecking for food in the center of town or outside the houses. These birds are integrated in *Satan's Tango*; they blend in with the rooting pig and the cows who wander about the village without human intervention, left to fend for themselves.

One counterexample of chickens found in an unusual location and therefore an index of something more than being a prop, however, are the chickens that appear in the opening shot of *Family Nest* despite the fact that of all Tarr's films this one is the most clearly situated in the capital (figure 5.3).

Chickens roam around the street of this major city mingling with the pigeons as though we were in the country, again signaling perhaps how out of place everything seems in this family nest filled with people who do not fit together. The film begins with a close-up of chickens pecking for food on the street in what is later confirmed as a completely urban setting. The camera pans out from there, as it had on the other animals that roam the streets in other films, the pigs, dogs, and cows. The camera angle is as tight against these animals as it is against the humans in the film. The yearning for a past life on the farm clashes with the violent realities of urban life. The family in *Family Nest* is certainly out of their element in the city, not able to adapt, badly fitting in an increasingly sophistical milieu. The Roma friend who is

Figure 5.3 Chickens in Budapest. Screen capture October 7, 2020. *Family Nest* DVD.

raped is described as someone from the country and she is derided for her seemingly un-urban ways. The film's inclusion of chickens in the opening scenes in unlikely to be an ironic comment on the title. Although the title includes the word "nest," the English translation is somewhat distant from Hungarian, which is closer to "family fires" or "home fires," a tinder box, a combustible situation. In the English translation, however, the idea of a family nest contains notions of warmth, coziness, and general satisfaction, even of comfort, all of which are lacking in the film. Even so, chickens pecking for food on Budapest streets provide a jarring prelude to the human relationships in this dysfunctional family.

An important avian presence in *Satan's Tango* remains the owl, as Samocki reminds us, the subject of a long traveling shot before the camera goes back into the ruined house:

> The animal gazes at the spectator, perched on a half-broken decorative stone. Still on its crumbled perch, it does not fly away. It affirms a promise that the internal night can be linked to nature's nocturnal power, that inside our being lies a non-judgmental, a non-verbal gaze, beyond human limits, which reaches the unhoped-for vacillation of the universe. (2016, 69)[2]

Peter Szendy also studies the owl, noting it as an example of what he calls "animal filmicum," a sort of meta-animal that stands metaphorically for ideas or other things in the film (2016, 101). The owl is only one example of how animals in Tarr, according to Szendy, transcend the merely earthly.

Other nondomestic birds appear in several Tarr films. When *The Prefab People* opens, birds fly across the screen with the camera angle pointing upward toward the sky. The public park under which the apartment window looms is empty, except for the birds flying above the surreal marching band playing in the center of the park to the sparse onlookers at the windows above of the gray, prefab housing blocks. The birds fly into what appears to be smoke belching from a chimney in a scene reminiscent of Antonioni's *Red Desert*. In that film, Giuliana walks through the swampy area near her husband's factory, carelessly holding her son's hand. She seems distant from her surroundings, the yellow, sulfurous belching towers appear menacingly out of focus in the background. Birds fly across the screen, partially blocking the view of these towers, but it is as if the birds were themselves going into the smoke and subsequently begin poisoned. The birds in *The Prefab People* seem to do the same, perhaps an homage to the Italian director's work. The similarity in these two films, produced about two decades apart, centers around the critique of industrialization on the one hand and capitalist culture that is linked to it on the other hand. For Antonioni, situating his film among an elite class in Ravenna, the family of an engineer in an oil refinery, allows the filmmaker to emphasize how the Italian boom was created largely without considering the consequences for the environment or for people. In the film, the couple's young son is surrounded by gadgets and robot toys but has little other interaction with people. His mother, depressed and distant, is not able to give him the affection he needs, rather trying to find it in the arms of another man. The father, never home, provides material goods but little interaction with his son. Similarly, the birds against the sky in *The Prefab People* provide a kind of surreal backdrop, in some ways, quite beautiful as sulfurous clouds billow from the smokestacks leaving a trail behind them. In Tarr's black and white universe, the birds fly against a gray backdrop, themselves a darker shade of gray. At a certain point, the camera follows them until they disappear, as though enveloped by the encroaching smoke.

Almanac of Fall, as we have seen filmed entirely within the walls of the suffocating patrician apartment, has no animals at all as might be expected from this interior landscape. The only suggestion of escape from this life remains the fluttering curtain on the open window letting in late fall warmth, and from that window the viewer can hear the unmistakable sound of birds, life outside this self-imposed prison. *Almanac of Fall* provides an interesting dilemma since birds are heard but never seen. Tarr uses extradiegetic sound rather sparsely, except for musical soundtracks. Here the birds outside the window bring the world of beauty and nature into the film, but without having any impact on this bleak human existence in the house.

Like in *Almanac of Fall*, birds in *The Man from London* are often heard but only rarely seen in the wild. Seagulls are part of the soundtrack at several moments in the film as would befit the seaside setting. They fly above Maloin as he moves toward the hut against the rock where the second murder takes place. They appear here as more a part of the setting than as part of the film's composition. However, this film is perhaps the only one in which an animal is kept and presumably taken care of by a human being in the house. Maloin has a caged bird in his apartment, which offers possibilities for exploration in this film of domesticity gone sour. Scenes in the interior of the house often prove tense due to the Maloin's constant bickering with his family about his newfound, ill-gotten wealth. The caged bird in Maloin's room, whose large window opens out on the central square, provides a respite within the scene's tension and intrigue (figure 5.4).

Maloin's domesticity has become a captivity, an entrapment that mirrors the web tightening around the family as the theft is being discovered. Humans are being entrapped by their greed and by their deceit, as the bird has lost its liberty. Its caged home is like the signal box out of which Maloin watches the world and where he is ultimately watched. There is no escape in this world of human greed and deception, as materialism corrupts everyone.

Figure 5.4 A Birdcage by a Window. Screen capture October 7, 2020. *The Man from London* DVD.

SEA CREATURES IN A LANDLOCKED COUNTRY

Given the setting of Tarr's films, the near absence of sea creatures is not surprising. However, the one appearance of sea life—the whale in *Werckmeister Harmonies*—remains significant. Neither domestic nor barnyard, it plays a central role. This dead animal is the only one that appears in the film and holds an important place in the narrative as it is directly tied to the future arrival of the prince who foretells destruction, and in the setting since the trailer is in the center of town. In an interview in 2016, Tarr said that *Werckmeister Harmonies* has three characters: the whale, Valuska, and Mr. Eszter. The same is true, incidentally, for the filmmaker, of the horse in *The Turin Horse* and the dogs in *Damnation*, since the latter occupy almost all the space. For Tarr, the animals represent a minimal level of life, similar to the inhabitants of the films (Maury and Zuchuat 2016, 18). As discussed previously, this carnival side show beast dominates the final scenes *Werckmeister Harmonies*, with the professor staring at its dead eye as it lies in the streets, its trailer-home broken by the rampaging mobs the night before. Mr. Eszter stares at the whale's eye, which seems to stare back blankly, but does not provide answers. Only the destruction the mob leveled on the city remains. Pfeifer dedicates much of his analysis to this creature. He notes that the whale's arrival just before the town's destruction could be construed as an allegory for post-Soviet capitalism. Like the cat in *Satan's Tango*, he sees the whale as an ambiguous moral signifier for the villagers:

It is János, the main character, who admires the whale like a religious idol. And it is one of the villagers that describes the whale as "horrible," and as a "mysterious, monstrous plague" before it even arrives. Another one says that it is "frightening," yet another predicts "trouble." It is difficult to think of a bigger contrast than between a divine being seen as a sign from the creator of the human race, and a diabolical underwater creature out to destroy it. (2013, n.pg.)

Although fairly rare in his films, animals, then, have precise meanings and are not simply accessories to liven or "ruralize" the scene. Domestic animals are present in films when they can mirror or highlight the desolate plights of the humans.

DOMESTIC ANIMALS MIRROR HUMAN LIVES

Desperate treatment of animals reflects the Anthropocene, man's influence on nature. Rancière even notes how some character become animals, perverse animals even: Anna in *Almanac of Fall*, for example, and how for Tarr many times hell is other people as it was for Jean-Paul Sartre in *Huis Clos* (2013, 19).

Tarr uses different types of animals in his films in completely unsentimental ways, in fact going so far as to have them undergo harm at the hands of humans—the cat, the dogs, even some chickens, cows, and pigs. The arrival of a dead sea animal is so out of place in the film and in general in Tarr's works that it stands for something more than human, an intrusion, a hulking behemoth from a totally different part of the world arriving already dead. Animals, part of the natural world that makes up the mise-en-scène, have a life of their own, a meaning beyond a simple creation of sets or mood as we saw was the case for Tarr's selection of types of interior and exterior spaces. Tarr intensely focuses on watching humans interact with each other, often to disastrous results, with animals caught in the middle who must endure like their human counterparts.

NOTES

1. La *contingence iconique* de Béla Tarr vise donc le douloureux constat que le cours des événements a depuis longtemps échappé au contrôle des créatures domestiquées et s'ancre dans le devenir de la pure durée.

2. L'animal regarde le spectateur, perché sur une dentelle de pierre, à moitié brisée. Fixe sur sa lisière effondrée, il ne s'envole pas. Il affirme une promesse, celle que la nuit intérieure puisse avoir un lien avec la puissance nocturne de la nature, qu'au fond de l'être se loge un regard sans jugement ni langage qui, par-delà la finitude humaine, atteint le vacillement inespéré de l'univers.

Chapter 6

Short Films and Segments
Further Experimentation

Tarr's feature films as we have seen present elements of nature, constructed man-made places, outdoor spaces that nevertheless replicate the decay of the human lives depicted, and are populated by animals whose existence reflects back the diminished human lives by their seeming indifference, marginality, or modeling of human behavior. Similar preoccupations that echo the geographic and ecological realities of the Anthropocene come to light even in other Tarr creations. I examine here non-feature films, which present Tarr with new narrative and filmic possibilities. Two short films, almost twenty years apart, *Hotel Magnezit* (Hotel Magnézit 1978) and *Journey on the Plain* (*Utazás az Alföldön* 1995), stand out in Tarr's production, both of which have at their core natural scenes and experiences that become poetic, almost Romantic, depictions.

From 1990, in between *Damnation* and *Satan's Tango*, Tarr contributed *The Last Boat* (*Az utolsó hajó*) to a collective film, *City Life*: an episode that does not quite present the city as do the other contributions. Tarr also contributed to a collective work, *Visions of Europe*, where twenty-five filmmakers representing all European nations celebrated the enlargement of the Union in 2004 with the addition of ten new members, among which Hungary. Tarr's short, *Prologue*, provides a sobering vision of what the new Europe might be, a clash between the haves and the have-nots. Even after retirement from producing feature films, Tarr has continued to work on installations. *Missing People* (2019) will be briefly introduced to round out this vision of "another Tarr." The short films have received less critical attention than Tarr's features but as we shall see they continue, and in one case at least provide a marked departure, from Tarr's dreary slow spaces.

Chapter 6

HOTEL MAGNEZIT

Hotel Magnézit is a short work, which continues the aesthetic of suffocation where close-up camera work dominates, as it did in *Family Nest* and to some extent *The Outsider*. The black and white film shows a transient hotel where one guest is being evicted for having stolen a motor. While only ten minutes long, and with a minimalist plot, the film squeezes the characters into the confined space of the hotel. This short film can be appreciated as a fairly successful theatrical unity of time and space. The matron tells György Kilián he has ten minutes to vacate the hotel, the film's only location, all unfolding in a film not much longer than ten minutes. In one or two scenes, the camera lingers on the hotel's outside door, but it does not venture farther out than the threshold. It is as though the camera attempts to escape but cannot.

In his interview with me, Tarr recalled that the word "magnézit" was the name of a company, although he could not recall what they made. He did however mention they ran a hostel of sorts for their workers and clearly this is the impetus for this film. Another student project like *Macbeth*, this short film concentrates human existence into a cramped room and the extreme close-ups intensify the interactions and hostility of the three men. When we spoke, Tarr refused to allow the label "parable" or "allegory" for films (although to me, in this short there were echoes of medieval morality plays where the character's conduct defines their role). The sparse treatment of the subject here, which distills human emotions in many ways, provides a prelude to his later work. The hotel itself, named for a forgotten company that made something we can no longer remember, seems to echo the loneliness and uselessness of so many elements in Tarr's work. Furthermore, the fact that the Hotel Magnézit is a hostel, a place for transient human beings, also reminds us of characters such as Valuska, moving from one place to the other, a messenger in a lost time and place. It also reminds us of Estike, abandoned, fed, clothed, but given no emotional sustenance until she ultimately can no longer endure. The men in this hostel who argue are really castaways of society, ostensibly living there because they work for the Magnézit company, but in really, just passing through life. The connection they might have had with others in their same situation is denied, and they remain lonely drifters. In some ways, the trajectory of Tarr's work begins here and ends with his recent installations such as *Missing People* during his post–feature film period, which brings to the fore and forces us to see the homeless. The residents in Hotel Magnézit are one step from that end.

As was the case in *Family Nest*, the principal interior spaces in this film are bedrooms, whether in private or public dwellings. Here too the camera often closes in on the characters as they argue and then watches as the accused thief prepares his meager belongings to move out. The destitution of this microcosm shows that although the claustrophobic interior suffocates the nameless characters, there is no outside, nowhere to escape, the interior becomes a trap. These characters exist in anonymity, cut off from their fellow citizens and relegated to the margins. Kilián had lived in the hotel for eighteen months, but only as he is being evicted do they verify who he is. He takes out his card from the Air Force Academy and they realize he has been telling them the truth all along about is heroic past. In this film, the ecology is entirely man-made, the interior of the hotel, the door, with only an occasional shot of the exterior as seen from across the street. There are no animals, even off camera sounds representing the presence of animals in the surrounding areas. The exterior shots also are essentially absent, with only the brief shot of the hotel's broken sign and the door of the hotel as seen from nearby outside.

The mise-en-scène remains indoors, as the residents themselves are shut into this hotel through their marginalization. The almost exclusive use of extreme close-up, especially at the beginning, brings the tightness of the quarters to bear on the viewers as well (figure 6.1).

The residents have a locker, a bunk bed, and we see little else on screen except for these features of the room. We see little of the walls, stairs, or other areas of the hotel because the residents' faces fill the screen. The bedposts often act as bars blocking the viewers' complete view of the faces arguing behind them, as though the residence and the residents were in a prison. This technique, as we have seen, returns in many other Tarr films such as the factory scene in *The Outsider*. The residents fight over the importance of their

Figure 6.1 Tension in the Hotel. Screen capture October 7, 2020. *Hotel Magnézit* in *The Turin Horse* DVD special features.

belongings as they jockey for space in the hotel. Similar to *Almanac of Fall*, this short film contains only scenes taken inside the destitute hotel to recreate a sense of claustrophobia although we see virtually nothing of the outside of the building. We also see little of the interior of the building because of the close-ups. The drama plays out in sight of the hotel matron who also chimes in that the character to be cast out is unfit. In this sense, the hotel becomes a microcosm where tensions and personalities wage against one another to take ownership of the establishment. Here, a group of presumed strangers acts to oust one of their own, similar to families that destroy one another in Tarr's feature films.

The film asks us to consider what happens to someone who is already marginalized if s/he is forced out of the last remaining refuge: where do the lonely people end up? It also asks us to consider the totality of context when deciding the fate of another fellow human being: the alleged thief tries to counter the charges by recalling he is a war veteran, to no avail. Although this film could only be considered a vignette, it poses the same themes of marginalization, dehumanization, and emotional disfunction that reappear in Tarr and initiates his lifelong search to show us those who often remain invisible.

JOURNEY ON THE PLAIN

Seventeen years later, Tarr produced another stand-alone short film that was out of the ordinary for him: *Journey on the Plain* (*Utazás az Alföldön* 1995), a solo production with similarities to *The Last Boat*, another short film that was part of a collaborative effort that we will discuss in subsequent pages. Two of Tarr's short films have no dialogue, *The Last Boat* and *Prologue*. In *Journey on the Plain*, there is a very definitive soundtrack. Mihály Víg narrates sixteen poems by Petőfi,[1] to whom the film is dedicated. This proves significant in understanding this short, which, along with *Hotel Magnezit*, is not part of a larger collective effort.

In his interview for this book, it seemed as though this film as well as *The Last Boat* elicit painful memories, both born in troubled times for the director and for his close friends. He remembers the genesis of this film: Víg's wife had died and they (presumable friends and collaborators) wanted to help him move away from his grief. They got into the car and drove back to the locations of *Satan's Tango*. This film, therefore, is very explicitly an epilogue for the longer one. The setting, the location, holds tremendous meaning in the creation of this film. It represents looking back in a new light, quite literally, to past creations, both Tarr's own films and the poems that were written more than a century before. The land, the landscape, becomes the reason for creation. Rereading the poet allows the grieving process to move forward.

In this respect, the poet is central to this film. Tarr says in our interview that Petőfi's poems are almost all about the lowlands and going back to that part of Hungary brings the poet to mind. Víg began reciting the poems during filming and that led to their inclusion as the exclusive narration of the film. This particular poet represents all of Hungary, in many ways. Petőfi (January 1, 1823, to July 31, [?] 1849) is considered Hungary's national poet, and was one of the key figures of the Hungarian Revolution of 1848. He tirelessly championed the Hungarian language, a radical notion in a country where the German-language Austrian side of the Austro-Hungarian Empire dominated. In many ways, Petőfi represents the introduction, the reaffirmation, of language, of the true expression of the nation, just as Dante Alighieri or Alessandro Manzoni hold a place as the "creators" of Italian. The poet is eulogized in this film as a way to bring the beauty of the language alongside the beauty of the landscape. The film uses the poems to create a hymn to Hungary. In this way, then, Tarr potentially unites very personal concerns—grief, friendship, artistic creation—with national concerns.

Journey on the Plain provides a quite different experience for Tarr's viewer, as though he had to examine the beauty of nature as the poet would have demanded. In this film, the fields are rich and ripe, the sun shines, and the warm summer breeze blows through tall wildflowers teeming with insects, filled with life. Víg, Tarr's primary musical score composer and occasional actor in his films, recites the poems, which provide the entire narrative. The empty dwellings, the house and ruined church, only serve to emphasize that human existence is absent from this bucolic reality (figures 6.2 and 6.3).

Víg journeys to the places of which the poet sang: the Plain refers to the Puszta, part of the Pannonian Steppe, a grassland ecosystem found in Hungary and a few other former Soviet satellite countries (as well as in Austria). The landscape appears primarily treeless and includes salt lakes, freshwater marshes, and floodplain of ancient rivers. It is thought this area is where the invading tribes of Magyars arrived after leaving the area around the Volga river sometimes toward the end of the ninth century. They settled possibly in the vicinity of the great Plain of Hungary, so in some respects, this location is the center of Hungarian history. The nostalgia that this area brings in the poems is echoed in the loving treatment Tarr gives to the scenery of the film.

The Petőfi poems in the film do not appear in chronological order. The choice follows a thematic unity where friendship, mostly lost, grief at the death of a loved one, and drunkenness as a way to forget provide common threads. In each case in the film, the poems are recited in their entirety. Nature provides a backdrop for the Romantic poet's grief, but in this case, Tarr's nature reflects the thematic thrust of the poem itself. In several scenes, the narrator moves from a dark space into the light, either from a shaded area or an interior toward an exterior filled with sunshine. This general movement

130   *Chapter 6*

Figure 6.2   The Open Road. Screen capture October 7, 2020. *Journey on the Plain* in *Satantango* DVD special features.

Figure 6.3   A Ruined Church and Field. Screen capture October 7, 2020. *Journey on the Plain* in *Satantango* DVD special features.

provides a hopeful context for the sadness inherent in the poems' texts. Yet even here, the narrator finds himself alone. In a few instances, the scene includes another person—a farmer working his field, an old man sitting in a room—but the narrator stands distant from them, lonely as were so many other characters in Tarr's films. They watch one another but do not communicate. In all case, the poems resonate as they are recited and echo in the landscape.

This short film allows Tarr to visually review his other film, but to show the surroundings to us in color and in sunlight. He returns to the locations we saw in *Satan's Tango*, but in the rain, in black and white: the village, the ruined manor, the bell tower, and the muddy road and fields now filled with life. The film opens with a still camera filming an open road in bright sunshine, the field green on both sides of the dirt road. We realize this is the same road we saw endlessly in *Satan's Tango*, but this time it is a light, summerly landscape. While reciting the poem "The Cellar Ramp Is Steep,"[2] Víg walks this same road toward the horizon, disappearing with the camera watching him from behind. A poem of drunken stupor, it had none of the conviviality of sharing a drink with friend, only the aftermath of disorder.[3]

In "My Candle Flutters Dimly," Víg finds himself inside a house, surrounded by darkness but with daylight coming through the window against the camera. He walks to the center left, then walks off camera, and walks around the interior, without, however, any candlelight. The loneliness in the poem resonates with the visual surroundings. He does not have a pipe but a cigarette as he muses about the candle flickering and the poet's loneliness in the face of lost friendship. "Here I Stand in the Middle of the Plain," and its reading positions Víg off camera as we see a man cutting grain with a scythe in the distance. In this poem, the gleaner acts out what the poems tell us, of grains that are like the bodies of two people who see one another but do not truly see. One of the rare moments in which two human beings are together, the poet ends lamenting that the sounds of the workman's scythe does not reach the poet/narrator. There is indeed no contact as the two watch each other, as so many characters in Tarr watch out windows, around corners, and here, from across a field.

Víg comes into close-up as the camera zooms very slowly on him reciting "Sort of Swan Song." We realize we are in the ruined house in *Satan's Tango*, where the unsuspecting group of swindled victims goes thinking they are moving to a better collective farm, only to be scattered. He begins to walk out of the building as the camera watches the corroded walls and floors. At the end of the recitation, he closes the door. A last will and testament of sorts, this poem has the sounds of a dirge as the narrator moves from darkness to light.

The mood brightens with "Let Us Drink," as Víg, dressed the same throughout the film in a white shirt and dark trousers, sits in an empty bar, possibly one of any of the kocsmas in Tarr's films, the public place where sorrows are revealed, where impending doom is foretold, where encounters sad and menacing happen, and where even dancing is joyless, just a movement of two bodies, an excuse to have some kind of human contact. The empty beer steins in front of him are neatly stacked as they are in so many Tarr features. He stares at the camera and it slowly moves out. The ironic ending announces there is no one to drink with, again emphasizing the loneliness of the poet and of the actor, but finds a "silver lining" in being able to drown his sorrows.

"Grief? It's a Great Ocean" brings back the mournful notes of many of both the poet's and the director's works. The camera rotates round the interior of a ruined tower belonging to the church in the forest clearing in *Satan's Tango*, and the camera moves 360 degrees in the interior until it finds Víg's face in close-up. The camera then moves to the open sky where the tower has lost its roof. The only light comes through the small pertuis windows. We see a close-up of Víg's face, but from profile. The poet cries out about grief, and the ruined tower and anguished face both tell the same tale. Here, too, the trope of the ocean's endlessness pointing to loneliness comes to the fore. The camera cuts to the interior of a train car as it looks out the window of the moving vehicle. The grain fields, lush and yellow, can be seen, with birds flying, perhaps disturbed by the motion. "The Birds Travel Away" becomes their narrative since we see nothing except this scene through the window. This poem too uses a theme found in literature, the flight of birds to imply the soul's flight after death, and the train car emphasizes the movement away, the flight, both metaphorically from something and toward an unknown.

Another strange interior appears, this time a beaten bench next to a closed shop window, a "penztar," money house, another scene from one of Tarr's films. Víg recites as the camera focuses on him reminding us that "This Is Too Good," that he is a "sad lad" abandoned by his love. This poem perhaps is the closest to the context in which Víg found himself. A particularly painful memory of a lost love, but with the curious visual addition of the closed money house. Here, the visual allusion may in some way indicate the bitterness of possibilities lost. This poem provides the most direct link to Víg's lived reality as it references the dead rose who is buried and can no longer appear. The contrast between the closed money house and the inaccessible lover creates an ironic tension that heightens the visual isolation implicit in Víg's on-camera presence.

"The Sun's Married Life," a satirical anthropomorphic poem, is the narrative backdrop while Víg travels in an open horse buckboard, with the camera positioned behind him and the driver. In front, the rosy sunset of which the poem speaks, pink and yellow, glows on camera. There is only one horse driving this carriage, perhaps Ricsi from *The Turin Horse*, alone, without the companion to help carry the load. This time, there are two younger horses frolicking in front of the carriage as it makes its way, the next generation, a sign of hope that all will not be lost in six days to the wind and the endless dryness. Another poem of love, bitterness, and loss despite its slightly humorous tone connects thematically to the previous one in its specific reference to the loss of a woman. The loveliness of the setting sun belies the melancholy tone. Here, Víg remains alone, although he sits next to the driver; they do not interact, as in so many scenes in Tarr's filmic kocsmas. The narrator looks at the camera while the driver stares ahead.

"Why Do You Look into My Room?" asks the poet as Víg sits in the corner of a room with light coming from a window partially shining on him. The old-fashioned, faded wallpaper is not a space that anyone would relish as "their room," and that is the point. The poet here shows us his faded existence in the room of the ruined house where the swindled, gullible crowd goes. And "Where Shall Man Finally Go?" poses another rhetorical question, answered by the camera lingering on bare fields of grass swaying, with the open road moving toward the distance, a journey that the camera suggest for us. The road bends, it takes us to unfamiliar places, and the camera moves off into the distance as the waving yellow grains dominate the screen. The paen to the moon, a common Romantic theme, here provides a contrasting vision of the setting sun, and impeding darkness, where dim light abounds. The black and white world of most Tarr films here becomes nuanced, imbuing a sadness that envelopes the viewer and recalls the loss.

In this continued alternation between indoor and outdoor mise-en-scène, Víg stands at a sink with synthesizer music as a soundtrack. The poet asks his friends to embrace him, as the face before us stares at himself in the mirror above the sink. The camera looks over his shoulder. Then the narrator goes to the table and we realize we are in a bar and two patrons are at another table drinking beer. We find ourselves here in one of the many kocsmas with the drinker, alone, with only a few fellow travelers. The poem recited, "My Friends, Embrace Me," provokes a striking cry for compassion that is ignored by the impervious patrons. The human contact implicit in the embrace is achingly denied. In fact, that is the dagger thrust into the poet's heart when he is betrayed by his friends. Our narrator goes to the bar and leaves money behind, as the camera slowly moves to show us the rotating fan keeping the room cool.

This scene is followed by an almost two-and-a-half-minute interlude of music, where Víg plays his primary role in Tarr's films, as musician and composer. He is sitting on the back of a moving truck, an open bed truck not unlike the buckboard seen in *The Turin Horse*. This same music we realize is heard in many films, variations of it in *Werckmeister Harmonies*, *Satan's Tango*, *The Man from London*, and finally in *The Turin Horse*. The truck rolls along a dusty road, passing yellow fields, and then a line of trees. The camera moves to the back of the truck and shows us the road we have already taken. We are at dusk. Several vignettes in the short film show Víg moving from place to place in a vehicle: a train, a buckboard, a truck, a boat. In a few others, he walks from or to a location, usually moving from a darkened indoors to a lighter outdoors. These moments of physical transition establish visual vectors that suggest hope for an emotional transition from grief toward acceptance. This musical moment provides a double transition, visually from place to place and narratively from poem to poem. This is one of two moments where sound connects to poems, here diegetically, as Víg reclaiming his primary role a musician and artist, an important step in moving forward from his loss.

"The Night" comes, with Víg in profile watching the river slowly move as the last hints of twilight fades before us. There is a close-up of his face, he looks out over water, we see an occasional boat, and we realize we are also on a very slow-moving boat. We hear ducks, and we see some orange lights in the distance and can tell they are fishermen. Do we hear the sound of impending thunder as the poems comes to its end? A continuation of the visual atmospheric references, here, too, we are bathed in twilight. The landscape envelopes us as we no longer can see, just as the doctor walls us off the screen at the end of *Satan's Tango*, to show us only a black screen, nothing. Not so severe here, the suggestion remains that soon there will be no way to make one's way in the world. Darkness will prevail.

A poem about loss, "What Happens to the Chuckle?" brings us to a dark interior as the camera focuses on an emaciated old man, shirtless, recalling perhaps the last man standing during the riots in *Werckmeister Harmonies*, the naked, old body in the hospital shower that finally reminded the thugs of their humanity, or so we may think, and inspired them to move away and end their rampage. In another room sits our narrator smoking as the camera moves slowly around his head in close-up. An ashtray on the table becomes the focus in the center of the frame, we hear a dog barking off camera, with the old man off in the distance, still hunched over on the bed. This short poem unites several thematic threads of the works cited as it echoes the pain of the transience of emotions, with two characters within site of one another but separated and disconnected.

"The Judgement" brings us again to the ruined tower, and the camera follows the narrator as he walks around the inside, in circles, repeatedly, in full sunshine. Birds chirp, we see plants growing in the distance outside the tower. The poet tells of rivers of blood, and terrible days, as the narrator walks through the ruin. He walks through an archway and continues to tell us the story of destruction as the camera stands still watching him move into the distance. This poem is the only one that moves from a highly personal tone and space to a more elegiac vision. The theme remains that of human failings but this time with violent overtones. Unlike many of the other poems, however, redemption arrives at the end.

As he ends his recitation, we begin to hear the creaking of a rusty machine of some kind. This second time a sound provides transition from one poem to the next, here with extradiegetic sound seems artificially generated until we realize the sound is a rusty swing when we see the outline of a girl swinging back and forth. "Life Isn't Worth Much" is recited after an intertitle: "Dedication," appears on the screen. In the opening credits, the entire film had been dedicated to Petőfi, so this second dedication appears superfluous. Unless here Tarr dedicates this last poem to the little girl, to another generation of lonely people who begin their lives alone on a swing in the sunshine. The girl gets off the swing, it continues to creak, and then Víg's voiceover comes as we watch the empty swing and see the old house in the distance, perhaps where the girl will go. The narrator tells us of the old beggar who licks off dried food from a pot, one of the discarded people, the missing people, of which Tarr tells us, and perhaps the little girl, alone is one of them. She may not be lost, as was Estike, watching the drunken dance in the rain outside the café, leading to a despair she could not shake. This little girl moves off and allows us to be alone with the words of the poet who has comforted us in the sun, with the green grass amid the ruins. The loneliness of the viewer is affirmed, abandoned by the little girl, the narrator and the poet bringing back the melancholy tone of loss, grief, and loneliness that had been the unifying thread of this poetic, episodic film.

Tarr's use of color brings a gaiety to the film that his usual black and white works downplay. Both *The Last Boat* and *Journey on the Plain* make ample use of the natural setting. We see close-ups of the grass, the insects buzzing on them, as the camera frames the road on the side of the screen. At several points, this could be a nature documentary, where the natural environment, or elements of it, takes center. The humans who inhabit the film are within the natural setting but still shape the environment to their concerns. Not merely a backdrop or a prop, nature becomes instead a repository for the human condition that it reflects, in some ways akin to the Romantic poet. For Tarr, nature reflects back at us even when we are immersed in it. The human condition does not allow nature to soothe us. In this short film melancholy replaces to some extent the desperation of the feature films but mitigated by the Hungarian lowlands landscape in the summer sun. In *Journey on the Plain*, occasional musical moments may provide connections to a Hungarian folk past, just as the landscape brings us back to the origins of the Hungarian people. In some ways, its loving gesture toward the lowlands of Hungary provides a hopeful counterpoint to the pessimism of Tarr's other shorts, contributions to collective films. He sees in this short, the real, lasting beauty of

Hungary, not through its people necessarily, who are often flawed, but rather to the land and to all it can and could provide.

THE LAST BOAT

Tarr's reputation brought him to be invited to contribute to two important and intriguing collective films, about fifteen years apart and made at crucially important historical junctures for Hungary. The first, *The Last Boat* (1990) was produced right after the Berlin Wall fell and the former satellite countries of the Soviet Union were freed. The collective film in which it appears, *City Life*, was created by Dick Rijneke and Mildred van Leeuwaarden, with participating directors representing cities: Alejandro Agresti (Buenos Aires), Gabor Altorjay (Hamburg), José Luis Guerín (Barcelona), Krzysztof Kieslowski (Warsaw), Clemens Klopfenstein (Bevagna), Tato Kotetishvili (Tbilisi), Ousmane William M'Baye (Dakar), Eagle Pennell (Houston), Carlos Reichenbach (Sao Paulo), Dick Rijneke and Mildred van Leeuwaarden (Randstad), Mrinal Sen (Calcutta), and Béla Tarr (Budapest) (City Life website). The article "City Life" explains the project:

> A kaleidoscopic panorama of the world. CITY LIFE is a visual anthology of twelve short stories by twelve innovative directors from all over the world. In each contribution each filmmaker presents his personal view of these cities he knows so well. In this way an inside view of the political, cultural, and social changes in the cities of the world of the 1990s is provided . . . . Each short is a separate and self-contained feature presented in an elaborate framework of sound and image. The sinking of the Titanic, a floating city of sorts, and the tower of Babel, symbolizing the diversity of cultures, serve as links between the various contributions. The cohesion of the episodes is intensified by the music, composed by Zbigniew Preisner, regular composer for Krzysztof Kieslowski. (n.pg.)

Tarr's segment shows a ferry boat that guides passengers from one small town on the Danube to the other. This choice of location for his segment—not depicting life in the city but a vacation spot frequented by those who live in the city—seems counterintuitive. Since it focuses on the last boat, and the segment ends with a shot taken from the interior of the last train car as the tracks pass behind us, this short film presents the extreme outskirts of the city, the place where urbanites go to unwind. Here the middle class is always behind the camera, recording their own versions of a counterpoint to "city life."

In the interview for this book, Tarr's explanation of this short film revealed another very personal moment in its genesis. Tarr had just finished

Damnation as an independent project, which only came to the attention of the Hungarian censors once it was awarded a prize in Berlin. Tarr, always an outspoken critic of the regime, was told he would no longer be allowed to return to Hungary after accepting the prize in person. He had been asked to do this collaborative project during this tumultuous time in his life. For this, *The Last Boat* represents a farewell to Hungary. The location on the Danube, the most iconic river in Hungary and in central Europe, which binds together countries and allows Hungarians to have access to the rest of Europe, becomes here a place for a last look back. This river trip becomes a gesture toward the homeland which is receding in the distance as the boat makes its stops. The sun sets as the boat moves forward, the twilight recalling the melancholy visions in *Journey on the Plain*. The boat, filled with merry makers we cannot hear because there is no sound, cannot lead us to happiness, but rather only reinforces our loneliness.

In opposition to *Hotel Magnezit*, this contribution is filmed entirely outdoors or on the bow of the ship. There are only limited domestic animals brought by their owners out for a stroll, and seagulls and other birds that accompany the boat as it makes its way around the lake. Whereas *Hotel Magnezit* continued emphasizing the claustrophobic atmosphere of Tarr's feature films, *The Last Boat* opens up the horizons almost exclusively with wide-angle lens shots, and lingering views of the calm waters through which the boat sails as it makes its way down the river. Tarr clearly wishes to distinguish his film through the use of color and the central place that the natural location occupies. Although quite brief, the film seems like a fairly radical departure for Tarr, a happy reminiscence of a lovely day on the water.

The film begins with the ship in motion, has no dialogue, and uses the natural light of the sun setting to great effect. A synthesizer provides music for this film as we have heard in many others, a kind of eerie soundtrack of electronically synthesized suspended notes, at times formed into melodic strings. The Hungarian flag flies prominently at the back of the boat. We could say there are characters, a young man and older woman—son and mother?—going from stop to stop on the boat, perhaps filming this voyage as a home movie. They get off to eat at a waterfront stand, they mug for the camera, they walk along the paths at certain stops. Although there is no dialogue per se, at times we realize the characters are talking because their mouths move without us hearing the sounds. The emptiness of their words, our deafness to their sounds, dominates. The only sound is the increasingly louder music. The camera remains on the boat deck, watches as passengers mostly get off with a few getting on to go to another stop on the route. The camera also lingers on the shorelines as the boat arrives, but never on the captain, the main crew members, or even on the majority of the passengers for any length of time. They are all temporarily inhabiting the space of the boat deck, but their paths will not cross for long. In a sense, the boat provides the same kind of transient environment as the worker's hostel featured in *Hotel Magnézit*.

The train ride at the end of this film closes the circle. We never see inside, nor where the car passengers are going. But we can assume from the context that they are going home. There are a few location markers as the ship docks at various small ports along the way, so we do have some identifiable locations in this film. But for the most part, it is an anonymous journey, to no special place and without a clear beginning or end.

This film lavishly and lovingly portrays the natural context of the journey, not only the locations and stops created by man on the way. Several scenes linger on the water, with the boat plying the calm surface. The camera points toward the setting sun, as an indication that this is indeed the last boat. As was the case in medieval literature, the boat here may be the ship of fools or as in Greek mythology, the ship that ferries the dead toward Hades, the last boat. The medieval ship of fools saw humanity as afloat on a boat, where all manner of humans come together, trapped together on this journey through life. In the Greek myth, the afterlife can only be accessed by crossing a river that divides the living from the dead. Charon is the boatman who will ferry over the dead going to their resting place but only in exchange for a coin under the tongue. Charon is a demanding master and like the boat in Tarr's film, he takes us from one side to the other but does not stop for long.

The Last Boat's layers of meaning become clear when contextualized through Tarr's own words of the reality surrounding the film's creation. Filmed as part of a collective effort bringing together filmmakers from throughout Europe, it visualizes one of Hungary's most recognizable landmarks, the Danube, but without visually highlighting its purely Hungarian reference points such as the Parliament Building built along its banks in Budapest. It is a river that binds Hungary to the other European countries just as the fall of the Berlin Wall provided the potential to reintroduce Hungary as a nation to Western Europe. The last boat, however, does not provide a starting point for the journey but rather an endpoint, a moment when the journey will end. Similar to *Prologue*, which as we shall see questions the optimism surrounding the enlargement of the European Union in 2004, it may be that Tarr here makes Hungary's journey toward Europe as a journey inward, questioning the movement forward. As in *Journey on the Plain*, journeys may end as the sun sets, slowly closing out the view.

Tarr insists on grounding film as a medium in reality, which allows for supplemental lawyer of meaning to emerge from this short film. It is the last boat of the filmmaker, who risked exile from Hungary for having dared to create outside the confines imposed on him. The passengers on the boat smile, enjoy the view, and speak but we cannot hear them. Their words mean nothing for they can no longer communicate. Speaking without begin heard continues the thematic separation between humans, destined to be lonely. All the while, the filmmaker records, takes a last look, and watches as the homeland recedes in the distance behind the train as it moves forward to the unknown. The boat is the last ride, the last look, a melancholy farewell. And the inability to hear or be heard isolates even further. It is the last boat of the day, the one where dreams have been made and then which fade along with the sunset.

PROLOGUE

Tarr's episode in *Visions of Europe* (2004) is almost the complete opposite of *The Last Boat*, where the camera remains inside looking out. In *Prologue*, the camera is outside, trained toward an exterior wall then on an interior. It represents a strange interlude, a collaboration between Tarr and other filmmakers who were providing visual understanding of the integration of ten European countries into the European Union in that year. This black and white segment explores class distinctions in the new Europe. *Journey on the Plain* and *The Last Boat* are in color, much more focused on natural surroundings. With this last short film, Tarr again moves to stark contrasts in black and white. The film includes the following directors, each representing their home country's "vision" of the new Europe, although they do not all create films about their countries: Faith Akin, Barbara Albert, Sharunas Bartas, Andy Bausch, Christoffer Boe, Francesca Comencini, Stijn Coninx, Tony Gatlif, Sasa Gedeon, Christos Georgiou, Constantine Giannaris, Peter Greenaway, Miguel Hermosa, Arvo Iho, Aki Kaurismaki, Damjan Kozole, Laila Pakalnina, Kenneth Scicluna, Martin Sulik, Malgosia Szumowska, Béla Tarr, Jan Troell, Theo Van Gogh, Teresa Villaverde, and Aisling Walsh. In *Variety*, Leslie Felperin has noted that some of the contributions are uneven, but that the overall production is interesting (2004, n.pg.).

In his interview for this book, Tarr noted a connection (although he seemed to resist it) between this film and *The Turin Horse*. The latter is a culmination of Tarr's manias—horse stalls, windows—liminal spaces where people watch out the window as the wind swirls and darkness arrives. I had made a connection between *Prologue* and *Macbeth*, which Tarr downplayed, although visually both films show characters huddled against walls as a way to create the claustrophobic feeling the viewer experiences watching so many Tarr films. *Prologue* is, he told me, a film to show Europe who the hell the Hungarians are in the context of this supposedly joyful reunion. For Samardzija, "Despite what he contends in his interviews, the compassionate miserabilism of his late films offer more than an abstract meditation on the cosmic condition of humanity. They also present a geopolitical aesthetic" (107). Shot in a single steadycam using Víg's score, the film is shot in medium close-up where we can only see the faces.

Tarr's contributions ask many questions in an almost surreal vision of society. What does it mean to be European from the perspective of important filmmakers? Tarr's segment continues with a long line of people waiting as the camera pans over the line. We realize that they are all waiting to arrive at a window of an aid station where food is being distributed to the needy. The men and a few women are lined against a wall outside, but no elements of an exterior landscape are visible. A glimpse of a quasi-official space can be seen at the end of *Prologue*, when the long line waiting for something is revealed to be a window where a functionary mechanically distributes one cup of coffee and one paper bag, presumably with bread or a sandwich, to each person, checks something off a list, and then moves to the next patron in assembly-line fashion. The camera never reaches the interior, only gazes fixedly from outside. This vision of the poor waiting for handouts has a political connotation given the film's timing.

Just as *City Life* could be read as an exploration and celebration of the possibilities of a Europe broken free from cold war divisions because of when it was released, *Visions of Europe* explores what it meant for the European Union to add ten new members at once in 2004. These states were largely former communist countries that had been able to integrate their political and economic trajectories to European Union specifications. Although the entire short film is shot outdoors, there is no feeling for the outdoors except for the obvious discomfort some of the people standing in line feel because of the weather. They huddle against the wall as they wait in line, really the only outdoors that the viewer sees to emphasize the people's misery (figure 6.4).

This vision of the wall that hugs characters shows us Tarr using exterior spaces to emphasize how they are trapped, either by institutional mechanisms, or by their own inability to have emotional connections with one another. The camera occasionally shows us the walls that people have built, to provide them with shelter, but which also, in the end at times, traps them in a situation from which they cannot escape.

This collaboration was to be:

Twenty-five countries, twenty-five visions from respected film directors from each of the respective countries that form the enlarged European Community. Each director was asked to give a personal vision of current or future life in this coming cultural melting pot. The hope was to have a powerful manifestation of the cultural diversity of Europe as opposed to the idea of globalization and conformity. The ambition was also to celebrate the artistic freedom and freedom

Figure 6.4 Waiting for a Handout. Screen capture October 7, 2020. *Prologue* in *Satantango* DVD special features.

of expression as these should be the key values of the European community. (Visions of Europe website)

Is Tarr's vision of the new Europe a handout, where some countries will come begging to others? It would seem that his contributions to two collective films marking seminal moments in history that directly impacted Hungary continue to provide somewhat pessimistic counterpoint to the overall enthusiasm of these moments.

AFTER RETIREMENT: *MISSING PEOPLE*

With *The Turin Horse* in 2011, Tarr announced he would no longer make films, which he has since clarified to mean no more feature films. He began his post-feature career by opening and teaching in a film school in Sarajevo. By the end of the decade, he had begun working on different types of constructions, but with the same theme, exploring neglect and cruelty in people, the forgotten. His subsequent work has been in the form of art installations, for example, the June 2019, opening of *Missing People* in Vienna. Richard Deming recounts the experience:

> Members of the audience were led by guides through a back alley of Vienna's Museumsquartier—an area almost never seen by the throngs of tourists visiting the city—into a medium-size hall, where we were made to sit on bleachers on either side of the space, above which hung two small movie screens. In the

middle of the hall stood several high tables on a red carpet, and the remnants of a lively party were everywhere evident. (2019, n.pg.)

The audience was alternately greeted with the debris after a party but also with the types of baggage that homeless people might need—sleeping bags, a suitcase, a dirty parka. With these interactive environments, Tarr brings the atmosphere and the meaning that he hoped to portray in his films to people's experiences.

David Katz notes that *Missing People* was the official commission "by the eminent multidisciplinary arts festival" (2019, n.pg). Deming continues that "*Missing People* is not exactly Tarr's coming out of retirement so much as it is an evolution, or at least an extension, of his negotiation of filmmaking's formal limits" (2019, n.pg.) The film was projected into a back alley of Vienna's Museumsquartier, and the film's hall resembled the space viewers were inhabiting. At the end, viewers were led to a space for conversation. Behind the tables hung portraits of the faces of people featured in the film who thus became part of the experience rather than just objects of the viewer's gaze. Jordan Raup notes that the film is made up of only a few shots (2019, n.pg.) like so many of Tarr's other contributions. A few very long takes to show us ourselves. Consistent with Tarr's view on people and their neglect for one another as mirrored in geographical spaces of the Anthropocene, *Missing People* brings viewers physically to a space where they must confront the neglected, hoping perhaps through this to make us see more clearly.

In our interview, Tarr mentioned several other projects stalled by COVID-19, but a general theme seems to emerge: homeless people. They represent the ultimate isolation, the ultimate landless people who belong and live nowhere. They are also those we choose to ignore, those who remain on the outside, as did Estike, looking at the dancers in the kocsma, as does Karrer, watching, as do those who are lonely and forgotten. These post-retirement projects, installations, container projects, casino projects, and various types of projections that are imbedded into the physical space rather than projected as light onto a two-dimensional surface use space to remind us of all those who have none of their own. These projects may be Tarr's "black canvas," the art that eliminates perspective, form, shape, light, and now color. They bring us to the end, as in *Satan's Tango*, as in *The Turin Horse*, where the light at the end of the film is extinguished as we know are the last characters we have seen on the screen. The art is the physical structure; however, it brings the viewer into the space along with the objects of our gaze. Perhaps this is the only possibility for a redemptive moment, for a journey unto the plain that is the heritage of all.

What to make of these short films in Tarr's career? They represent extremely concentrated moments, like distilled representations of human emotion, suffering, alienation, and redemption. In the way that a short story provides the nucleus that longer novels expand, so too these short films contain in them elements of Tarr's worldview and map out his ecology that will be developed in his longer feature films.

NOTES

1. The poems recited in this film, and their English translations, appear in the appendix.

2. In this section, I will refer only the English translations of the titles. Please refer to the appendix for the Hungarian original.

3. A contrast here might be with Alexandre Dumas Fils' *La Dame aux camélias* (*The Lady of the Camelias*) from 1848, contemporary to Petőfi. Turned into an opera in 1853, Verdi's rousing drinking song "Beviamo" provides a carefree, but foreboding, context for the lovers' quarrel.

Chapter 7

Conclusion

Visions of Loneliness

"No parables. No allegories."
"No."

Those words exchanged during our interview guide me here to allow the places to speak for themselves as I hoped to provide a map of patterns in Tarr's physical universe. The concrete unity that Tarr said separates film as an art form from literature hopefully provided a structure for this work. Even Tarr's loneliness is concrete, as are the taverns, the dwellings, and even the forest and the empty roads. Tally and Battista note that "most of the time, it seems, 'nature' stands in the background, a more-or-less picturesque backdrop to the main drama of human activity" (2016, 5). Tarr's physical locations become a backdrop and indexical markers of the frayed human existences in his lonely universe.

The films we have discussed have similar locations that create a physical universe with emptiness and foreboding, a mirror of human lives. The locations, both rural and urban, at times identifiable at times not, remain mostly anonymous. The public places that could encourage contact such as kocsmas become lonely and dreary. The outdoors is filled with empty squares, or when they are filled with people they tremble with violence. The natural world is desecrated: coal pits and empty, muddy roads. And the forces of nature continue to add to the misery, with wind, rain, and fog. All of these places when viewed through the slow camera become objects in themselves, a kind of itinerary through a ruined landscape. Animals, too, provide little comfort, or nourishment. They exist oblivious or at times abused, one more element that watches us indifferently just as we watch each other from afar.

The short films provide a contrast and were born out of heartbreak. Some such as *Journey on the Plain* or *The Last Boat* are melancholy journeys that say goodbye to a love lost or to the homeland. Others continue the themes of hostility and neglect that often characterizes human relations, such as *Hotel Magnezit* and *Prologue*. Tarr continues to create projects that show us those who have no dwellings but who are all around us, watching us watch them. The absence of a place to call one's own continues the exploration of how physical spaces, the reality on which Tarr insists, shows the fissures in human relationships.

In the interview, one gleans the overarching preoccupation Tarr has with loneliness, with our inability to connect to one another. Parting and departures fray the fabric of human connections. Even the greetings, the arrivals, the possibilities to join a union such as the EU may be fraught with suspicion about how we are: Who are these newcomers? Newcomers are greeted with suspicion, even perhaps with hostility: the sausage factory colleagues in *Family Nest*, the swindlers in *Satan's Tango*, the prince in *Werckmeister Harmonies*. Hostilities can make those who are different into outcast of sorts: András in *The Outsider*, or Valuska in *Werckmeister Harmonies*. Végső reminds us that the Hungarian title of *The Outsider* is *Szabadgyalog*, a technical expression borrowed from chess referring to a pawn whose movements is not opposed by the opponent's pawn. This underscore the duality between the freedom of the pawn to move forward and the predetermined path of its movement that is not free (Végső 316). Tarr's characters are often trapped in this way, confined by their spaces and in turn allowing spaces to weather and decay.

Space blurs in Tarr: "attributes of 'inside' and 'outside' lose their significance in the face of the ubiquitous arbitrariness of events" (Sierek 2016, 117).[1] For Rancière, space and time are material realities (2016, 248). Tarr's techniques—black and white film, lack of montage—are not merely technical effects but rather devices that appear as interesting experiments, part of a system of visualizing human relationships and in turn their relation to the environment. The long take brings Tarr's films in contact with the slow pace of literature, and Damien Marguet understands this as an essential element in Tarr's translating Krasznahorkai's novels into film. The long takes and the long, clause-filled sentences provide breathing room for author and filmmaker (Marguet 2016, 79). In the 2016 interview, Tarr himself notes that black and white eliminates the possibility that a viewer could mistake what is on screen for reality, for black hides things while white shows them, and the entire gamut of gray can be used to create nuance (Maury and Zuchuat 2016, 17). When discussing the arc of his films, whether or not there were "periods" to his work, Tarr says in the same interview that there is no rupture between his films, only evolution with increasing attention given to details (Maury and Zuchuat 2016, 13–14). All this leads us to understand Tarr's work as a continuum, like a dance, a testament to the many dances in his films (tangos and others) that Térésa Faucon reflects upon, where the body is weighed down, and falls, an exchange between bodies, the elements, objects, and time (2016, 95). That is the premise on which this exploration of slow spaces takes place, a geographic and Anthropocentric continuity through the slow camera lens.

The complete length of a thirty-five-millimeter film is eleven minutes. Tarr has noted that this physical and technical limitation has guided many of his aesthetic choices. He knows how much visual information can be included in one film and works toward a narrative that can be contained in that time. The long, slow camera work punctuates the action and the film itself bears witness to how life unfolds. Tarr has noted in interviews (2019 and before) that digital cinema has changed the aesthetic potential of film, with its ability to allow filming to continue. And yet, many critics have noted that Tarr edits as did Godard; he says he edits in the camera. The scene appears on film and makes its way into a universe, revealing the lives of desperate people before our eyes. For Tarr demands that we see other people, that we recognize that they exist, as they bring their pain and their uneven ways of dealing with the world with them. We cannot hide. They will not, and Tarr tells us should not, be "missing people," the people we do not see but who, as he shows us in the 2019 installation in Vienna, are everywhere in the background of our lives.

Those missing people appeared already in a drab communist-era flat in Budapest in *Family Nest*, a husband, a desperate housewife who works in a salami factory to make ends meet, who wants to leave her abusive father-in-law's place but just can't because the bureaucracy does not see their desperation. They must remain, brutal inmates who rape those even less fortunate out of a kind of boredom, and who find no real joy even at the fairgrounds. For *The Outsider*, there is not enough joy in playing the violin to escape the world of the institution—political, mental. In the prefab world, there is no joy at the pool, on a sunny day, in two children who seemingly have everything. There is certainly no joy in *Almanac of Fall*, in a bourgeois household where families plot against one another, where the young take advantage of the old. Even company hostels provide no diversion from men fighting amongst themselves; even years later men and women wait endlessly in line for bread. The world is so cold, so bleak, that Estike kills herself, that erudite young postmen like Valuska who study the planets are institutionalized. This is a world of swindles and of thieves, even good men get seduced by the lure of a briefcase from London that no one sees fall into the water. This is finally a world (outside Turin?) where only wind, potatoes, and darkness remain once the stable door is closed and the well runs dry. Tarr's world shows us the most bleak of possibilities, a true Beckettian "end game," where there is no God(ot) in the end.

And yet the Romantic poet will bring light into the world's summer fields, reciting lines from long ago, that speak of love of the land, that lilt into the sunshine streaming through a ruined wall. The rays of sunshine on a silent boat ride where only the sound of the water and birds can be heard. In the end, is there something onto which we can hold? Is it Europe? The Hungarian lowlands? Is it a chance for humans to see one another, to find those who are missing?

Slow Cinema and its techniques provided the ideal mechanism for Tarr to decrease the speed at which we look away, try to change the subject, strive to make life invisible. Jaffe, quoting Bordwell, notes that the long take postpones the exit or escape afforded by a cut and

> conveys a feeling of confinement rather than freedom. In addition, the tendency of the long-take style to forgo or limit point-of-view shots and shot/reverse shots perhaps reduces the sense that characters possess narrative agency—or distinctive visions and perspectives conducive to effective action. The characters instead become passive victims of "forces compelling them," or captives of the overall design of the film. Tarr's evolution as a filmmaker perhaps bears on this question of human agency in relation to the length of the shot. For his embrace of the long take, in conjunction with slow, intricate camera movement, seems to have coincided with his growing perception of human frailty and limitation. (2014, 164)

Tarr's spaces could be a "huis clos," an enclosed space, and also the title of Sartre's play translated in English as *No Exit*. The claustrophobia of these films, of these universes, do not allow characters to move beyond unless they are swindled into leaving, only to find themselves in a ruined building. There is no exit, because, as Sartre concluded, "l'enfer, c'est les autres"—hell is other people. Tarr's characters have made it so, by their get-rich-quick ideas, their infidelities that give us the illusion of being loved, of not reaching out in a real fashion, even to children, who are smothered in capitalist culture and detached, or who end their lives in the hopes the angels will come. Tarr's overarching film project shows weaknesses but not really the way to get out of our difficulties. The end is only darkness and a raw potato.

Tarr's use of slow cinema to show lives unfolding could have become the sleek, cool emptiness of Antonioni, Tarkovsky's endlessly swirling waters that make geometric shapes, Bergman's game with death overlooking the unfeeling sea, Angelopoulos's wailing mother whose cry falls only on the waves as they did millennia ago in those other tales of human woes when gods and men collided. They all used a slow camera style to show us a side of ourselves that no action film could. In many slow cinema masters, characters are disconnected, for only a camera that forces us to slow down allows us to see past the blur of what modern, industrial society has become, no matter what the political regime in power.

Rancière provided us with a calendar of Tarr's time, the time after, telling us that for Tarr, "it is always the same film that he makes, the same reality of which he speaks; he simply delves a little deeper into it each time. From the first film to the last, it is always the story of a broken promise, of a voyage that returns to its point of departure" (2013, 4). Time, then, as a guiding principle for a lifetime of films about the human condition, where time is made to stand still, to slow down, so we can concentrate on it.

Geography in Tarr, space, demands slowness too. Through geography and slow cinema combined, he leads us to the inevitable downfall of man. Ecological interpretations could help us understand that this downfall is partially due to, or made symptomatic by, our destruction of the world itself, with coal pits, squeaking buckets covering the horizon, muddy fields, and roads that go on forever. In this intersection of geography and ecology, the landscape can be inhospitable, where the despoliation of the land (or is the land despoiled a mirror of a people despoiled?) remains. Space and the city, space and the country, space in places that are hard to define, everything comes together in a black and white starkly contrasting universe.

The claustrophobic indoors began his trajectory, *Family Nest* (where the nurturing nest is only a sarcastic reminder of disfunction), *Hotel Magnezit* (a transient place for disposable people), *The Outsider* (where even the love of music is only another form of madness that cannot bring us closer), *The Prefab People* (where the desire for the good life creates a wedge so that living together is just a form of huis clos), to *Almanac of Fall* (where Sartre's hell arrives in Hungary).

With *Damnation*, we have, as we did in Geoffrey Chaucer's "Pardoner' Tale," a tired, trying triangle where man's bestiality is on display. Shakespeare's *Macbeth* brought greed and its consequences to eternal recognition and Tarr brings the claustrophobia of murderous intent to bear on the story as the walls wedge the couple in.

Satan's Tango and *Werckmeister Harmonies* bring us village streets, squares, swindlers, and princes who threaten social unrest, upheaval, and disorder, only to be stopped by walling oneself up or looking leviathan in the eye to find only emptiness. Even the prologue to our "visions of Europe" shows a skepticism about Europe's hymn, the Ode to Joy—final movement in Beethoven's "Ninth Symphony."

Tarr's *The Man from London* transformed the Belgian novel, faithful in many details, but with emphasis on the thief's loneliness. All that is left, then, is a stable door closing on a horse, two people not even looking at each other anymore, waiting for the end in *The Turin Horse*. And many times, in many place, an endless rain, a wind that makes it impossible to put down roots, except for one lone tree on the horizon, a place where there might have been escape but from where one inevitably turns back, defeated.

What does endure then, once it has all been washed away by the rain? Is it the open fields, the sunlit grass and wheat growing tall on the Plain that provide life and nourishment? It may be the poetry to which a film was dedicated, verses about grief, about love lost, about loneliness: the endless, the poet's Romantic, maybe romantic longing. The ruins show us what was, what we inevitably always do: destroy, take advantage, neglect. But they also show that there was a time when beauty was possible, when we could band together and build, stone by stone, by hand, without gear factories, nor salami factories, without shipyards. Where it would be possible to make slow spaces that could become our resting place.

NOTE

1. Les attributs de "dehors" et du "dedans" perdent leur signification face à l'ubiquité et à l'arbitraire de l'événement.

Appendix A
Petőfi Poems

I here reproduce the sixteen Petőfi poems Tarr has Víg recite as the narration for the short film *Journey on the Plain*. Poems cited here in the original Hungarian have been provided from various sources, with reference to their origin in the bibliography. Translations come essentially from Frank Szomy's complete English translations of the poems (in the bibliography under "Petőfi," with page numbers included here). In our interview, Tarr noted that the film's subtitles provide accurate translations of the poem. The very few instances where the subtitles deviate from Szomy's printed translation are highlighted in endnotes. Punctuation and versification appear here almost exclusively as they do in the printed text except for one or two instances where the subtitle punctuation allows for greater clarity.

The poems are reproduced in the order in which they appear in the credits rather than in alphabetical order so as to provide a more exact understanding of their narrative impact in the film.

1. "Meredek a pincegádor . . ."

Meredek a pincegádor,
Nehéz teher az a mámor.
Hazafelé mendegéltem,
Terhe alatt összedőltem -
Összedőltem!

Elnyúltam a föld színére,
Megeredt az orrom vére.
Ha ott tégla nem lett volna:

Orrom vére nem folyt volna -
Nem folyt volna!

Nem járnék én a pincébe
Jó időbe', rosz időbe'. . .
De tehetek is én arról,
Hogy oly igen jó az a bor -
Jó az a bor!

Dunavecse, 1844. April–May.

"The Cellar Ramp is Steep"

The cellar ramp is steep
A heavy load is intoxication
Slowly I meandered homeward,
Under the load I collapsed,
Collapsed!

I stretched out on the ground,
The blood from my nose began,
If there would not have been a brick
The blood from my nose would not have flowed.—
Would not have flowed!

I would not go to the cellar, either
During nice days or bad days . . .
But can I help it
If that wine is so good—
That wine is so good! (page 63)

2. "Gyertyám homályosan lobog . . ."

Gyertyám homályosan lobog . . .
Magam vagyok . . .
Sétálok föl s alá szobámban . . .
Szájamban füstölő pipám van . . .

Multam jelenési lengenek körűlem . . .
Sétálok, sétálok, s szemlélem
A füst árnyékát a falon,
És a barátságról gondolkodom.

Szalkszentmárton, 1846. Before March 10.

"My Candle Flutters Dimly"
My candle flutters dimly . . .
I am alone . . .
I walk up and down my room . . .
In my mouth is my smoking pipe . . .
My past's apparitions wave about me . . .
I walk, I walk, and I watch
The shadow of the smoke on the wall,
And I think about friendship (page 280)

3. "Itt állok a rónaközépen . . ."

Itt állok a rónaközépen,
Mint a szobor, merően.
A pusztát síri csend födé el,
Mint elfödik a halottat szemfödéllel.
Nagymessze tőlem egy ember kaszál;
Mostan megáll,
S köszörűli a kaszát . . .
Pengése hozzám nem hallatszik át,
Csak azt látom: mint mozog a kéz.
És most idenéz,
Engem bámul, de én szemem sem mozdítom . . .
Mit gondolhat, hogy én miről gondolkodom?

Szalkszentmárton, 1846. Before March 10.

"Here I Stand In the Middle of the Plains . . ."

Here I stand in the middle of the plains,
As a statue, stiffly.
The prairie is covered by a grave-like silence,
Just as a corpse is covered with an eyecover[1]
Far away from me a man mows;
Now he stops,
He sharpens his scythe . . .
The ringing does not reach me,
I see only the movement of his hands.
And now he looks this way,
He stares at me, but I don't even move my eyes . . .
What does he think that[2] I think about? (page 278)

4. "Hattyúdalféle"

Bizony, bizony csehül vagyunk!
Mellem szorúl, majd megfulok,
S szivem táján valami rág . . .
Belőled én, árnyékvilág,
Aligha el nem patkolok.

Hányszor kivántam a halált!
És most midőn már közeleg,
Midőn félig rám lehele:
Olyanformán vagyok vele,
Mint a mesében az öreg.

Hiába! bármi a halál,
Az élet nála többet ér.
Van ottan béke - semmi más;
Van itten bú - de vígadás
Kéjében is pezsg ám a vér.

S én már maholnap elhagyok
Örömeket, fájdalmakat.
Most gomblyukamban a virág,
S ha újra zöldül a világ:
Talán sirom halmán fakad.

S ti majd, ti jó fiúk, kiket
Hozzám barátság lánca köt,
Kikkel most annyi éjszakát
Fölségesen virasztok át:
Gyászoltok a halott fölött.

De én azt mondom, társaim,
Hogy engem ne gyászoljatok;
Természetünktől az elüt -
Mert tudjátok, velem együtt,
Ti mind víg fickók voltatok.

Jertek ki hozzám legfölebb,
S ha állotok sírom körűl:
Vigan hangoztassátok itt

Holt cimborátok dalait
A múlt idők emlékeűl!

Dunavecse, 1844. April-May.

"Sort of a Swan Song"

Truly, truly, I am nearly croaked!
My chest tightens, I nearly choke,
And something chews about my heart . . .
From you, shadowy world,
It seemed I may chug off.

How often I yearned for death!
And now when it is near,
When it breathes on me halfway:
I am now as the elder was
In the story.

Regardless! Whatever death is
Life is worth more than it.
There is peace there—nothing else:
There is grief here—but in the pleasures
Of merriment the blood bubbles.

In a short time
I shall leave joy and pain,
The flower is now in my button hole
And if the world greens again:
Perhaps it shall bloom on my gravemound.

And then, good fellows,
You who are tied to me by friendship's chain
And with who,[3] together, we kept
Wide awake so many nights:
You may mourn over my corpse.

But I say, my companions,
Do not mourn me:
You know, that with me,
You as were all gay chaps,
And mourning would strike against our normal selves.

Most assuredly, come out to me,
And as you stand above my grave:
Cheerfully sound out
Your dead buddy's songs
Of the happenings of bygone days! (page 58-59)

5. "Igyunk!"
Akinek nincs szeretője,
Bort igyék,
S hinni fogja, hogy minden lyány
Érte ég.

És igyék bort az, akinek
Pénze nincs,
S az övé lesz a világon
Minden kincs.

És igyék bort az, akinek
Búja van,
S a bú tőle nyakrafőre
Elrohan.

Sem szeretőm, sem pénzem, csak
Bánatom;
Másnál háromszorta többet
Ihatom.

Pest, 1844. September.

"Let Us Drink!"

One who has no sweetheart
Should drink wine,
And he shall believe
That every girl burns for him.

And wine should drink he,
Who does not have any money
And to him will by then belong
Every treasure of the world.

And wine should drink he,
Who has grief,
And then, from him,
Grief shall rush away.

I have no sweetheart, I have no money,
I have only grief;
Thus, compared to others,
I can drink three times as much. (page 113)

6. "A bánat? Egy nagy óceán"

A bánat? egy nagy óceán.
S az öröm?
Az óceán kis gyöngye. Talán,
Mire fölhozom, össze is töröm.

Szalkszentmárton, 1846. Before March 10.

"Grief? It's a Great Ocean"

Grief? It's a great ocean,
And joy?
It's the little pearl of the ocean. Perhaps
By the time I bring it up I may even break it. (page 280)

7. "Elvándorol a madár . . ."

Elvándorol a madár,
Ha őszre jár
Az idő.
(Tavasszal azonban ismét visszajő.)
Száll . . . száll . . . száll . . . viszi szárnya;
Azon veszed észre magad, hogy már a
Távolság kék levegőit issza.
Olyan sebesen száll,
Hogy eltünő álomnak véled. –
A madárnál
Mi száll tova még sebesebben? . . . az élet!
De, mint a madár, ez nem tér többé vissza.

Szalkszentmárton, 1846. Before March 10.

"The Birds Travel Away"

The birds travel away
If the weather
Turns to autumn.
(In spring they return again)
They fly . . .fly . . .fly . . .their wings carry them;
Suddenly you notice that they already
Drink of the distant blue sky.
They fly so swiftly
That one takes them as disappearing dreams.—
What flies more swiftly
Than the birds? . . .life!
But unlike the birds, it never comes back again. (page 275)

8. "Igy is jó"

Megkopott a mentém préme,
A sarkantyúm rozsdás, görbe,
Nincs a kucsmám félrecsapva,
Nincs a bajszom kipödörve.
Így is jó ily bús legénynek,
Akit elhagyott rózsája,
És lement a földbe mélyen,
Hogy ne is nézhessek rája.

Pest, 1845. February-March.

"This Is Too Good"

My cloak's fur is worn,
My spurs are rusty, bent,
My cap is not cocked to one side,
My mustache is not twirled.

This, too, is good for such a sad lad,
One who has been left by his rose,
She went down deep into the earth,
So that I cannot even look on her. (page 192)

9. "A nap házasélete"

A nap házas legény,
Tudjátok?
Hanem szegény
Fején
Ez épen a nagy átok,
Mert a papucskormány terhét nyögi;
Rosz felesége annyi bút szerez neki.
Természetes hát, hogy a jó öreg
A bort nem veti meg.
A bort, mely minden bajnak orvoslója.
A bort, mely a szívből a bút kiszórja.
De otthon inni nem merészel,
Mert ekkor kész a pör a feleséggel.
Azonban tud magán segíteni.
Midőn az égen a szokott utat teszi:
Csak arra vár,
Hogy fellegekbe öltözzék a láthatár.
Ekkor nem félve,
Hogy őt meglátja felesége,
Bebaktat egy közel eső
Kocsmába,
S iszik, mint a kefekötő,
Bújába'! -
Ha jön az est,
S a felleg oszlani kezd,
Látjátok őtet, amint mámorosan
Piros pofával az égről lezuhan.

Pest, 1844. October.

"The Sun's Married Life"

Did you know
That the sun is a married lad?
But then this is
The big curse
On his head,
For he strains under the load of a puppet government;
His bad wife makes grief for him.[4]
It is natural then, that the good elder

Does not sow the wine material;
Wine, which doctors every trouble,
Wine, which scatters every grief from the heart.
But at home he dares not drink
For then the fight would be ready with his wife.
Meanwhile, when he does his familiar travel
Across the sky:
He waits that
Clouds should dress the horizon.
Then he is not afraid
That his wife may see him;
He hobbles into a
Nearby saloon
And drinks, in his grief,
Like a brush maker! —
When the night comes
And the clouds start to disperse
You can see him with his red face
As he crashes from the sky. (page 118-119)

10. "Miért tekintesz be szobámba?"

Miért tekintesz be szobámba?
Kiváncsi hold!
Nem úgy foly már itt a világ, mint
Hajdanta folyt.

Egykor ha pillantásod hozzám
Betévedett:
Látád a szívben meg nem férő
Lángéletet.

Bú, kedv között élet-halálra
Látál csatát,
De győzedelmeskedni a bút
Nem láthatád.

Ez akkor volt, - ha megtekinted
Most arcomat,
Azt vélheted: tükörben látod
Tenmagadat.

Hideg vagyok és szótalan, mint
- Ahonnan jő
E hidegségem, szótlanságom, -
A temető.

Budapest 1845. January.

"Why Do You Look Into My Room?"

Why do you look into my room,
Inquisitive moon?
The world no longer goes here
As it did in days of old.

Once, when your glance stumbled
Into me:
In my heart you saw a flaming life
For which there was no room.

Between grief and joy you saw
A life or death battle,
But you could not see
Grief become victorious.

This was then—if you would now
Look at my face
You could assume that you see yourself
In a mirror.

I am cold and wordless as—
From where my coldness
And wordlessness comes—
The graveyard. (page 178)

11. "Az ember ugyan hova lesz ?"

Az ember ugyan hova lesz? . . .
Sokrates,
Ki a mérget megitta,
S hóhéra, ki a mérget neki adta,
Egy helyre mentek mind a ketten?

Oh lehetetlen!
És hátha . . .hátha . . .
Mért nem láthatni a másvilágba!

Szalkszentmárton, 1846. March.

"Where Shall Man Finally Go?"

Where shall man finally go? . . .
Socrates,
Who drank the poison,
And his executioner, who gave him the poison,
Did both of them go to the same place?
Oh, impossible!
Yet perhaps: . . .perhaps . . .
Why can not one see into the world beyond! (page 281)

12. "Barátaim megölelének"

Barátaim megölelének . . .
Szivökhöz nyomták szívemet;
Bennem mi boldog volt a lélek! . . .
Később tudám meg: mért öleltek? -
Azt tapogatták, míg öleltek:
Hol van legfájóbb része e kebelnek?
Hogy gyilkukat majd oda döfjék . . .
És odadöfték!

Szalkszentmárton 1846. Before March 10.

"My Friends Embrace Me . . ."

My friends embrace me,
They have pressed their hearts to my heart;
How happy the soul is in me! . . .
Later I found out: why do they embrace me? —
While they embraced me they felt out:
Where is this bosom's most painful place?
That is where they will stab their daggers . . .
And they stabbed it there. (page 286)

13. "Az éj"

Feküdjetek
Már le,
Emberek!
Vagy ha jártok,
Halkan
Lépjetek.

Lábujjhegyen
Lassan
Járjatok,
S durva zajt ne
Üssön
Ajkatok.

Tisztelni kell
A gyászt,
Mert az szent . . .
Éj, a gyászos
Ifju,
Megjelent.

Kedvese volt,
És az
Meghala;
Azért gyászol,
Szegény
Éjszaka.

Csendesen a
Földre
Leborúl,
Hull a fűre
Könnye
Szomorún.

Most egyszerre
-Vajjon
Mi dolog? -

Búsan bár, de
Mégis
Mosolyog.

Im, sírjából
A hold
Feljöve:
Holt kedvese
Halvány
Szelleme.

Találkoznak
Édes
Keservvel,
Ölelkeznek
Kínos
Gyönyörrel.

És beszélnek . . .
De ki
Tudja, mit?
Amit senki
Nem sejt,
Nem gyanit.

Nem is volna
Ezt jó
Tudnotok,
Mert e beszéd
Örök
Nagy titok.

Csak az őrült
Hallja,
Amidőn
Rá a lázas
Rémes
Óra jön;

S a haldokló,
Ha már

Csak egy-két
Pókhálószál
Tartja
Életét;

Még egy hallja,
Még egy
Harmadik:
A költő, ha
Ébren
Álmodik,

A merengő
Költő
Érti még
Ama szellem-
Hangok
Rejtelmét,

De nem szólhat
Róla,
Ne kérdezd . . .
Elfelejti,
Mire
Fölébred.

Pest, 1847. December.

"The Night"

Lay down
Now,
Men!
Or if you move about,
Step
Softly.

Go about
Slowly
On tiptoe,
And do not let

Your lips
Strike rough noises.

You must respect
Mourning . . .
For that is sacred . . .
Night, the
Mourning youth,
Has arrived.

It had a love,
And that
Died,
That is why
The poor night
Mourns

Quietly
It falls
Onto the earth,
Sadly
Its tears
Fall on the grass.

Now suddenly
--What
Is it?
Though sadly,
But still
It smiles.

Behold, the
Moon comes up
From its grave:
It is the pale ghost
Of its
Dead loved one.

They meet
With sweet
Bitterness,
They embrace

With torturous
Beauty.

And they talk . . .
But who knows
What?
What no one
Suspects,
Supposes.

But then
It would not be good
For you to know this,
For this talk
Is an eternal,
Great secret.

Only the lunatic
Hears it,
When the feverish,
Terrible
Hour comes:

And the dying,
When his life
Is held
By only
One-two
Spiderweb strands:

One more hears it,
A third
One:
The poet,
If he dreams
While he is awake.

The wistful
Poet
Understands
The mysteries
Of these

Ghostly voices,

But he cannot
Speak of it,
Don't ask him . . .
He forgets
By the time
He comes to. (page 519-521)

14. "Hová lesz a kacaj . . ."

Hová lesz a kacaj,
Hová lesz a sohaj,
Ha hangja elenyész?
S hová lesz az ész,
Midőn már nem godolkodik?
S a gyűlölet,
Ha a szívből kiköltözik?

Szalkszentmárton, 1846, March 10.

"What Happens To the Chuckle . . ."

What happens to the chuckle,
What happens to the sigh,
When their sound's perished?
And what happens to the brain
When it no longer thinks?
And love,
And hate,
When it goes from the heart? (page 282)

15. "Az itélet"

A történeteket lapozám s végére jutottam,
És mi az emberiség története? vérfolyam, amely
Ködbevesző szikláibul a hajdannak ered ki,
És egyhosszában szakadatlan foly le korunkig.
Azt ne higyétek, hogy megszűnt már. Nincs pihenése
A megeredt árnak, nincsen, csak a tenger ölében.
Vértengerbe szakad majd a vér hosszu folyója.
Rettenetes napokat látok közeledni, minőket

Eddig nem látott a világ; s a mostani béke
Ez csak ama sírcsend, amely villámnak utána
A földrendítő mennydörgést szokta előzni.
Látom fátyolodat, te sötét mélytitku jövendő,
És, meggyujtván a sejtés tündéri tüzét, e
Fátyolon átlátok, s attól, ami ott van alatta,
Borzadok, iszonyodom, s egyszersmind kedvre derűlök
És örülök szilajan. A háboru istene újra
Fölveszi páncélját s kardját markába szorítván
Lóra ül és végigszáguld a messze világon,
És a népeket, eldöntő viadalra, kihíja.
Két nemzet lesz a föld ekkor, s ez szembe fog állni:
A jók s a gonoszak. Mely eddig veszte örökké,
Győzni fog itt a jó. De legelső nagy diadalma
Vértengerbe kerűl. Mindegy. Ez lesz az itélet,
Melyet igért isten, próféták ajkai által.
Ez lesz az ítélet, s ez után kezdődik az élet,
Az örök üdvesség; s érette a mennybe röpűlnünk
Nem lesz szükség, mert a menny fog a földre leszállni.

Pest, 1847. April.

"The Judgement"

I have leafed through history and I have come to the end,
And what is the history of man? A river of blood, which
Long ago came forth from the fog-lost boulders,
And in one length, without an interruption, flows down to our time.
Do not believe that it has now stopped. The started flood
Has no rest, not until it reaches the ocean's lap.
The long river of blood shall stop in an ocean of blood.
I see terrible days approaching, such that the world
Till now hasn't seen: and the present peace
Is only that grave stillness which follows the lightning
And comes before the earthshaking thunder.
I see your veil, you dark secret future,
And lighting the fairy fire of predictions, I see
Through this veil, and from what is under it,
I shudder, I am horrified, and at the same time, I rejoice
And I am wildly happy. The War-God again puts on his
Armour, and taking his sword into his hand
He sits on a horse and scouts the far world,

And he calls out the far world,[5]
And he calls out the people for a decisive struggle.
The world then will become two nations and they will face each other:
The good ones and the bad ones. That one, which till now always lost,
The good ones, will win here. But the first big battle shall result
In an ocean of blood. But regardless. This shall be the judgement
Which God has promised, as it has been described by the prophets,
This shall be the judgement and after this life shall begin,
Eternal salvation; and it shall not be necessary for us
To fly to heaven for heaven shall come down to earth. (page 393)

16. "Annyit sem ér az élet"

Annyit sem ér az élet,
Mint egy eltört fazék, mit a konyhából
Kidobtak, s melynek oldaláról
Vén koldús nyalja a rászáradt ételt!

Szalkszentmárton 1846. Before March 10.

"Life Isn't Even Worth As Much . . ."

Life isn't even worth as much
As a broken pot that is thrown from the kitchen
And from whose sides
The old beggar licks off the dried-on food. (page 276)

NOTES

1. The subtitles include the more idiomatic "shroud."
2. The subtitles do not include "that" here, allowing for greater flow.
3. The subtitles include the correct word: "whom."
4. The subtitle includes the more idiomatic "gives him grief."
5. This verse is not in the subtitles.

Appendix B

Transcript of Interview with Béla Tarr

Sunday, January 24, 2021, 11 am CST

CO: Clara Orban BT:Béla Tarr
BT: Tell me what can I do, or what do you want to do.
CO: Well, it would be very helpful to me if you could answer a few questions that have come up as I have been writing a book about spaces in your films.
BT: Give me the questions.
CO: First, some of the questions are factual because I found some information in articles but only once, so I wanted to confirm with you if it's OK.
BT: Yes.
CO: So I found one article that mentions that *Sátántangó* and *Werckmeister Harmonies* were both filmed in the same town.
BT: *Sátántangó* had eighteen different locations and *Werckmeister* had I think three but they were different. It's only one place that I liked that we used in both films, the main square of Baja. Both films are there.
CO: What was it about that location in Baja that attracted you?
BT: This is the main square, beautiful buildings, plus a kind of Hungarian Classicism and the city hall was very big and very . . . I like it. That's all.
CO: It is beautiful.
BT: Yes.
CO: Just to confirm *Macbeth* was filmed in Buda castle?
BT: Yeah.
CO: Thank you.
BT: There was a kind of labyrinth under the castle and that's what we were using.
CO: Thank you. And the village in the film *Journey on the Plain* is the same location as *Sátántangó*?

BT: Yeah, because the *Journey on the Plain* is a kind of epilogue for *Sátántangó*.

CO: Thank you. And was this particular area or village also the location of other films?

BT: No. Just for *Sátántangó* and *Journey on the Plain*. For this short stuff, we went back with Mihály because during the shooting of *Sátántangó*, sometimes we had a lot of breaks and he was just reading the poems of Petőfi and after the film, he had some really deep, deep trouble in his life. His wife died. And we just wanted to push him a little bit away from this situation by the end. We just jumped into the car and went back to the locations and he was just reading Petőfi.

CO: Is this near Debrecen?

BT: No, it's a lot of different places in the Hungarian lowlands, not connected to Debrecen.

CO: Thank you. OK. Now one of the things for an American reader that I mention is that the locations for some of the indoor places where people go to drink is in Hungarian a "kocsma," not a "csárda," correct?

BT: Yes, kocsma.

CO: OK. Because I make kind of, well not really a big deal.

BT: It's not a csárda it's a kocsma.

CO: Thank you. Does the word "magnézit" mean something?

BT: It was a kind of company, and they were just producing some . . . I don't know what, anyway, the company's name was magnézit and they had a kind of hostel where the workers were living and I kept only the name because I was selecting the different places, the people, and by the end, it was a project for the film school. And we had to do a ten-minute-long TV play and I just remembered this name and I used just the title. But there wasn't any connection with this company.

CO: Thank you. So, the book that I am writing on your films includes a chapter on the short films, so I have one or two questions on some of the longer films, the feature films but my few questions are mainly about the short films. So, if I could begin with the longer films maybe.

BT: Yes.

CO: And since I'm a literature professor, I'm very intrigued by your literature connection, so my first question: What attracted you in particular to *Macbeth* over other Shakespeare plays or international literature?

BT: I have to tell you the truth, it's very simple. I was doing my movies and it was during the film school, and they . . . and I did not care about the film school but I had a professor who said to me "now you are in the third year and you have to do a classical adaptation," because I was just using my manias, and he said if I don't do the classical stuff, in this case, they will kick me out. And because I had to fulfill—it was a kind of exam—I said,

OK. Yesterday night (the night before), I prepared myself for the literary exam and my job was to read all of Shakespeare within two days, and I did it.

CO: Oh!

BT: And I did it. And the last piece was *Macbeth* and I was standing with my professor who was the boss of the school—and on the floor, because I went up, he just came down and all the discussion was on the floor, the corner—and he said he will kick me out if I don't do it. And I watched him. And I remembered only *Macbeth*. And I said to him "*Macbeth* is good for you or not?" He said "of course it's good!" I said, OK I will do it. And it was twenty-five minutes long. But I love Shakespeare very much, and I was really . . . and I understood a lot of things when I was reading. Then I decided, the exam is done, but this man, who was my professor, he loved it very much and on the other hand, he was one of the bosses of the Hungarian television. And he said to me, "OK, you did a part of the play for the exam. But I would like to ask you to do the whole drama for Hungarian television," and I said to him "give me five days." I was reading again, reading, reading, and I said, "OK. I will do it, but we have to cut off half the play." Because there were too many things in it. And for me the most important thing was this couple, the Lady and Macbeth, how their relationship goes. And by the end, I decided I will do it for Hungarian television, and this is what you can see now. And we did it with only two takes, one take five minutes, but it was the same location and the same casting, almost the same casting, but it was a bigger production. For the school project we just did it I think in three days and for the television it was fifteen days. It was very difficult to do because of the weather and it was cold and technical things, because it was only two long takes. And the cameras were frozen, and we had to interrupt. By the end, it was fifteen days.

CO: Thank you. And then another question I have is about the Simenon novel, for *The Man from London*. What was it about that particular novel that interested you?

BT: The title is the same, *The Man from London*. You know I was reading . . . let's see . . . almost thirty years ago, or maybe longer, I don't remember when I read it the first time and I just remembered all the time the atmosphere. A man is sitting in a tower, in his cage, alone, watching the dead town, and all the time working, on the night shift, and it's somehow very, very important for me to talk about his loneliness. And it was very interesting, his revolt, how he wants to change his life, the family's life, and generally life. But by the end, unfortunately, I forgot the novel because I just remembered the atmosphere. And then we saw a lot of new things, but again half of the characters, half of the story line, everything (was eliminated) . . . I was just focusing on these two questions, really, that is his revolt, how he wants to change his life and that's all that was important. But the most funny thing—and it was a big honor for me—the son of Simenon, because he owns the rights, he came to see the movie. He came to Budapest it was, you know they have three different—we paid a lot of money, it was a horrible amount of money (for the rights)—but he came and he saw the movie and he said he was deeply sorry that his father did not see this movie because he said it was the most authentic Simenon adaptation around the world. And he allowed us to write in the credits that it's based on his novel.

CO: Because I saw others, was it Henri Decoin, that did *L'Homme de Londres*, and then there was *Temptation Harbor* by Lance Comfort. So I think you partially answered my follow up question on *The Man from London*, because of course the novel ends—because as I was writing I had the pleasure of reading the novel—so the last line is "Il suivit docilement les gendarmes." He's just completely passive, and your film ends with the extreme close up and the tear so you are, your film is focusing on this family rather than on his defeat. I mean his defeat is almost, I don't know, almost something out of Verga, from the 1800s in Italy, you know, "I vinti," this concept of the ones who would . . . .

BT: Yes, I told you what was important for me. And it was clear. For me, the two women and the two guys, and this kind of duel which by the end is full of respect and time. Nobody wants bad things, but by the end, they found them.

CO: Thank you so much, thank you for the information on the longer films. So just a few questions, then, on the shorter films. So, I have a chapter on *Hotel Magnezit*, *Journey on the Plain*, and the two films which are part of collaborative efforts, *The Last Boat* and *Prologue*. So you've said something already about the circumstance around *Hotel Magnezit*, that it was a school project. How did *Journey on the Plain*, how was that, how was the project born?

BT: I told you, the main issue was Mihály and how he was reading Petőfi and this is *Journey on the Plain*. *The Last Boat* is a little bit more complicated because, you know it was, the idea was to do a kind of episode film about city life and different directors would do something. And the idea was . . . and by the end the Dutch producer finished it. That was the moment after filming *Damnation*. And *Damnation* was the first independent Hungarian movie. We did it out of the system and it was a real underground production. We shot in a publicity studio that was doing advertisements, usually. But they had cameras, they had some technical equipment and by the end we did it, but it was out of the system and at this time, there was still communist censorship in Hungary. And we were out of the censors and everything and by the end we got an invitation to the Berlinale. And the Hungarian officers, they got the invitation officially and they did not know what this movie was. And it was a shock for them. And they called it a "comedy" for the censors, and by the end, they came to see the film and they did not want to allow the film to leave Hungary. But we had already received the invitation. And by the end, they did not take the risk of the scandal and they allowed us to show the film at the Berlinale. And it was a big success but they were really, really angry with me. And by the end, they said, "You did this movie, but you will never do any movie in Hungary in your life." And I got an invitation from the DAAD, this German (artists in residence), and they had this Berliner Künstlerprogramm, and I got an invitation . . . . By the end, it was a year. They said to me very clearly "OK, we allow you to go out of the country, but you cannot come back anymore." And before we left we had this short production, and *The Last Boat* I was thinking what can I do? I combined two novels—two short stories—by László Krasznahorkai, and by the end, I just said, OK, I have to say goodbye to my homeland this is my saying goodbye. I was 100 percent sure I would never, ever come back. And the funny thing was we were in the Berlinale, I was registered, and my accreditation was like a Dutch film director. They did not allow me to have a Hungarian accreditation. And that was my relationship with the Hungarian state and the Hungarian communist shit. It was not funny and somehow painful.

CO: I was thinking how the movie is, it's on Lake Balaton, no?

BT: No, it's the Danube.

CO: OK, so you see, it's almost like a home movie, the people on the boat . . .

BT: Yeah, yeah.

CO: And I was thinking *Hotel Magnezit*, it feels, sorry to come back to *Hotel Magnezit* for one minute, but it feels almost like a parable, or like an allegory.

BT: No, I don't know what is an allegory, what is a parable. No.

CO: No.

BT: Films are all the time concrete, there are no symbols, no allegories of any kind. . . . You know those categories that you are using are coming from literature and I'm sorry, but film is more simple, very concrete, and really for simple thing. Everything is concrete. It's not, it's not an allegory, it's surely not. . . .

CO: OK, I'll be careful when I'm writing . . . .

BT: Yeah, no symbols, no nothing. What you see is real.

CO: You mentioned, I just wanted to get back to Petőfi.

CO and BT discussed poem translations and the Journey on the Plain*'s subtitles.*

CO: For Mihály, was there a particular importance with Petőfi?

BT: You know Petőfi wrote almost all his poems, not all, but almost all, but mostly about the Hungarian lowlands and when we were shooting in the lowland, of course we were thinking a lot about Petőfi. And Mihály discovered for everyone Petőfi and he was just reading between the lighting and preparing the next scene and he was just standing. . . . It was a nice nineteenth-century scene, very Romantic.

CO: I noticed that the poems that you use are not in chronological order. Is there a thematic order? I tried to find one but . . . .

BT: I don't know. The logic was mostly the way of the thinking, not chronology.

CO: Thank you. About the film. You've discussed *The Last Boat* as a collaborative project and about *Prologue*, which is from *Visions of Europe*. How did that collaboration begin, your participation in that project?

BT: It was just an idea. It was . . . the German television ZDF had an idea, and they wanted to do a kind of celebration that the whole Europe is all together, and they were asking me to do a short five minutes long (piece). And I was just thinking how can I celebrate letting Hungary in the European Union? And that was *Prologue*. I just wanted to show where we are, how we are, and what the hell we are doing. And that's all. But anyway, I love very much this movie.

CO: Me too. One of the things that, one of the connections, I think I saw was between *Macbeth* and *Prologue* because in *Macbeth*, the characters are mostly hugging the wall, very close to the wall, and in the same way . . . but not standing in a line. And in *Prologue*, the characters, again we see the wall, we see the line of people and the camera just moves along, and we watch each one come, gets his sandwich and his coffee . . . . So is there a link between *Macbeth* and *Prologue*?

BT: No. If you say *The Turin Horse* I have some things to say. I have some manias. The door of the stall. A lot of small things. Looking out the window. And it's, this is my manias. I was just doing *The Turin Horse*. But it's not . . . . Just take some pictures, some situations . . . .

CO: So the link would be *The Turin Horse* and *Prologue*?

BT: No. In *The Turin Horse*, I was collecting all my manias. I just wanted to say goodbye to all my manias. And the repetitions and a lot of things.

CO: One last thing, I've read a little bit about *Missing People* and some of the recent projects. Are there projects that you would be interested in talking about that you are working on now?

BT: You know, after the *The Turin Horse*, there were a few years when I was doing this film school in Sarajevo. This film factory. Then after, when I stopped, I got this invitation from the Eye Museum in Amsterdam which was a big, big, big, very big exhibition. Thirteen thousand square meters. And it was really kind of retrospective, but not a retrospective. A different way. We were touching the subject of refugees. I got this invitation from the Vienna Festwochen to do this *Missing People*, which was a kind of installation, theater and motion picture, and live music show, and all together it was a big project and it was about homeless people. And now I had an invitation from Locarno. They wanted me to do a kind of casino project, but now Locarno is changed. And of course I am a faithful person I am going out (of Locarno) with Lilly who was the director who invited me and I am really thinking with her to build up this project, this casino, somewhere in France. I have an invitation now from Barcelona, but it's stuck. This is a kind of container project and also a kind of exhibition. It is a museum, a contemporary art museum. I am just waiting for the end of this COVID-19 and I can start this shit. And I have some new ideas. I got a question (query) from Greece, and I'm just trying to do something. And I have some invitations from some countries. I have an invitation, from Princeton, but . . . Because, you know, the last time I was in the States, it was 2011, and I had to give my fingerprints. What kind of a fucked-up country is this? Afraid of my 60 kilograms. Such an idiotic situation and I decided I won't go to the States. You know, I had a huge retrospective in Lincoln Center and I did not go there. Because of the fingerprints. Mentally killing me. When a big, uneducated 200 kilogram fucking police guy is saying "What do you want to do?" You know, I really loved the States. I really love New York. I know a lot of people there. I have a lot of friends in New York, and there was a time when every year, minimum twice a year, I went back to New York to do something there. I had a huge retrospective at MOMA. I had really a lot of things in the States. I went to Chicago.

CO: I know. I saw you at Facets when *Werckmeister Harmonies* came out.

BT: And I was there, and I was there really a lot of times, a lot of cities. But I don't know. I am waiting. This fingerprint is . . . .

CO: I agree.

BT: I am not a criminal. I didn't do anything. I am totally transparent. Anyway, I don't care about the states. I care. Of course, and for me it was very important, the end of the elections.

CO: Yes. Thank goodness.

BT: Like everybody around the world, I was crossing my fingers, and I was watching everything on the screen. But I'm still waiting.

CO: I understand. Should you every come to Chicago . . .

BT: Yeah, yeah. We will see what's going on. But anyway, they release there a lot of thing. The people know me, some of them love me. It's fine.

CO: I want to thank you so much for taking this time to answer some of my questions.

Filmography

FAMILY NEST (CSALÁDI TŰZFÉSZEK 1977)

Music: János Bródy, Mihály Móricz
Cinematography: Ferenc Pap
Editing: Anna Kornis
Production: Balázs Béla Stúdió

Cast:
- Lászlóne Horváth as Irén
- László Horváth as Laci
- Gábor Kun as Laci's father
- Gáborné Kún as Laci's mother

After leaving the army, Laci returns home to his father's crowded apartment, where his wife, Irén, and daughter, Kristi, live with several other family members. The (unnamed) father's verbal abuse makes the living situation very tense, and the mother (also unnamed) and her passive manner do not help the situation.

The film opens with Irén leaving a salami factory after her shift, where workers are checked for smuggled goods. The film takes us through the family's meals, their sleeping arrangements, and their tense conversations. In the background, a TV blares news establishing atomic power and the threat of conflict. The father tries to convince Laci that Irén cheated on him while he was away. As they play chess in an outdoor area, the father insinuates she was going out late after her shift had ended. Irén brings home a colleague, a Roma woman, who works alongside her in the factory. Laci and his brother

Gábor accompany her down the stairs and rape her as the violence just under the surface in this household unleashes itself.

Laci and Irén wish to find their own apartment but the film centers around the bureaucratic nightmare this entails. Irén goes to the housing office to plead for an apartment, but continues to be turned down.

One of Laci and Irén's few moments of joy takes place when they take their child to the carnival fairgrounds. But this moment becomes overshadowed by the family tension. The film ends with the family still trying to achieve their housing independence. Irén leaves as the couple separates as she faces a precarious living situation as a squatter.

HOTEL MAGNÉZIT (1978)

Cast and other specifications unknown

This short film takes place entirely within the walls of a tired and worn hotel for guest workers. One of the residents has been accused of stealing a motor from the factory and is then asked to leave the hostel. The matron in charge and the other guests berate him as they oust him from the premises.

THE OUTSIDER (*SZABADGYALOG* 1981)

Music: András Szabó
Cinematography: Barna Mihók, Ferenc Pap
Editing: Ágnes Hranitzky
Production: Mafilm

Cast:
- András Szabó as András
- Jolán Fodor as Kata
- Imre Donkó as Csotesz
- István Bolla as Balázs
- Ferenc Jánossy as the artist
- Imre Vass as a workman

András is a talented but irresponsible musician who ekes out an existence in a town outside the capital. He gets fired from his job as a hospital orderly for creating a disturbance among the patients. He plays his violin at events such as in the town's café. He had been gifted enough to attend the music academy but was thrown out for his undisciplined behavior. After leaving the hospital, he gets a job working in a gear factory. At the end of the film, however, a labor crisis ensues when foreign machines have increased production making fewer workers necessary and overtime pay impossible.

András moves from relationship to relationship and we see him eventually get married to Kata, who also was involved with his brother Csotesz. Balázs, one of the more well-off people of the village lives in a disorganized house containing symbols of faded elegance such as his own paintings and objets d'art. He tries to convince András to become serious once again about his music. Instead, András continues to drift, only dreaming of breaking out and breaking away. Several scenes focus on András' still great talent—he plays the violin in bars and for small events. In a fantasy/dream sequence, dressed in tie and tails, he air-conducts Beethoven's "Seventh Symphony" as music plays on a record player in an otherwise almost entirely bare room. His married life becomes more tense as financial pressures weigh on Kata who has become the breadwinner of the family. Helped by a loan, András manages a disco in the town and seems to finally be doing well. He has, however, surrendered to the capitalist encroachment of low culture and we assume thrown away his talents to make a buck. The couple breaks up, and the film ends with a band in a restaurant playing Liszt's "Second Hungarian Rhapsody" for a group of foreign patrons. This is one of Tarr's rare films in color.

THE PREFAB PEOPLE (PANELKAPCSOLAT 1982)

Music: Not available
Cinematography: Barna Mihók, Ferenc Pap
Editing: Ágnes Hranitzky
Production: Balázs Béla Stúdió, Mafilm, Magyar Televízió Fiatal Müvészek Stúdiója (MTV-FMS)

Cast:
- Judit Pogány as wife/Judit
- Róbert Koltai as gusband/Robi
- Kyri Ambrus as singer
- Gábor P. Koltai as son Gábor Koltai
- Józsefné Sothó as teacher
- András Udvarhelyi as works manager

A man, his wife, and children live in a prefab housing development, surrounded by other equally monotone dwellings. Their relationship is strained in the small apartment because the wife longs for larger quarters, comparing their situation to that of others around them. She feels trapped into the household role while the husband goes out every day to work and to socialize. The man's lack of ambition is highlighted when he plays soccer with colleagues, all seated at their desks with rolling chairs.

The man has the chance for career advancement when the opportunity arises to go abroad for a year or two. The wife will not allow him to leave her in Hungary caring by herself for their house and children. He gives up his dream and their dream for improved living conditions.

The film intersperses scenes of daily activity, often strained because of differing views of the domestic situation. The flat is furnished with decorative elements, a fridge, a TV, but these signs of comfortable existence are contrasted to the otherwise cramped quarters. A few signs of the family's modest living include the pull-out bed in the living room the couple uses and the can of hairspray that the husband gives his wife for their ninth anniversary. The couple bickers about finances and the wife unfavorably compares herself to other housewives at the hairdresser's as she prepared for the celebratory dinner her husband's workplace is organizing at a local restaurant. The other women discuss travel, but she cannot join in. At the restaurant, the husband dances with another woman as his wife seethes with jealousy. Their increasing bitterness boils over at the public pool when the husband lags behind the family to share a beer with his tavern-owning friend, a farewell drink, for he plans to leave. Instead, the husband proceeds to the pool where his wire yells at him for his tardiness.

At the end of the film, the couple buys a German washing machine, the sign of their inevitable plunge into middle-class existence. They ride in the back of the delivery truck on their way home with the machine, blank expressions on their faces as the empty streets, and seemingly deserted apartment blocks move past them in the distance.

MACBETH (1982)

Music: András Szabó and Gépfolklór
Cinematography: Buda Gulyás, Ferenc Papp
Editing: Not available
Production: Magyar Televízió Drámai Főosztály

Cast:
- György Cserhalmi as Macbeth
- Erzsébet Kútvölgyi as Lady Macbeth
- Also starring:
  - Ferenc Bencze
  - Imre Csuja
  - János Derzsi

- István Dégi
- Pál Hetényi
- Tamás Jordán
- Attila Kaszás
- Gyula Maár
- Đoko Rosić
- József Ruszt
- Géza Rácz
- János Ács
- Lajos Őze

This Hungarian filmic representation of Shakespeare's play is composed of only two shots: the first shot (before the main title) is five minutes long, the second, fifty-seven minutes long. This film was an interlude in Tarr's career, a class project started while he was still a student and later completed and aired on Hungarian television. It is a rare example of Tarr's adaptation of non-Hungarian source materials.

ALMANAC OF FALL (ÖSZI ALMANACH 1985)

Music: Mihály Víg
Cinematography: Buda Gulyás, Sándor Kardos, Ferenc Pap
Editing: Ágnes Hranitzky
Production: Társulas Filmstudio with Magyar Television Drama Department

Cast:
- Hédi Temessy as Hédi
- Erika Bodnár as Anna
- Miklós B. Székely as Miklós
- Pál Hetényi as Tibor
- János Derzsi as János, Hédi's son

Hédi, a rich elderly lady whose home is decorated in a fading, elegant style, filled with dainty, fragile objects, lives with her abusive son. She is tended by Anna, a helper who slowly infiltrates herself into the home, using sex to gain acceptance with the son and with other male members of the extended household (a new lodger, and her own lover who wants to take everything he can and leave the house). The film takes place entirely in the dwelling, with only a suggestion of the outside coming through the open window and fluttering curtains. The film's use of saturated colors gives a psychedelic feeling to the interior and gives off mood suggestions as well. This represents a departure from Tarr's earlier, more documentary-style filmography. Hédi realizes she is being taken advantage of by her son as well as all the other inhabitants.

After raping her in the kitchen, János marries Anna, and the film ends with the inhabitants dancing to "Che Sarà" on a phonograph in the parlor in a mournful celebration. The camera often pans on objects in the rooms, glassware, furniture, curtains, signs of a wealthier lifestyle than that afforded most characters in Tarr's films. Unusual camera angles also at times accentuate the sense of disorientation (e.g., the camera positioned below a glass floor).

DAMNATION (KÁRHOZAT 1988)

Music: Mihály Víg
Cinematography: Gábor Medvigy
Editing: Ágnes Hranitzky
Production: Jozsef Marx for Hungarian Film Institute, Mokep, and Hungarian Television

Cast:
- Miklós B. Székely as Karrer
- Vali Kerekes as the Lounge singer
- Gyula Pauer as Willarsky, the bartender at the *Titanik* bar
- György Cserhalmi as Sebestyén, the singer's husband

This film was cowritten with László Krasznahorkai who would collaborate on many of Tarr's works. Karrer, a depressed engineer in a mining town, is in love with a married singer from a local bar, the Titanik. The singer breaks off their affair, wanting to free herself of the town and its stifling confines to become famous. Willarsky offers Karrer a smuggling job, the swindle at the center of the characters' lives. Karrer offers the job to the singer's husband, Sebestyén, to get him out of the way of his relationship with the singer. The swindle, however, does not materialize and the characters continue, trapped in their provincial nightmare. A visual marker of the tawdry, inexorable degradation of these characters is a line of coal buckets, suspended above ground, moving to and from the coal pit just on the town's outskirts. The coal buckets move inexorably forward, squeaking all the way to the pit.

The town's interiors include Karrer's flat, whose window looks out on the buckets, the Titanik bar and the lounge where the singer performs, and a crowded dance hall featured in a scene where drunken couples slosh around the floor together. They form a circle at the end of the evening in a line dance that may be reminiscent of the final scene of Fellini's *8 ½*. But the joy Guido finds in dancing with all the people he has known is nowhere in Tarr's barren dance where weary patrons join together but remain apart. In the final scene, after having been seen inside a police station perhaps reporting the swindle, Karrer becomes completely dehumanized as he gets down on his hands and knees in the mud near the coal pit where a pack of stray dogs rummage for food. His howls mix with theirs, and with the sound of the coal buckets.

CITY LIFE (1990) SEGMENT: *THE LAST BOAT (AZ UTOLSÓ HAJÓ)*

Cast and other specifications unknown

This short segment, Tarr's contribution to a longer film, represents an almost silent journey by boat on the Danube, with the vessel making several stops along the way. The sun slowly sets on the horizon as the boat docks and the camera peers through the last door of a train presumably on its way back home.

SÁTÁNTANGÓ (1994)

Music: Mihály Víg
Cinematography: Gábor Medvigy
Editing: Ágnes Hranitzky
Production: Gyorgy Feher, Joachim von Vietinghoff, and Ruth Waldburger for Mozgokep Innovacios Tarsulas and von Vietinghoff Filmproduktion, Vega Film.

Cast:
- Mihály Víg as Irimiás
- Putyi Horváth as Petrina
- László Lugossy as Schmidt
- Éva Almássy Albert as Mrs. Schmidt
- János Derzsi as Kráner
- Irén Szajki as Mrs. Kráner
- Alfréd Járai as Halics
- Miklós Székely B. as Futaki
- Erzsébet Gaál as Mrs. Halics
- Erika Bók as Estike
- Peter Berling as the Doctor

This seven-plus hour film is based on Krasznahorkai's novel of the same name. A dreary collective farm village has collapsed, which leads to divisions, swindles, and deception. Futaki is having an affair with Mrs. Schmidt. Mr. Schmidt steals the villagers' money and flees. Futaki discovers the plan and decides to take part in it. This scene plays out in front of the Doctor, whose house with its one large window looks out over the village "square," such as it is. The conspiracy ends when rumors spread that Irimiás, a charismatic charlatan, is returning. Irimiás and his friend Petrina make a deal with the police captain of a nearby urban community to watch the village.

The Doctor leaves his house to buy pálinka in the town kocsma despite the lashing rain and darkness. Estike, a young girl from the village, comes up to him on his way to the kocsma begging for his help. At first he reacts harshly, then tries to make up for it, but she runs off. Chasing after her, the Doctor passes out and collapses in nearby woods, and is found in the morning by the town's conductor who takes him to a hospital.

Before this encounter, Estike's brother, Sanyi tricks her into burying her small savings so that a "money tree" will sprout. He subsequently steals the money from her, and she wanders in desperation. During her nocturnal ramblings she stares at a joyless, drunken dance resembling a tango taking place in the kocsma, looking through the window as the rain continues to soak her. In these central scenes from the film, she goes to the barn and first seems to befriend a cat there, then poisons it in a seemingly senseless act. She encounters the Doctor entreating him to help her cat. After he rebuffs her, she takes the lifeless cat with her to an abandoned, ruined church where she takes the same poison she used on the animal.

Irimiás arrives in the village as the villagers watch over Estike's corpse lying on a pool table in the upper floors of the kocsma. He exploits their grief and in a funeral oration tells them to hand over their money to him so he can establish a new collective farm for them in another place. The villagers comply, and he takes them to an abandoned villa. Irimiás and Petrina meet with an accomplice in a nearby city to acquire explosives after having left the villagers. Irimiás returns to tell the villagers there has been a delay in the establishment of the farm community and they must go to different parts of the country to wait for instructions. Schmidt and Kráner demand their money back, but ultimately relent. They travel by truck to the city where the villagers are separated and must complete tasks. Futaki instead wants a job as a watchman, and leaves on his own. Irimiás's police report contains details of the villagers' habits and descriptions, but the police rewrite the report in a more bureaucratic language.

The Doctor returns from the hospital to find the villagers gone. Bells start to ring in the distance and the Doctor goes to investigate their source: a ruined church. A madman is ringing the bells and shouting that Turks are coming. The Doctor returns home as the bells continue. The final scenes show him barricading himself in the house, boarding up the one large window through which he had witnessed the goings-on of the village, as the screen becomes increasingly black. When the final board is nailed in, the screen goes dark. The voiceovers in this scene are the words the Doctor penned as witness to the demise, swindle, rebirth, and destruction of the collective farm.

This film's length makes a structure necessary for cohesion. Each section is titled as follows (with Hungarian translations):

- A hír, hogy jönnek (The News Is They Are Coming)
- Feltámadunk (We Are Resurrected)
- Valamit tudni (Knowing Something)
- A pók dolga I. (The Job of the Spider I)
- Felfeslők (Comes Unstitched)
- A pók dolga II (Ördögcsecs, sátántangó) (The Job of the Spider II [The Devil's Tit, Satan's Tango])
- Irimiás beszédet mond (Irimiás Gives A Speech)
- A távlat, ha szemből (The Perspective From the Front)
- Mennybe menni? Lázálmodni? (Going to Heaven? Having Nightmares?)
- A távlat, ha hátulról (The Perspective from The Rear)
- Csak a gond, a munka (Just Trouble and Work)
- A kör bezárul (The Circle Closes)

The twelve-part structure replicates the novel, and would be in the form of a tango: six steps forward and six steps back.

JOURNEY ON THE PLAIN (UTAZÁS AZ ALFÖLDÖN 1995)

Music: Mihály Víg
Cinematography: Fred Keleman
Editing: Gábor Csövi, László Bolga, János Zentay, Győző Kicsiny, György Kovács, László Priska, Balász Vajna, János Rédei
Production: Magyar Televízió

Cast:
- Mihály Víg

This short film was produced separately and not, as was the case for some other Tarr ventures, as part of a longer film. The text is composed entirely of poems by Sándor Petőfi, Hungary's Romantic National poet. Tarr's camera follows Víg as he recites the texts in fields, ruined castles, and other suggestive locations, all under brilliant sunshine or starry skies. This film, in color, evokes a quiet beauty in both text and image where we revisit *Satan's*

Tango's locations. The poems are reproduced in Hungarian and English in appendix A. Understanding these texts provides important information for appreciating this work.

WERCKMEISTER HARMONIES (*WERCKMEISTER HARMÓNIÁK* 2000)

Music: Mihály Víg
Cinematography: Emil Novák, Patrick de Ranter, Rob Tregenza, Jörg Widmer, Gábor Medvigy
Editing: Ágnes Hranitzky
Production: Miklós Szita, Franz Goess, Joachim von Vietinghoff and Paul Saadoun for Goess Film and Von Vietinghoff Filmproduktion

Cast:
- Lars Rudolph as János Valuska
- Peter Fitz as György Eszter
- Hanna Schygulla as Tünde Eszter
- János Derzsi as Man in the Broad-Cloth Coat
- Đoko Rosić as Man in Western Boots
- Tamás Wichmann as Man in the Sailor Cap
- Ferenc Kállai as Director

This film is based on Krasznahorkai's 1989 novel *The Melancholy of Resistance*. The film's title refers to the baroque musical theorist Andreas Werckmeister. János Valuska, the postman in a desolate faded town, leads drunken bar patrons in a dance in imitation of the total eclipse of the sun, but ends when sunlight returns. György Eszter is a composer and one of the intelligentsia who provides a monologue on the imperfections of the musical scale as defined by Werckmeister, who had proposed a change to the scale to make it more harmonious. Tünde, György's estranged wife, is plotting a political coup to clean up the town with the blessing of her lover, the police chief. In the meantime, a dead whale in a trailer rumbles into the town square in the middle of the night, its arrival witnessed only by Valuska as he wanders the streets. The whale presages the mounting rumors of a Prince who will destabilize the political landscape with threatened mob action.

As Valuska goes about his rounds, he hears workers unsettled by events. A list of "recruits" for the political "clean up" effort circulates, and gets into the hands of the mob. The circus master breaks rank with the Prince as the latter becomes more dictatorial and his rhetoric more enflamed. The Prince is now free to incite the masses, who rampage through the village, raping post office workers, beating hospital patients, and looting stores. They stop when confronted by a naked frail, elderly man in a hospital shower, and they slink away.

After the riot, Valuska comes across the diary of a rioter. It explains that the rioters did not know what they were angry with; so they were angry at everything. Valuska tries to escape the now-ruined village ruled presumably by the triumphant Prince but is intercepted by a helicopter while running in a field. This suspenseful scene is filmed with a tracking shot in front of Valuska as he runs toward it, empty fields, and sparse trees all around, with the helicopter hovering in the distance, reminiscent of Alfred Hitchcock's *North by Northwest*. He is sent to a mental institution while Mr. Eszter is evicted to live in a shed in the garden. Tünde's political triumph is complete. Mr. Eszter retuned the piano so that it is now like any other, the imperfect order restored. The final scene shows Mr. Eszter alone in the vacant square, the whale outside the trailer abandoned after the riot. He stares directly at the vacant, giant eye before slowly wandering away as the fog begins to lift.

VISIONS OF EUROPE SEGMENT: *PROLOGUE* (2004)

Music: Not available
Cinematography: Not available
Editing: Not available
Production: T. T. Filmmühely

Cast:
- Kristina Tomka as the serving woman at the window
- A cast of dozens of men who are all mentioned in the final credits

Visions of Europe is a film consisting of twenty-five short segments by twenty-five European directors to celebrate the European Union's adding ten new member states, including Hungary. Each director was to present an idea about Europe, the new, the old and in between. Some segments are hopeful, others wary, others whimsical. Tarr's five-minute contribution has the camera track across a line of people standing next to a stone wall, moving forward very slowly. We come to see they are standing in line for a meal and a drink, as the clock on the wall behind the server shows twelve o'clock. This "handout" may be Tarr's view of what the new Europe will end up having to do to integrate the ten countries, so different from each other and from the countries that were already members.

THE MAN FROM LONDON (A LONDONI FÉRFI 2007)

Music: Mihály Víg
Cinematography: Fred Kelemen
Editing: Ágnes Hranitzky
Production: Gábor Teni, Paul Saadoun, Miriam Zachar, Joachim Von Vietinghoff, Cristoph Hahnheiser, a TT Filmműhely (Hungary) 13 Production, Cinéma Soleil (France), Von Vietinghoff Filmproduktion, Black Forest Films (Germany)

Cast:
- Miroslav Krobot as Maloin
- Tilda Swinton as Maloin's wife
- Erika Bók as Henriette
- János Derzsi as Brown
- István Lénárt as Morrison
- Gyula Pauer as the barkeep
- Kati Lázár as the butcher's wife
- Ági Szirtes as Brown's wife

This filmscript is Tarr and Krasznahorkai's adaptation of Georges Simenon's 1934 *L'Homme de Londres*. Maloin, a railway worker who switches trains at the Dieppe wharf where boats arriving from London dock, recovers a briefcase filled with British pounds. Maloin witnessed one courier kill the other on the wharf before throwing the briefcase into the shallow water by the dock. He cannot decide what to do with the money, and his secret creates friction in the house between him, his wife, Camélia, and daughter, Henriette. The killer remains in Dieppe and begins a cat and mouse game with Maloin. Brown shadows Maloin's home, and searches the area around the tower for clues. Later at the tavern, a police inspector from London, Morrison, arrives, claiming to be working on behalf of a theater owner named Mitchell from whose office safe the money was stolen.

Meanwhile, Maloin begins to spend the money on expensive gifts for his family, especially his daughter. The fact that Henriette works for a butcher who has her washing the floors makes Maloin indignant. He takes her out of her job but neither his wife nor daughter understand what seems like a financially reckless act. Morrison meets Brown's wife and asks for her help in finding her husband, accused of murder. Someone has been found in a hut Maloin keeps by the seaside to store fishing gear and he goes there assuming it is Brown, hiding. He comes out, composes himself, and locks the door. He brings the briefcase to Morrison, confesses to killing Brown in the hut, and returns the briefcase. Morrison gives a small amount of cash to Brown's widow and to Maloin, telling him it was self-defense. The camera focuses on the widow's face as the film fades to white.

THE TURIN HORSE (A TORINÓI LÓ 2011)

Narration: Mihály Ráday
Music: Mihály Víg
Cinematography: Fred Kelemen
Editing: Ágnes Hranitzky
Production: T. T. Filmműhely

Cast:
- János Derzsi as Ohlsdorfer
- Erika Bók as Ohlsdorfer's daughter
- Mihály Kormos as Bernhardt
- Mihály Ráday as narrator

This film is another cowritten script from Tarr and Krasznahorkai. The title refers to the story of Nietzsche's breakdown in 1899 upon witnessing a horse being beaten in the northern Italian city. The film is shot in only thirty long takes. A narrator begins by explaining the context of the title, an incident after which Nietzsche becomes mute and demented.

A potato farmer and his daughter eke out a meager existence with their horse, the wind constantly blowing around them, with thick dust everywhere. Each segment of the film refers to a day, until the sixth day when they stop even eating and we presume they will soon die. Each day sees repetitions, with nuances. They get dressed, sit at the window, sometimes clean, sometimes sew or mend tools, eat facing each other at the table, sleep, and begin again the next day.

Progressively, their lives become even more bleak because of outside circumstances. The horse refuses to budge so they cannot leave. They tie it up again in the barn, it stops eating and will presumably die. A neighbor arrives to buy some pálinka from them because the town, he says, has been destroyed. In the only long verbal sequence of the film, he blames the town's demise on God and on man. A band of Roma arrives on white horses and Ohlsdorfer and his daughter send them away, not wanting to share their water. The Roma put a curse on them and the next day their well goes dry. They decide to leave because they cannot continue there, but as the camera watches them almost disappear on the horizon above the hut, we see them return, defeated. They then begin the last inevitable decline. In the last scene, they cannot even muster the strength to eat the raw potato they cannot cook for lack of water. The scene goes dark as they stare at the table.

Bibliography

Allen, William S. "The Cracks in the Surface of Things: On Béla Tarr, Rancière, and Adorno." *Screening the Past*. 2015. Accessed 14 January 2021, http://www.screeningthepast.com/issue-39-first-release/the-cracks-in-the-surface-of-things-on-bela-tarr-ranciere-and-adorno/.
Angelopoulos, Theo. *To livadi pou dakryzei* (*The Weeping Meadow*). 2004. DVD.
———. *Topio stin omichli* (*Landscape in the Mist*). 1988. DVD.
Antonioni, Michelangelo. *L'avventura* (*The Adventure*). 1960. DVD.
———. *La notte* (*Night*). 1961. DVD.
———. *L'eclisse* (*The Eclipse*). 1962. DVD.
———. *Deserto rosso* (*Red Desert*). 1964. DVD.
Aristotle. *Poetics*. New York: Penguin, 1997.
Bacsó, Péter. *A Tanú* (*The Witness*). 1968. DVD.
Bálint Kovács, András. "The World According to Béla Tarr." *Kinokultura*, Special Issue No. 7: Hungarian Cinema. February 2008. Accessed 18 February 2021, http://www.kinokultura.com/specials/7/kovacs.shtml.
———. *The Cinema of Béla Tarr: The Circle Closes*. New York: Columbia University Press, 2013.
———. "Un *outsider* au centre." In *Béla Tarr. De la colère au tourment*. Edited by Corinne Maury and Sylvie Rollet. 25–33. Crisnée, Belgium: Editions Yellow Now, 2016.
Bayon, Estelle. "Un désastre écologique." In *Béla Tarr. De la colère au tourment*. Edited by Corinne Maury and Sylvie Rollet. 47–57. Crisnée, Belgium: Editions Yellow Now, 2016.
Beckett, Samuel. *Waiting for Godot*. New York: Grove, 2011.
Bergman, Ingmar. *Det sjunde inseglet* (*The Seventh Seal*). 1957a. DVD.
———. *Smultronstället* (*Wild Strawberries*). 1957b. DVD.
Bondanella, Peter. *Italian Cinema from Neorealism to the Present*. New York: Continuum, 1995.

Botz-Bornstein, Thorsten. *Organic Cinema: Film, Architecture, and the Work of Béla Tarr.* New York and Oxford: Berghahn, 2017.
Carmichael, Deborah A. "The Living Presence of Monument Valley in John Ford's *Stagecoach.*" In *The Landscape of Hollywood Westerns.* Edited by Deborah A. Carmichael. 212–228. Salt Lake City: Utah University Press, 2006.
Carr, Jeremy. "Tarr, Béla." *Sense of Cinema.* 22 June 2017. Accessed 14 January 2021, http://www.sensesofcinema.com/2017/great-directors/bela-tarr/.
Chaucer, Geoffrey. "The Pardoner's Tale." In *The Complete Works of Geoffrey Chaucer.* Edited by F. N. Robinson. Second Edition. 148–215. Oxford: Oxford University Press, 1957.
"City Life." Film Website Information. Accessed 18 February 2021, http://www.citylifefilm.com/.
Comfort, Lance. *Temptation Harbor.* 1942. DVD.
Corneille, Pierre. *Œuvres complètes.* 3 vols. Paris: Gallimard.
Crutzen, Paul, and Eugene F. Stoermer. "The 'Anthropocene.'" IGBP (International Geosphere-Biosphere Programme) Newsletter #41 (May 2000): 17–18.
Cunningham, John, *Hungarian Cinema from Coffee House to Multiplex.* London and New York: Wallflower Press, 2004.
Decoin, Henri. *The London Man.* 1943. DVD.
De Luca, Tiago, and Nuno Barradas Jorge. "Introduction: From Slow Cinema to Slow Cinemas." In *Slow Cinema.* Edited by Tiago de Luca and Nuno Barradas Jorge. 1–21. Edinburgh: Edinburgh University Press, 2016.
Deming, Richard. "Now and Then: View of Béla Tarr's *Missing People*, 2019, Wiener Festwochen." *Vienna.* 13 June 2019. Accessed 14 January 2021, https://www.artforum.com/film/richard-deming-on-bela-tarr-s-missing-people-2019-80180.
De Sica, Vittorio. *Sciuscià (Shoeshine).* 1947. DVD.
Eisenstein, Sergei. *Alexandre Nevsky.* 1939. DVD.
Esposito, Joan. "Antonioni and Benjamin: Dialectical Imagery in *Eclipse.*" *Film Criticism* (Fall 1984): 25–37.
European Association for the Study of Literature, Culture, and the Environment. Organization Website. Accessed 18 February 2021, http://www.easlce.eu/about-us/what-is-ecocriticism.
Farkas, György. "Zártkörő előadás Tarr Macbethjéről." In *Filmszem II./2. Tarr-újratöltve.* Translated by Andrea Nemeth-Newhauser. 54–61, 12 July 2012a.
———. "Beszélgetésmorzsák: interjú Tarr Bélával." In *Filmszem II./2. Tarr-újratöltve.* Translated by Andrea Nemeth-Newhauser. 62–65, 12 July 2012b.
Faucon, Térésa. "Du geste quotidien à l'extra-quotidien: où commence la danse?" In *Béla Tarr. De la colère au tourment.* Edited by Corinne Maury and Sylvie Rollet. 85–95. Crisnée, Belgium: Editions Yellow Now, 2016.
Fellini, Federico. *8 ½.* 1960a.
———. *La dolce vita.* 1960b. DVD.
Felperin, Leslie. "Visions of Europe." *Variety.* 27 September 2004. Accessed 18 February 2021, https://variety.com/2004/film/reviews/visions-of-europe-1200530699/#!.
Frankel, David. *Marley and Me.* 2008. DVD.

Friel, Brian. *Translations*. New York: Farrar, Straus, and Giroux Faber Drama, 1995.
Ginn, Franklin. "When Horses Won't Eat: Apocalypse and the Anthropocene." *Annals of the Association of American Geographers* 105, no. 2 (2015): 351–359.
Golding, William. *Lord of the Flies*. New York: Capricorn Books, 1954.
Gosnell, Raja. *Beverly Hills Chihuahua (#1)*. 2008. DVD.
Grønstad, Asbjørn. "Slow Cinema and the Ethics of Duration." In *Slow Cinema*. Edited by Tiago de Luca and Nuno Barradas Jorge. 273–284. Edinburgh: Edinburgh University Press, 2016.
Hallström, Lasse. *A Dog's Purpose*. 2017. DVD.
Hames, Peter. "The Melancholy of Resistance." In *Kinoeye: New Perspectives on European Film* 1, no. 1 (n.d.). Accessed 14 January 2021, http://www.kinoeye.org/01/01/hames01.php.
Hitchcock, Alfred. *North by Northwest*. 1959. DVD.
Hoberman, J. "Welcome to His World: Béla Tarr's First Meteorological Event." *The New York Times*. 29 October 2020. Accessed 14 January 2021, https://www.nytimes.com/2020/10/29/movies/bela-tarr-damnation.html.
Horton, Andrew. "The Master of Slow Cinema: Space and Time—Actual, Historical, and Mythical—In the Films of Theo Angelopoulos." *Cinéaste* 36, no. 1 (Winter 2010): 23–27.
Ingram, David. *Green Screen: Environmentalism and Hollywood Cinema*. Exeter: University of Exeter Press, 2000.
Ivakhiv, Adrian J. *Ecologies of the Moving Image: Cinema, Affect, Nature*. Waterloo, Ontario: Wilfred Laurier University Press, 2013.
Jaffe, Ira. *Slow Movies: Countering the Cinema of Action*. London and New York: Wallflower Press, 2014.
Jancsó, Miklós. *Szegénylegények* (*The Round Up*). 1966. DVD.
———. *Csillagosok, katonák* (*The Red and the White*). 1967. DVD.
———. *Szerelmem, Elektra* (*Electra My Love*). 1974. DVD.
Jones, Jonathan. "Painting Icons." *The Guardian*. 1 July 2004. Accessed 14 January 2021, https://www.theguardian.com/film/2004/jul/02/features.jonathanjones.
Kalmár, György. *Formations of Masculinity in Post-Communist Hungarian Cinema: Labyrinthian Man*. Cham, Switzerland: Springer Nature, 2017.
Katz, David. "Béla Tarr to Premiere New Film *Missing People* at this Summer's Wiener Festwochen." *Cineuropa*. 4 October 2019. Accessed 14 January 2021, https://www.cineuropa.net/en/newsdetail/370729/.
Koepnick, Lutz. *On Slowness: Towards an Aesthetic of the Contemporary*. New York: Columbia University Press, 2014.
Krasznahorkai, László. *Satantango*. Translated by George Szirtes. New York: New Directions Books, 2012 (original Hungarian 1985).
Kubrick, Stanley. *2001: A Space Odyssey*. 1968. DVD.
Kuzma, Konstanty. "The End: Béla Tarr's *The Turin Horse* (*A torinói ló*, 2010)." *Berlinale 2011*. 17 February 2011. Accessed 14 January 2021, https://eefb.org/perspectives/bela-tarrs-the-turin-horse-a-torinoi-loi-2010/.
Lamoure, Jean-Marc. *Tarr, Béla. I Used to be a Filmmaker*. DVD.
Landy, Marcia. *Italian Film*. Cambridge: Cambridge University Press, 2000.

Levine, Matt, and Jeremy Meckler. "Listening to the World: A Conversation with Béla Tarr." *Magazine*. Walker Arts Center. 20 March 2012. Accessed 14 January 2021, https://walkerart.org/magazine/bela-tarr-turin-horse.
Marguet, Damien. "*Sátántangó* ou les ellipses de la traduction." In *Béla Tarr. De la colère au tourment*. Edited by Corinne Maury and Sylvie Rollet. 73–83. Crisnée, Belgium: Editions Yellow Now, 2016.
Maury, Corinne. "De l'habitat d'état à l'errance damnée." In *Béla Tarr. De la colère au tourment*. Edited by Corinne Maury and Sylvie Rollet. 35–45. Crisnée, Belgium: Editions Yellow Now, 2016.
Maury, Corinne, and Olivier Zuchuat. "Tout lieu a un visage: entretien avec Béla Tarr." In *Béla Tarr. De la colère au tourment*. Edited by Corinne Maury and Sylvie Rollet. 13–21. Crisnée, Belgium: Editions Yellow Now, 2016.
Moore, Kevin. "Eclipsing the Commonplace: The Logic of Alienation in Antonioni's Cinema." *Film Quarterly* (Summer 1995): 22–34.
Nagib, Lúcia. "The Politics of Slowness and the Traps of Modernity." In *Slow Cinema*. Edited by Tiago de Luca and Nuno Barradas Jorge. 25–46. Edinburgh: Edinburgh University Press, 2016.
Noonan, Chris. *Babe*. 1995. DVD.
Orban, Clara. "Antonioni's Women, Lost in the City." *Modern Language Studies* 31, no. 2 (Autumn 2001): 11–27.
———. "Contextualizing History in Hungarian Films of the New Millennium." *AHEA E-Journal of the American Hungarian Educators Association* 6 (Fall 2013). Accessed 18 February 2021, http://ahea.net/e-journal/volume-6-2013/7.
———. "When Walls Fall: Families in Hungarian Films of the New Europe." In *Popular Cinemas in East Central Europe: Film Cultures and Histories*. Edited by Dorota Ostrowska, Francesco Pitassio, and Zsuzsanna Varga. 248–260. London and New York: I.B. Tauris, 2017.
Petőfi, Sándor. *Sándor Petőfi: His Entire Poetic Works*. Translated by Frank Szomy. Copyright Frank Szomy, 1972.
———. *Petőfi*. English and Introduction by Anton N. Nyerges. Edited by Joseph M. Értavy-Baráth. Buffalo, New York: Hungarian Cultural Foundation, 1973.
———. *Összes Költeményei*. Budapest: Szépirodalmi Könyvkiado, 1974.
Following is a list of poems taken from various sources, reproduced in the appendix. Translations in the appendix come from Szomy's text, above. They are reproduced here in the order in which they appear in the credits to the short film *Journey on the Plain*.
———. "Meredek a pincegádor..." Accessed 31 July 2019, https://www.arcanum.hu/hu/online-kiadvanyok/Verstar-verstar-otven-kolto-osszes-verse-2/petofi-sandor-DFB2/1844-E2C7/meredek-a-pincegador-E3FD/.
———. "Gyertyám homályosan lobog..." Accessed 31 July 2019, http://magyar-irodalom.elte.hu/sulinet/igyjo/setup/portrek/petofi/gyertyam.htm.
———. "Itt állok a rónaközepen..." Accessed 31 July 2019, http://magyar-irodalom.elte.hu/sulinet/igyjo/setup/portrek/petofi/gyertyam.htm.
———. "Hattyudalféle." Accessed 31 July 2019, https://www.arcanum.hu/hu/online-kiadvanyok/Verstar-verstar-otven-kolto-osszes-verse-2/petofi-sandor-DFB2/1844-E2C7/hattyudalfele-E3BE/.

———. "Igyunk!" Accessed 31 July 2019, https://www.arcanum.hu/hu/online-ki advanyok/Verstar-verstar-otven-kolto-osszes-verse-2/petofi-sandor-DFB2/1844-E2C7/igyunk-E58C/.

———. "A bánat? Egy oceán." Accessed 31 July 2019, http://magyar-irodalom.elte.hu/sulinet/igyjo/setup/portrek/petofi/banatoce.htm.

———. "Elvándorol a madár..." Accessed 31 July 2019, http://magyar-irodalom.elte.hu/sulinet/igyjo/setup/portrek/petofi/elvandor.htm.

———. "Így is jó." Accessed 31 July 2019, http://www.vers-versek.hu/petofi-sandor/igy-is-jo/.

———. "A nap házasélete." Accessed 31 July 2019, http://www.vers-versek.hu/petofi-sandor/a-nap-hazaselete/.

———. "Miért tekintesz be szobámba?" Accessed 31 July 2019, http://kiskoros.hu/petofi_vers/miert-tekintesz-be-szobamba.

———. "Az Emberugyan hova lesz?" *Petőfi Összes Költeményei*, 453–454.

———. "Barátaim megölelének..." Accessed 31 July 2019, http://kiskoros.hu/petofi_vers/barataim-megolelenek.

———. "Az éj." Accessed 31 July 2019, http://www.vers-versek.hu/petofi-sandor/az-ej/.

———. "Hova lesz a kacaj?" *Petőfi Összes Költeményei*, 455.

———. "Az itélet." Accessed 31 July 2019, http://www.vers-versek.hu/petofi-sandor/az-ej/.

———. "Annyit sem ér az élet…" Accessed 31 July 2019, http://kiskoros.hu/petofi_vers/annyit-sem-er-az-elet.

Pfeifer, Moritz. "Bad Animals: Some Ideas on the Meaning of Béla Tarr's Animals." *East European Film Bulletin*. 3 January 2013. Accessed 18 February 2021, https://eefb.org/perspectives/some-ideas-on-the-meaning-of-bela-tarrs-animals/.

Prieto, Eric. "Geocriticism Meets Ecocriticism: Bertrand Westphal and Environmental Thinking." In *Ecocriticism and Geocriticism: Overlapping Territories in Environmental and Spatial Literary Studies*. Edited by Robert Tally Jr. and Christine M. Battista. 19–35. New York: Palgrave MacMillan, 2016.

Racine, Jean. *Œuvres complètes: Théâtre Poésie*. Paris: Gallimard, 1999.

Rancière, Jacques. *Béla Tarr, The Time After*. Translated by Erik Beranek. Minneapolis: Univocal Press, 2013.

———. "Béla Tarr: The Poetics and the Politics of Fiction." In *Slow Cinema*. Edited by Tiago de Luca and Nuno Barradas Jorge. 245–260. Edinburgh: Edinburgh University Press, 2016.

Raup, Jordan. "Béla Tarr to Premiere New Film *Missing People* this Summer in Vienna." *The Film Stage*. 9 April 2019. Accessed 14 January 2021, https://thefilmstage.com/bela-tarr-to-premiere-new-film-missing-people-this-summer-in-vienna/.

Ray, Man. *Emak Bakia*. 1926. DVD.

Remes, Justin. *Motion(less) Pictures: The Cinema of Stasis*. New York: Columbia University Press, 2015.

Renoir, Jean. *La Grande Illusion (The Grand Illusion)*. 1932. DVD.

"Rethinking the Anthropocene." The Editors. *Scientific American* (December 2018): 10.

Robbe-Grillet, Alain. *La Jalousie*. Paris: Minuit, 1957.

Roberts, Phillip. "Control and Cinema: Intolerable Poverty and the Films of Béla Tarr." *Deleuze Studies* 11, no. 1 (2017): 68–94.

Rollet, Sylvie. "L'étoffe rythmique du monde: une théorie à l'œuvre." In *Béla Tarr. De la colère au tourment*. Edited by Corinne Maury and Sylvie Rollet. 127–137. Crisnée, Belgium: Editions Yellow Now, 2016.

Romney, Jonathan. "Gone with the Wind: Interview." *Sight and Sound* 22, no. 6 (June 2012): 34–39.

Rosenbaum, Jonathan. "Commentary." *The Turin Horse*. DVD.

———. "A Place in the Pantheon." *Chicago Reader*. 9 May 1996. Accessed 14 January 2021, https://www.chicagoreader.com/chicago/a-place-in-the-pantheon/Content?oid=890479.

Rucekert, William. "Literature and Ecology: An Experiment in Ecocriticism." *Iowa Review* 9, no. 1 (1978): 71–86.

Ruttman, Walter. *Wochenende (Weekend)*. 1930. DVD.

Samardzija, Zoron. *Post-Communist Malaise: Cinematic Responses to European Integration*. Rutgers, New Jersey: Rutgers University Press, 2020.

Samocki, Jean-Marie. "Ce que devient la nuit lorsque le jour s'effondre." In *Béla Tarr. De la colère au tourment*. Edited by Corinne Maury and Sylvie Rollet. 59–69. Crisnée, Belgium: Editions Yellow Now, 2016.

Sartre, Jean-Paul. *Huis clos suivi de Les Mouches*. Paris: Folio, 2000.

Schwägel, Christian. *The Anthropocene: The Human Era and How It Shapes Our Planet*. Santa Fe, New Mexico: Synergetic Press, 2014. Kindle edition, introduction.

Scott, A. O. "Facing the Abyss with Boiled Potatoes and Plum Brandy. Béla Tarr's Final Film, *The Turin Horse*." *The New York Times*. 9 February 2012. Accessed 14 January 2021, https://www.nytimes.com/2012/02/10/movies/the-turin-horse-from-bela-tarr.html.

Selyem, Zsuzsa. "How Long and When: Open Time Interval and Dignified Living Creatures in *The Turin Horse*." *Acta University Sapientiae, Film and Media Studies* 10 (2015): 105–120.

Shakespeare, William. *Macbeth*. New York: Simon and Schuster, 1959.

Sibertin-Blanc, Guillaume. "De la mélancolie à la résistance: communautés et désœuvrement." In *Béla Tarr. De la colère au tourment*. Edited by Corinne Maury and Sylvie Rollet. 151–164. Crisnée, Belgium: Editions Yellow Now, 2016.

Sierek, Karl. "Durée et contingence. Une révision du plan-séquence." In *Béla Tarr. De la colère au tourment*. Edited by Corinne Maury and Sylvie Rollet. 113–125. Crisnée, Belgium: Editions Yellow Now, 2016.

Simenon, Georges. *L'Homme de Londres*. Paris: Gallimard Livre de Poche, 2013.

Stevenson, Robert. *Old Yeller*. 1957. DVD.

Stojanova, Christine. "The Damnation of Labor in the Films of Béla Tarr." In *Work in Cinema: Labor and the Human Condition*. Edited by Ewa Mazierska. 169–187. London: Palgrave MacMillan, 2013.

Strausz, László. "The Politics of Style in Miklós Jancsó's *The Red and the White* and *The Lord's Lantern in Budapest*." *Film Quarterly* 62, no. 3 (Spring 2009): 41–47.

Szabó, István. *Apa (Father)*. 1966. DVD.

Szendy, Peter. "Animal filmicum." In *Béla Tarr. De la colère au tourment*. Edited by Corinne Maury and Sylvie Rollet. 97–109. Crisnée, Belgium: Editions Yellow Now, 2016.

Szöts, István. *Emberek a havason (People of the Mountain)*. 1942. DVD.

Tally, Robert T. Jr, and Christine M. Battista. "Introduction: Ecocritical Geographies, Geocritical Ecologies, and the Spaces of Modernity." In *Ecocriticism and Geocriticism: Overlapping Territories in Environmental and Spatial Literary Studies*. Edited by Robert T. Tally Jr and Christine M. Battista. 1–15. New York: Palgrave MacMillan, 2016.

Tarkovsky, Andrei. *Andrei Rublev*. 1966. DVD.

———. *Solaris*. 1972. DVD.

———. *Zerkalo (The Mirror)*. 1975. DVD.

———. *Stalker*. 1979. DVD.

Tarr, Béla. "Interview." *Cork Film Festival*. October 2000. With Furgus Daly and Maximilian Le Canh. Reproduced in Facets video jacket to accompany *Damnation* DVD.

———. "Group Interview." *Berlin Film Festival*. 2011. *The Turin Horse*. Reproduced in Facets video jacket to accompany *Damnation* DVD.

———. "Interview." *Berlinale International Film Festival*. 16 February 2019. Accessed 18 February 2021, https://www.youtube.com/watch?v=dfxzAC3CvLo.

Tőke, Lilla. "The Outsider Within: Béla Tarr and the Hungarian National Cinema." *Hungarian Cultural Studies, E-Journal of the American Hungarian Educators Association* 9 (2016): 90–99. Accessed 18 February 2021, http://ahea.pitt.edu.

Tomasulo, Frank P. "The Rhetoric of Anti-Closure: Antonioni and the Open Ending." In *Purdue University Seventh Annual Conference on Film*. 133–139. Purdue, Indiana: Purdue University Department of English, 1983.

———. "The Architectonics of Alienation: Antonioni's Edifice Complex." *Wide Angle* (July 1993): 3–20.

Van Radvány, Géza. *Valahol az Europaban (Somewhere in Europe)*. 1947. DVD.

Végső, Roland. "Towards an Aesthetic of Worldlessness: Béla Tarr and the Berlin School." In *The Berlin School and Its Global Context*. Edited by Marco Abel and Jaimey Fischer. 317–334. Detroit: Wayne State University Press, 2018.

Vincze, Teréz. "Nézem, érzem: Tarr Béla a 'lassú mozi' és a befogadói folyamat." In *Filmszem II./2. Tarr-újratöltve*. Translated by Andrea Nemeth-Newhauser. 5–33. 12 July 2012.

Visconti, Luchino. *La terra trema (The Earth Trembles)*. 1948. DVD.

Visions of Europe. "Film Website." Accessed 18 February 2021, https://www.inkasfilms.com/movie/visions-of-europe/.

Westphal, Bertrand. *Geocriticism: Real and Fictional Spaces*. Translated by Robert J. Tally Jr. New York: Palgrave Macmillan, 2007.

Wetherall, Greg. "'Time is Very Cruel, Only Some Films Survive'—Béla Tarr on *Sátántangó* at 25." *Little White Lies. Truth and Movies*. 26 February 2019. Accessed 5 July 2019, https://lwlies.com/interview/bela-tarr-satantango-berlin-film-festival.

Wincer, Simon. *Free Willy*. 1993. DVD.

Index

Note: *Italic* page numbers refer to figures and page numbers followed by "n" denote endnotes.

The Adventure (*L'avventura*) (Antonioni), 20, *22*, 39n3; emptiness and urban setting in, 21–22; interior space in, 24
Agresti, Alejandro, 136
Akin, Faith, 139
Albert, Barbara, 139
Alexander Nevsky (Eisenstein), 26, 39n7
Allen, William S., 112
Almanac of Fall (*Őszi Almanach*) (Tarr), 35, 37, *57*, 70, 79n12, 83–84, 124, 128, 147, 149; birds in, 122; dwellings in, 48, 55–57; geographical location in, 46; outdoor spaces in, 84; story of, 183–84
Altorjay, Gabor, 136
Andrei Rublev (Tarkovsky), 26, 27, 39n6; horse in, 113; Jones on, 39n7
Angelopoulos, Theo, 1, 9, 30, 148; and Tarr compared, 32
animals, 107; domestic, in town and on farm (birds, 119–23; cats, 108–10; cows, 115–16; horses, 103, 113, 116–19; pigs, 114–15); domestic, mirroring human lives, 124; sea creatures in landlocked country and, 123–24
Anthropocene, 1–2, 8, 34, 107, 124, 125; as framework, 3; Ginn on, 2, 118–19; indoor spaces and, 47, 49, 65, 78
Antonioni, Michelangelo, 1, 9, 39n3, 45, 121–22, 148; loneliness in films of, 21–25; outdoor urban landscapes in films of, 20–24; and Tarr compared, 20, 25

Babe (Noonan), 109
Bacsó, Péter, 34
barns, 9, 186, 191; animals and, 108, 114; indoor spaces and, 42, 46, 62, 70, 75–77; outdoor spaces, 87, 95, 101
Bartas, Sharunas, 139
Battista, Christine, 7, 26
Bausch, Andy, 139
Bayon, Estelle, 5, 48, 81
Beckett, Samuel, 79n13, 97
Béla Tarr, The Time After (Rancière) (book), 13n10
Beranek, Erik, 13n10

Bergman, Ingmar, 1, 9, 19–20, 148
Berlin Film Festival, 63, 65, 103
Beverly Hills Chihuahua (Gosnell), 109
birds, 119–23
black and while films, 46, 87, 146, 149; animals and, 122; empty outdoors and, 105; short films and, 126, 131, 133, 135, 139; slow cinema and, 25, 32, 39n3
Boe, Christoffer, 139
Bondanella, Peter, 22, 23
Bordwell, David, 43, 148
Botz-Bornstein, Thorsen, 43, 58, 60, 83, 86

capitalism, critique of, 26
Carmichael, Deborah A., 5
Carr, Jeremy, 52, 78n4, 79n9
cats, 108–10
Chaucer, Geoffrey, 149
chickens, 119–21
City Life (Tarr) (documentary), 11, 140; segment: *The Last Boat* (*Az utolsó hajó*), 11, 42, 99, 105n2, 125, 128, 136–39, 145, 174, 185
claustrophobic indoors, 41–45, 148, 172, 183, 184; animals and, 107, 110, 122, 124; Anthropocene and, 6, 9, 11; dwellings and, 47–65; as geographic location, 42, 43; loneliness and, 149; outdoor spaces and, 81–85, 91, 95–98, 102, 104, 105; short films and, 126–29, 131, 132–34, 136, 139, 140; signal boxes and barns and, 75–78; slow cinema and, 15, 24, 25, 34, 35, 38; urban leisure spaces and, 65–72; urban *versus* rural, 45–47; workspaces and, 72–75
coal pit, 98–99
Comencini, Francesca, 139
Comfort, Lance, 78n4
Coninx, Stijn, 139
Cork Film Festival, 28, 39n6, 106n5
Corneille, Pierre, 16

cows, 115–16
Crutzen, Paul J., 2
csárda (roadside inn/tavern), 43–44
Cunningham, John, 32, 36, 83

Damnation (*Kárhozat*) (Tarr), 10, 17, 25, 35, 79n9, *98*, *111*, 149, 174–75; coal pit in, 98–99; dogs in, 110–12; dwellings in, 57–58; forest in, 96; geographical location in, 46; Hungarian taverns in, 66, 68–69; open fields in, 94, 95; outdoor spaces in, 82; parking lot in, 92; public square in, 86; rain in, 100; Rancière on, 42, 98, 99; story of, 184–85
Dante Alighieri, 129
Decoin, Henri, 78n4
Deming, Richard, 141–42
De Sica, Vittorio, 33
deterritorialization, 43
A Dog's Purpose (Hallström), 109
dogs, 86, 108–10
drunkenness, 67, 68, 129, 135
dwellings, 77–78; in *Almanac of Fall* (*Őszi Almanach*), 48, 55–57; in *Family Nest* (*Családi Tűzfészek*), 48–50, 61; in *The Prefab People* (*Panelkapcsolat*), 51–54, 77; in *The Turin Horse*, 60–65; in *Werckmeister Harmonies* (*Werckmeister harmóniák*), 58–61

The Earth Trembles (*La terra trema*) (Visconti), 21
The Eclipse (*L'eclisse*) (Antonioni), 20, *24*, 39n3; emptiness and urban setting in, 23–24; interior space in, 24–25
ecocriticism, 4–6, 9, 81–82; link with geocriticism, 7
ecologies, of moving image, 6
ecology and outdoor spaces, 104–105
Eisenstein, Sergei, 26
Electra My Love (*Szerelmem, Elektra*) (Jancsó), 39n11

Emak Bakia (Ray), 4
emptiness, 21, 145, 149; of human lives, 105; of material search, 53–54; modern consumeristic, 31; public parks and, 93; public squares and, 86, 90; space as loci of, 8
Esposito, Joan, 23
European Association for the Study of Literature, Culture and Environment, 6
exterior spaces. *See* outdoor spaces

Family Nest (*Családi Tűzfészek*) (Tarr), 35, 45, *49*, 106n9, *120*, 126, 147, 149; chicken in, 120–21; dwellings in, 48–50, 61; factory in, 75; Hungarian taverns in, 66, 68; pig in, 114; public park in, 93; story of, 179–80; workspaces in, 72–73
Farkas, György, 35, 55
Fassbinder, Rainer Werner, 37
Father (*Apa*) (Szabó), 34–35
Faucon, Térésa, 147
Fellini, Federico, 31, 59, 79n13
Felperin, Leslie, 139
Fils, Alexandre Dumas, 143n3
Flanagan, Matthew, 17
Ford, John, 5
forest, 95–98
Free Willy (Walker), 109
Friel, Brian, 12n7

Gatlif, Tony, 139
Gedeon, Sasa, 139
geocriticism, 6–9; link with ecocriticism, 7; mapping of, 8
Georgiou, Christos, 139
Giannaris, Constantine, 139
Ginn, Franklin, 2, 8, 118–19
Golding, William, 34
Greenaway, Peter, 139
Green Screen (Ingram) (book), 82
Grønstad, Asbjørn, 18
Guerín, José Luis, 136

Hames, Peter, 83
Hermosa, Miguel, 139
Hoberman, J., 25
Holocene, 2
horses, 103, 113, 116–19, 132–33
Horton, Andrew, 30
Hotel Magnézit (Tarr) (short film), 10, 43, 83, 125, *127*, 146; claustrophobic feeling in, 126–28; flophouse in, 66; story of, 180
Huis Clos (Sartre) (play), 124, 148
Hungarian film spaces, 3–4, 9, 11, 146, 174, 183; indoor spaces and, 43, 45, 48, 51, 54, 77; short films and, 135–38; slow cinema and, 18, 28, 32–38; urban leisure spaces and, 65–72. *See also individual* films

Iho, Arvo, 139
indoor spaces. *See* claustrophobic indoors
Ingram, David, 15
interiors. *See* claustrophobic indoors
isolation, 107, 110; Anthropocene and, 1, 3, 7, 8, 12; indoor spaces and, 44, 45, 50, 53, 65, 78, 79n14; outdoor spaces and, 83, 86, 87, 90, 102, 105; short films and, 132, 139, 142; slow cinema and, 17, 20, 32, 33
I Used to Be a Filmmaker (documentary) (Lamoure), 62, 97–98, 118
Ivakhiv, Adrian J., 6

Jaffe, Ira, 17, 18, 101, 104–105, 148
Jancsó, Miklós, 1, 4, 9, 28, 39–40n11; as model for Tarr, 28; and Tarr compared, 30
Jones, Jonathan, 39n7
Jorge, Nuno Barrados, 16
Journey on the Plain (*Utazás az Alföldön*) (Tarr) (short film), 10–11, 125, 128–35, *130*, 145, 172, 174; dwellings in, 48; Petőfi poems in,

129, 131–35, 151–70; story of, 187–88

Kalmár, György, 77
Katz, David, 142
Kaurismaki, Aki, 139
Kieslowski, Krzysztof, 136
Klopfenstein, Clemens, 136
kocsma space (Hungarian taverns), 41–43, 65–72, 91
Koepnick, Lutz, 18
Kotetishvili, Tato, 136
Kovács, András Bálint, 19, 27, 37, 58–59, 83
Kozole, Damjan, 139
Krasnahorkai, László, 48, 86, 184
Kubrick, Stanley, 27

La dolce vita (Fellini), 31, 59, 79n13
La Grande Illusion (*Grand Illusion*) (Renoir), 34
La Jalousie (Robbe-Grillet), 63
Lamoure, Jean-Marc, 97
Landscape in the Mist (*Topio stin omichli*) (Angelopoulos), 30–31
leisure space, 41–42
Levine, Matt, 62
L'Homme de Londres (Simenon) (novel), 13n10, 46, 90
Literature and Ecology (Rucekert) (book), 5
loneliness, 3, 8, 11, 12, 173; empty outdoors and, 86, 90, 93; indoor spaces and, 73, 76, 78; short films and, 126, 131, 132, 135, 137; slow cinema and, 21–25, 32; visions of, 146–50
long takes, 49, 79, 142, 173, 191; Anthropocene and, 1, 4; empty outdoors and, 83, 101; loneliness and, 146, 148; slow cinema and, 15, 17, 19, 20, 21, 24, 26, 29, 30, 32, 35, 36, 40n11
Lord of the Flies (Golding), 34
Luca, Tiago de, 16

Lyell, Charles, 2

Macbeth (Tarr), 35, *56*, 76, 78n3, 79n11, 99, 126, 139, 149; dwellings in, 54; horses in, 116; outdoor spaces in, 84–85; story of, 183
The Man from London (*A londoni férfi*) (Tarr), 10, 13n10, 36, 37, 91, *123*, 149, 173; birds in, 122; dwellings in, 61; film and novel compared, 90; geographical location in, 45, 46; interior spaces in, 42, 44, 79–80n14; ocean in, 99–100; public square in, 89–90; signal box in, 75–76; story of, 190–91
Manzoni, Alessandro, 129
Marguet, Damien, 146
Marley and Me (Frankel), 109
Maury, Corinne, 3, 48, 50, 79n12, 86
M'Baye, Ousmane William, 136
Meckler, Jeremey, 62
Mirror (*Zerkalo*) (Tarkovsky), 26, 27
mise-en-scène, 4, 5, 45, 83, 114, 124, 127, 133
Missing People (Tarr) (documentary), 9, 11, 36, 125, 141–42, 177
modernity, 18
Moore, Kevin, 25
Motion(less) Pictures (Remes) (book), 16

Nagib, Lúcia, 18
natural locations, 5
natural world, 1
New York Café (Budapest), 44
Night (*La notte*) (Antonioni), 20, 39n3; emptiness and urban setting in, 22–23; interior space in, 24

ocean, 99–100
official spaces, 44
Old Yeller (Gipson) (novel), 109
open field, 94–95
outdoor spaces, 81–85, 145, 179; animals and, 107, 108, 110,

124; Anthropocene and, 6, 10; domesticated, 85–94; ecology and, 104–105; indoor spaces and, 42, 43, 46, 48–49, 54–58; short films and, 125, 127, 129, 133, 134, 137, 139, 140; slow cinema and, 15, 20, 23, 25, 34, 38; wilderness and, 94–104

The Outsider (*Szabadgyalog*) (Tarr), 35, 45, *51*, *74*, 79n9, 106n9, 126, 127, 147, 149; disco in, 71; dwellings in, 50–51; factory in, 75; horse in, 116; hospital in, 73–74; Hungarian taverns in, 66, 67; open fields in, 106n7; parking lot in, 91–92; story of, 180–81; workspaces in, 72

owl, 121

Pakalnina, Laila, 139
"Pardoner Tale" (Chaucer) (novel), 149
parking lots, 90–92
Pennell, Eagle, 136
People of the Mountains (*Emberek a havason*) (Szőts), 33
Petőfi, Sándor, 11, 129, 176; poems, in *Journey on the Plain* (*Utazás az Alföldön*), 129, 131–35
Pfeifer, Moritz, 112, 113, 123
pigs, 114–15
Poetics (Aristotle), 16
Porumboiu, Corneliu, 101
The Prefab People (*Panelkapcsolat*) (Tarr), 35, 45, *52*, *54*, 60, 74, 79n9, 149; birds in, 121, 122; dwellings in, 51–54, 77; forest in, 106n9; hairdresser in, 71, 78n1, 93; Hungarian taverns in, 66–68; public park in, 93, 94; story of, 181–82
Prieto, Eric, 7
public park, 92–94
public square, 85–90

Racine, Jean, 16
Radvány Géza van, 33
rain and wind, 100–104

Rancière, Jacques, 13n10, 15, 18–19, 90, 98; on animals, 108, 115, 124; on *Damnation*, 98; on dwellings, 48; on interior spaces, 42, 44–45; on political reality, 53; on rain, 100; on space and time, 146, 148
Raup, Jordan, 142
Ray, Man, 4
The Red and the White (*Csillagosok, katonák*) (Jancsó), 29–30
Red Desert (*Deserto rosso*) (Antonioni), 39n3, 56, 121–22
Reichenbach, Carlos, 136
Remes, Justin, 16
Renoir, Jean, 34
Rijneke, Dick, 136
Robbe-Grillet, Alain, 63
Roberts, Phillip, 61
Rollet, Sylvie, 35
Romney, Jonathan, 36
Rosenbaum, Jonathan, 35, 62, 83
Rossellini, Roberto, 33
The Round Up (*Szegénylegények*) (Jancsó), 28–29
Rucekert, William, 5
Ruttmann, Walter, 16

Samardzija, Zoran, 26
sameness, 45–47
Samocki, Jean-Marie, 28, 36, 46–47, 121
Sarte, Jean-Paul, 124, 148, 149
Satan's Tango (*Sátántangó*) (Tarr), 10, 11, 36, 42, 74, *96*, *115*, 134, 149, 172; barn in, 76; cat in, 113–14; chickens in, 120; cows in, 115–16; dogs in, 112; dwellings in, 48, 58; forest in, 96–97; geographical location in, 45–46; horses in, 117; Hungarian taverns in, 69, 88; open fields in, 94, 95; outdoor spaces in, 81, 86; owl in, 121; pig in, 114–15; public squares in, 87–88; rain in, 100; story of, 185–87; workspaces in, 72, 73

Sátántangó (Krasznahorkai) (novel), 86
Schwägel, Christian, 2
Scicluna, Kenneth, 139
Scott, A. O., 65
sea creatures, 123–24
Seasons of Monsters (*Szörnyek évadja*) (Tarr), 28
Selyem, Zsuzsa, 103
Sen, Mrinal, 136
The Seventh Seal (*Det sjunde inseglet*) (Bergman), 19
Shoeshine (*Sciuscà*) (De Sica), 33
Sibertin-Blanc, Guillaume, 77
Sierek, Karl, 81, 109
Sight and Sound Magazine, 62
signal boxes, 9, *10*, 13n10, 42, 61, 99, 122; barns and, 75–78
Simenon, Georges, 13n10, 46
slow cinema, 15; examples, before and beyond Tarr, 19–32; Hungarian film spaces and, 32–38; meaning and significance of, 16–17; political implications of, 18; Rancière on, 18–19. See also individual entries
Slow Cinema (Luca and Jorge) (book), 16
Solaris (Tarkovsky), 26, 27
Somewhere in Europe (*Valahol az Europaban*) (Radvány), 33–34
space: interior, 24; as loci of emptiness, 8; significance of, 7; three-dimensional, 8
Stagecoach (Ford), 5
Stalker (Tarkovsky), 25–28, 39n6
Stoermer, Eugene F., 2
Strausz, László, 30
Sulik, Martin, 139
Szabó, István, 4, 34
Szendy, Peter, 121
Szomy, Frank, 151
Szőts, István, 33
Szumowska, Malgosia, 139

Tally Jr., Robert T., 7, 26

Tarkovsky, Andrei, 1, 9, 39n6, 148; critique of capitalism in films of, 26; and Tarr compared, 25, 27, 28
Tarr, Béla: and Angelopoulos compared, 32; and Antonioni compared, 20, 25; and Jancsó (compared, 30; as model, 28); human dignity in films of, 37–38; Hungarian film spaces and, 32–38; interview with, 171–77; Rancière on, 44–45; and Tarkovsky compared, 25, 27, 28. See also individual entries
timelessness: animals and, 116; empty outdoors and, 83, 91, 94, 102; indoor spaces and, 46, 59, 62, 76, 77; slow cinema and, 27, 30, 31
Tőke, Lilla, 37
Tomasulo, Frank P., 21, 23
Translations (Friel) (play), 12n7
Troell, Jan, 139
The Turin Horse (Tarr), 10, 35, 36, 38, 42, *64*, 75, *101*, 139, 149, 176; barn in, 76–77; cyclical temporality in, 62–64, 102; dwellings in, 60–65; ecology and outdoor spaces in, 104–105; forest in, 97; furniture in, 64–65; geographical location in, 46; Ginn on, 2, 8, 118–19; horses in, 103, 117–19; Hungarian taverns in, 70–71; Jaffe on, 17, 104–105; Nietzsche reference in, 103; poverty depiction in, 61–62; story of, 191; wind in, 101–104
12:08 East of Bucharest (Porumboiu), 101
2001: A Space Odyssey (Kubrick), 27

urban leisure spaces, 65–72

Van Gogh, Theo, 139
van Leeuwaarden, Mildred, 136
Variety (magazine), 139
Végső, Roland, 50
Villaverde, Teresa, 139

Vincze, Teréz, 8, 17, 20, 25, 38
Visconti, Luchino, 21
Visions of Europe (Tarr) (short film), 11; segment: *Prologue*, 11, 42, 105n3, 125, 128, 138, 139–41, *141*, 146, 176, 189

Waiting for Godot (Beckett) (play), 79n13, 97–98
Walsh, Aisling, 139
Weekend (*Wochenende*) (Ruttman), 16
Weeping Meadow (*To livadi pou dakryzei*) (Angelopoulos), 31–32
Werckmeister Harmonies (*Werckmeister harmóniák*) (Tarr), 10, 36, 43, *70*, 83, *89*, 134, 149; barn in, 77; dwellings in, 58–61; geographical location in, 45, 46; hospital in, 74; Hungarian taverns in, 69–70; open fields in, 95; poverty depiction in, 61; public square in, 88; rain in, 100; Rancière on, 18; story of, 188–89; whale as metaphysical in, 59, 60, 88–89, 95, 123; workspaces in, 73
Westphal, Bertrand, 7, 43
Wetherall, Greg, 37
whale: ambiguous moral signifier, 123–24; as metaphysical, 59, 60, 88–89, 95
wilderness: coal pit and, 98–99; forest and, 95–98; ocean and, 99–100; open field and, 94–95; rain and wind and, 100–104
Wild Strawberries (*Smultronstället*) (Bergman), 19–20
The Witness (*A tanú*) (Bacsó), 34
workspaces, 13n10, 42, 72–75
Wright, Frank Lloyd, 58

About the Author

Clara Orban is professor of French and Italian at DePaul University. She received her PhD at the University of Chicago in Romance Languages. She has published books, book chapters, and articles, and presented papers on surrealism, futurism, language pedagogy, AIDS literature, sports, TV, and Italian film. She published her first novel, *Terra Firma*, in 2006. She is also a certified sommelier and teaches Geography 350: The World of Wine at DePaul with a Study Abroad component. Her book *Wine Lessons: Ten Questions to Guide Your Appreciation of Wine* is in its third edition. Her eighth book *Illinois Wines and Wineries: The Essential Guide* was published in 2014. Her interest in Hungarian cinema has led to several presentations, published articles, as well as the current book on Béla Tarr.